The Forces of Economic
Growth and Decline

The Forces of Economic
Growth and Decline

Paolo Sylos-Labini

The MIT Press
Cambridge, Massachusetts
London, England

This book was set in Apollo by Asco Trade Typesetting Ltd., Hong Kong and printed and bound by Halliday Lithograph in the United States of America.

Library of Congress Cataloging in Publication Data

Sylos Labini, Paolo.
  The forces of economic growth and decline.

  Includes bibliographical references and index.
  1. Economic development—Addresses, essays, lectures. 2. Technological innovations—Addresses, essays, lectures. 3. Industrial organization (Economic theory)—Addresses, essays, lectures. 4. Income distribution—Addresses, essays, lectures. I. Title.
HD75.S95 1984   338.9   84-9699
ISBN 0-262-19224-1

Contents

Introduction:
Innovations, Market Structures, Income Distribution, and the Process of Economic Growth

Innovations, changes in market forms, and changes in income distribution are the three specific processes that constitute the general process of economic growth. This is the unifying conception behind the essays collected here, which are grouped into different parts depending on the emphasis given to one of the three said processes. They are treated sequentially, however, only after an introductory part that discusses the problem of economic growth as posed by the classical economists. In one way or another the tripartition of economic growth that I have just mentioned goes back to the classical theory. To clarify my approach, I must start with a short autobiographical note.

When I was a young student at the University of Rome in 1940, I chose to prepare a dissertation on the economic consequences of inventions. My knowledge of economic theory was extremely limited. I was fascinated by the great technical inventions of our time, and this was the reason for my choice. In starting my work, I believed that I was going to find a huge bibliography, and I was a little scared by the prospect of studying a large number of books and articles. To my surprise both the bibliography that was suggested to me and the one that I was able to find myself were incredibly scanty: I discovered that Joseph Schumpeter's *Theory of Economic Development* was the only important book analyzing that problem systematically (his treatise on business cycles was not yet available in Italy). Important chapters could be found in John Bates Clark's *Essentials of Economic Theory* and in Dennis Robertson's *A Study of Industrial Fluctuations*. Chapters and sections could be found in the books of other economists, together with a number of articles, treating that problem directly or indirectly, but the treatment was never systematic. My surprise in finding this state of research, I must confess, was great. The importance of innovations for all aspects of society, both in peace and in war, should have been obvious to anyone. Why was it, then, that economic theory had largely neglected this category of problems?

It is true that after the second world war the situation to some extent improved.[1] However, it is still very surprising to realize that the main body of economic theory is static in nature. It is surprising, nay unbelievable, to realize that the central economic problem, both in theory and in practice, is considered the problem of the optimal allocation of given resources, whereas it is evident that the central problem, both in advanced and even more in backward countries, is the problem of how to develop available resources. It is surprising to observe that many economists of our time, who are trying to leave the static ground, conceive the movements of the economy as the result of a sort of comedy of errors, in which people are systematically fooled or else are capable of neutralizing even important economic changes if only they succeed in predicting them. At the same time such economists simply ignore those powerful agents of economic and social change, technological innovations.

The explanation is, I think, a very complex one, implying logical, ideological, and social aspects. As for the purely logical aspects, I only recall that in the development of economic theory two ideas, which are to be related to the aspiration of many economists to acquire a status similar to that of natural scientists by applying certain techniques of mathematics and of theoretical physics that were developed in the late nineteenth century, have had a particularly important role: the idea of applying differential calculus to economics, where it is natural to analyze problems of maximum and minimum in instantaneous terms, and the idea of using certain analogies—especially the analogy between the economic system and a static mechanical system—borrowed from a concept of physics. The result has been paradoxical, however: the static approach has come to dominate economic theory precisely in the historical period when technological change and economic growth have become the characteristic features of an increasing number of societies.

Yet directly or indirectly the problem of economic growth has been the main concern of the classical economists, including Marx, and their analysis was by no means "static."

In view of the cultural interests I have just mentioned, it was natural for me to study Schumpeter and, through him, to go back to the classical economists, especially to Adam Smith, David Ricardo, and Karl Marx. I had just started on this itinerary when I had the good fortune of meeting Alberto Breglia, who was my guide in my formative years. He encouraged me to go to Harvard and to complete my studies under Joseph Schumpeter, whose work I had become familiar with in preparing my doctoral dissertation. I was awarded a scholarship in 1948 to be spent in the United States. After three months in Chicago, where I came to know Franco Modigliani, I went on to spend about nine months at Harvard, where I was able to obtain Schumpeter as my supervisor.

Then in 1950 I won another scholarship, this time for an academic year at Cambridge University. There I was lucky enough to have Dennis Robertson as my supervisor. The new and the old Cambridges were two great experiences for me: in both academic communities I had the privilege of meeting and associating with some of the most illustrious economists of our time.

Although written fairly recently (in 1976), the essay on Adam Smith presented in chapter 1 logically precedes that on Marx and Schumpeter (chapter 2), originally written in 1954. Smith emphasizes the importance of technological change in the process of economic growth: expansion of the market provides new possibilities for the division of labor and therefore for technological change, which can promote an expansion of production by reducing its costs and in this way lead to a further expansion of the market itself; a sort of chain reaction is thus put into motion. At the same time Smith emphasizes that the only market structure consistent with economic growth is competition, which he conceives of not as a fixed state—a market with a great number of producers—but as a process—a market where free entry and free exit tend to create a continuous expansion of production and trade. For Smith monopoly is a serious obstacle to growth; it is well to remember that for him monopoly is essentially the result of legal and institutional barriers that were typical of the stage of commercial capitalism in his time. Smith does not attach great importance to the changes in the distribution of income. Although he is sometimes described as the ideologist of the emerging bourgeoisie, Smith is very critical of high profits which, among other things, he associates with high prices and with low, or even zero, growth. As I will argue in chapter 8 ("On the Concept of the Optimum Rate of Profit"), this is not so strange or contradictory as it may appear. In any case Smith does not see the danger that declining profits could put an end to the accumulation process; rather, the end of this process would occur when the society under consideration would have "acquired that full complement to riches which the nature of its laws and institutions permits to acquire." For Smith, then, the end of accumulation and the ensuing stationary state would be a consequence of institutional rather than purely economic causes.

Contrary to Smith, Ricardo is preoccupied not with profits being too high but too low; for him the end of accumulation would precisely be the consequence of profits being too low. Ricardo derives such a notion from his conviction that the diminishing returns from land would push up the share of rents and pull down the share and the rate of profits.

Ricardo agrees with Smith on the issue of competition and in his *Principles* discusses technological changes partly with regard to the problem of relative prices and partly in the chapter on machinery added to the third edition.

On the whole he concentrates his attention on the changes in the distribution of income, not because he does not attach importance to the process of accumulation but because he takes it for granted that, if the tendency of the rate of profit to fall were offset, accumulation would meet with no other obstacles (see the appendix to chapter 1).

Marx too attaches great importance to the changes in the distribution of income and believes that in the long run the rate of profit tends to fall, thus creating increasing obstacles to the process of accumulation; for him, however, this tendency was not due to diminishing returns from land but to the rise in the "organic composition of capital" (a very controversial thesis that seems to have no supporters nowadays).

Marx is the first economist to place great emphasis on technological innovations, without which the process of enlarged reproduction (i.e., of accumulation) would be impossible. He is also the first economist, before Schumpeter, to conceive of the process of capitalist development as a cyclical process, development and growth being viewed as two aspects of the same process which is carried out by innovations and conditioned by changes in income distribution. For Marx, as for Smith, competition is an essential part of this process. Marx, however, differently from his predecessors, is able to see as another aspect of the same process the tendency of firms in many important branches to increase in size and decrease in number, which implies an increasing concentration of productive units.

Schumpeter distinguishes economic growth, which tends to take place gradually and, in principle, continuously, from economic development, a process by its nature discontinuous, originated as it is by innovations. (In this book I use the term "growth" in a broad sense, covering the two Schumpeterian meanings, and the term "development" when I wish to emphasize Schumpeter's second meaning). In fact Schumpeter gives the greatest importance to the economic consequences of innovations. He was one of the first economists to point out that the large enterprises, which are obviously in a position to influence prices and therefore do not fit in the classical or neoclassical model of competition, are not necessarily an impediment to the process of development but under certain conditions, as I have argued in several works of mine and as I show in chapter 5, can even speed up this process. (In different terms Maffeo Pantaleoni maintained a similar thesis in an essay published in 1909.) In a certain sense Schumpeter agrees with Marx on the particular view that modern large enterprises fall in between the capitalist and the socialist economic order, but on grounds that are very different from those of Marx: Schumpeter emphasizes the bureaucratization of innovations; Marx, the increasing separation between ownership and administration. Moreover Marx points out that the spread of large enterprises makes government control inevitable. These two concepts—the separation between ownership and administration and the question of government control proposed by Marx more than a century ago—are the same concepts to be found in the famous 1926 pamphlet of Keynes, *The End of Laissez-Faire*.

The appearance of large enterprises greatly modifies the structure of modern industrial economies. However, this is but one of many structural changes of our time. Another one consists of the increasing differentiation of products, a phenomenon related to the development of the mass media, transportation, and advertising, which can assert itself only when per capita income rises well above the subsistence level. Both the concentration process and the increasing differentiation of products have determined the spread of noncompetitive market structures in industrial and tertiary activities, though not in agriculture and mining. (Oligopoly in its three varieties—concentrated, differentiated, and mixed—emerges as the most frequent market structure in industry and services.)

These structural changes require new theoretical models that analyze the process of economic growth. Several stages in the evolution of modern capitalism have to be distinguished, and correspondingly, several theoretical models have to be worked out. As frames of reference we can consider the Smithian model for the premodern stage, and the Marxian and the Schumpeterian models for the competitive stage. As for the third stage—the "trustified," as Schumpeter terms it, or, as I prefer to say, "oligopolistic" capitalism—Schumpeter does not really supply a new model, but in *Business Cycles*, and to a greater extent in *Capitalism, Socialism, and Democracy*, he presents many elements that can be used to work out such a model. It could be argued that after World War II we entered into a stage that suggests still another model to be worked out, one that should give due emphasis to technological and organizational changes in the service sector and to the direct and indirect role of government in promoting applied scientific research. At present little is available in the literature concerning this development.

Some aspects of the problems just mentioned are discussed in chapter 3, and the factors affecting changes in productivity are analyzed in chapter 4. Productivity increases constitute the main effect of technological progress, although such increases can be determined also by organizational innovations. Technological progress, however, does not only determine an increase in productivity, it also gives rise to new products which can be seen as a source of an increase in productivity when we consider the economy as a whole. Among the factors affecting productivity changes, I consider investment, changes in output, and changes in the relative cost of labor, that is, the ratio between wages and the price of machines. This ratio has important theoretical implications that are discussed in the first part of chapter 4; in the final part of that chapter a few estimates of the productivity equation are presented for Italy and the United States.

One might ask, How have the changes in the structure of modern industrial economies affected the productivity trend? The answer, though somewhat paradoxical, is: Such changes do not seem to have had any discernible effect at all on that trend, which is almost always upward. Although in certain periods we have noticed an acceleration or, as in the last ten years, a deceleration of productivity increases, the fundamental trend does not show significant modifications. To understand this fact, one has to reflect on the views of Schumpeter on large enterprises. Stated generally, in the period of oligopolistic capitalism the conditions of economic progress vary with respect to those of competitive capitalism. The overall performance in terms of production and productivity does not need to change, however. Under certain circumstances this performance can even be, and often has been, superior. Moreover there is no reason to think that the factors directly affecting productivity have changed, rather the determinants of such factors, particularly output, investment, and what I call the relative cost of labor, have changed. The said determinants as well as the relationships of large firms' price policies, financial requirements, and investment policies in the times of oligopolistic capitalism are discussed in chapter 5. In chapter 6 the analysis is focused on the problem of price variation both in oligopolistic markets and in markets where a situation close to competition still prevails—the former situation being frequent in industry and services, the latter in agriculture and mining. Certain relationships then are discussed between world inflation and the slowdown of growth in industrial economies.

The last three chapters are concerned mainly with the relationship between economic growth and changes in income distribution. In chapter 7 I show that the theoretical and empirical analyses of price changes can be expanded into an analysis of the changes in the distribution of income. The conclusions reached in this chapter have an important methodological implication: if changes in prices necessarily determine changes in income distribution, and if in turn the changes in income distribution affect the rate of growth of income as well as the level of employment, then it is radically wrong to treat real and nominal quantities as if they are fundamentally independent of each other. The analysis worked out in this chapter may help to explain the recurrent postwar stagnation or even recession accompanied by inflation, which is regarded by many economists as a paradox. In chapter 8 the relationships between investment and the rate of profit are discussed, and it is argued that from the point of view of economic growth this rate can be "too low" as well as "too high," hence the concept of the optimum rate of profit. What emerges is that, whereas in the last ten years or so in the manufacturing industry of certain advanced countries the average rate of profit appears to have been "too low," in the twenties in the United States it was "too high," and this was one of the causes of the Great Depression. This thesis is elaborated further in chapter 9, which consists of part of an essay written recently for a volume on the current state of Keynesian theory. I thought it fitting to include it for the reason that my discussion there of the diagnosis of the Great Depression is based on the conception of the three processes mentioned at the beginning of this introduction and appearing in all nine chapters, though in different ways and with different emphases. This is why chapter 9, which makes use of such a conception to try and clarify one of the most important historical events of our time, concludes this volume.

I have edited some of the essays to render the whole collection more homogeneous but have not introduced substantial changes. To this end a section on Ricardo and diminishing returns is appended to chapter 1 and the postscript to chapter 2 enlarged.

Chapter 1 reproduces a report presented at the conference organized in 1976 by the University of Glasgow for the bicentenary of *The Wealth of Nations*; the Proceedings were collected in the volume *The Market and the State: Essays in Honour of Adam Smith*, edited by Thomas Wilson and Andrew S. Skinner (Oxford University Press, Oxford, 1976).

Chapter 2 appeared originally in Italian in the volume *Teoria dello sviluppo economico*, edited by G. U. Papi (1954; reprinted in *Problemi dello sviluppo economico*, Laterza, Bari, 1970). It was translated into English by Joseph Halevi and revised by Peter Groenewegen for *Altro polo*, a book containing essays of Italian scholars published annually by the F. May Foundation of Italian studies in Sydney.

Chapter 3 gives the text of the Eleventh R. C. Mills Memorial Lecture at the University of Sydney on 21 October 1980; it was first published in the August 1981 issue of *Economic Papers*, which is the journal of the Economic Society of Australia and New Zealand—New South Wales and Victorian Branches, edited by Peter Groenewegen.

Chapter 4 is an essay published in the Winter 1983 issue of the *Journal of Post Keynesian Economics*.

Chapter 5 is an article originally published in French in the *Revue d'économie politique*, March 1971.

Chapter 6 combines two papers: one published in March 1982 in *Banca Nazionale del Lavoro Quarterly Review* and the other, the modified text of a report presented in February 1982 before the World Conference on Gold held in Rome, published in the volume *The Gold Problem: Economic Perspectives*, edited by Alberto Quadrio Curzio (Oxford University Press for the Banca Nazionale del Lavoro and Nomisma, 1982).

Chapter 7 was originally published in the Fall 1979 issue of the *Journal of Post Keynesian Economics*.

Chapter 8 is a short essay published in the volume *Studies in Economic Theory and Practice: Essays in Honour of Edward Lipinski*, edited by J. Łoś et al. (North-Holland, Amsterdam, 1981).

Chapter 9 is part of a chapter appearing in *Attualità di Keynes*, a collection of essays edited by Fausto Vicarelli (Laterza, Bari, 1983; the English edition of this book will be published in 1984 by Macmillan, London).

All the papers in this volume are reprinted with the kind permission of the publishers concerned. I should like to express my gratitude to Mrs. Gisele Podbielski, who translated from the French the essay constituting chapter 5 and made emendations in the English of this introduction, the appendix to chapter 1, and chapter 9.

Notes

1. See F. H. Hahn and R. C. O. Matthews, "The Theory of Economic Growth: A Survey," *Economic Journal* 74 (1964): 826–832; reprinted in the volume *Survey of Economic Theory: Growth and Development* (prepared for the American Economic Association and the Royal Economic Society, New York: St. Martin Press, 1965). See also R. F. Harrod, *Towards a Dynamic Economics* (London: Macmillan, 1948); W. E. G. Salter, *Productivity and Technical Change* (Cambridge: Cambridge University Press, 1960). L. Robbins, *The Theory of Economic Development in the History of Economic Thought* (New York: Oxford University Press, 1968); N. Kaldor, *Essays on Economic Stability and Growth* (London: Duckworth, 1960); *Growth Economics: Selected Readings*, ed. by A. Sen (Baltimore: Penguin Books, 1970); M. Kalecki, *Selected Essays on the Dynamics of Capitalist Economy 1933–1970* (Cambridge: Cambridge University Press, 1971); C. Freeman, *The Economics of Industrial Innovation* (Baltimore: Penguin Books, 1974); R. Goodwin, *Essays in Economic Dynamics* (London: Macmillan, 1982). For a more general critical appraisal of contemporary developments in economic theory, see the essays included in *The Crisis in Economic Theory*, ed. by D. Bell and I. Kristol (New York: Basic Books, 1981), especially the essay by P. Davidson, "Post Keynesian Economics." See also the bibliography appended to chapter 4 and, in particular, the important book by L. L. Pasinetti, *Structural Change and Economic Growth* (Cambridge: Cambridge University Press, 1981).

A dynamic analysis of a peculiar type is the one concerning business cycles, an analysis that has got an old tradition, in which we find several great economists like Juglar, Spietoff, Robertson, Pigou, Mitchell, Fanno—Schumpeter has already been mentioned. However, this tradition developed laterally with respect to the main body of economic theory, from which it remained largely separated.

I The Problem of Economic Growth in Classical Theory

1   Competition and Economic Growth in Adam Smith

In this chapter I contrast Smith's view of the competitive process with modern developments and compare his expectations with what happened in the next two centuries. To do this, I isolate the appropriate measure of value in which to make meaningful intertemporal comparisons of prices and incomes. Therefore the first part of the chapter is concerned with this fundamental problem, the understanding of which is necessary before an appraisal can be attempted of Smith's conception of competition and economic growth. The main analytical lines for such an appraisal are discussed in the second part.

1.1 Competition and Monopoly

The distance between the static conception of competition prevalent in our time and that of Smith is very great indeed: in *The Wealth of Nations* competition and economic growth are two aspects of one and the same process. More precisely, according to economists belonging to the marginalist tradition, the essential characteristic of competition is the large number of suppliers, each of whom is so small as not to be able to modify the conditions of the market, and in particular not the price. For Adam Smith, as well as for the other classical economists, competition is characterized by free entry; conversely, monopoly implies obstacles to entry. In Smith's time such obstacles were primarily institutional or legal, such as "the exclusive privileges of corporations, statutes of apprenticeship, and all those laws which restrain, in particular employments, the competition to a smaller number than might otherwise go into them" (*WN* I. vii. 28), or the privileges granted to certain companies in the colonial trade (*WN* IV., viii., III), or the high duties and prohibitions on foreign manufactures (*WN* IV., iii., II).[1] Such obstacles were to be attacked on the political and legislative plane. Smith, however, also considers other types of obstacles to entry: those determined by natural scarcities in agriculture and mining, those determined, in his time, temporarily by secrets in manufactures, and most important, those determined by high costs of transport. Still, other obstacles to entry can be found in certain activities carried on in the towns, where, for technical reasons or for reasons of geographic location, the number of manufacturers, workers, or tradesmen is small and cannot easily increase. In such a situation the people concerned, just because they are very few, are likely to enter into a combination in order to raise the price of their products or their labor. Here again the important element is not the smallness of the number but the obstacles to entry, that is, the impossibility or the great difficulty for "new rivals" to enter the market. The tendency toward equality of wages and profits in different employments (apart from the inequalities arising from the nature of the employments) presupposes free entry or, as Smith sometimes says with reference to both the product and labor markets, "perfect liberty" (*WN* I., x., a. 1).

The obstacles to entry can keep the market price of particular commodities above the natural price and maintain not only profits but also wages above their natural rates for a long time.

> When the quantity brought to market is just sufficient to supply the effectual demand and no more, the market price naturally comes to be either exactly, or as nearly as can be judged of, the same with the natural price . . . . (*WN* I., vii., 11)

The effectual demand, according to Smith, is the quantity demanded by all "those who are willing to pay the natural price of the commodity, or the whole value of the rent, labor and profit" at their natural rates (*WN* I., vii., 8). The market price will rise above the natural price when the quantity of a given commodity which is brought to market falls short of the effectual demand, and it will fall below the natural price when the opposite is the case. Under competition the market price can be higher than the natural price only for a limited period.

The concepts of natural price and natural rate are inseparable from the concept of competition: in this respect "natural" and "competitive" can well be considered as synonymous.

1.2 The Natural Price and the Natural Rate of Wages, Profits, and Rent

To understand correctly Smith's conception of the natural price, it is necessary to realize that, unlike the point of view prevailing today among economists, Smith is considering not only the distinction between the short and long run but also what we today would call—for different analytical purposes—"stages of development" which are indistinguishable from long historical periods. (When speaking of the short run, Smith says "occasionally" or "temporarily"; when referring to the long run, he uses either this expression or other equivalent ones, like "considerable time"; when referring to the stages of development, Smith speaks of "states," "conditions," "general circumstances of the society," or "different periods of improvement.")

According to Smith, the basic stages are three: progessive, stationary, and declining. (It should be clear that these three stages refer to a society that has already developed an exchange economy.) The progressive stage, on which Smith concentrates his attention, is often divided further. In brief, in discussing the behavior of the natural and market prices, Smith is using three, and not two, terms of reference: short run, long run, and stage of development. In the short run, the market price depends on supply ("quantity brought to the market") and demand. In the long run, under conditions of monopoly, it depends on the same forces; under competition it tends to coincide with the natural price or, we may say, with the cost of production, with the proviso that, in a given historical period or subperiod the natural price varies only if technology varies, whereas the natural rates of wages, profits, and rent are to be considered as constant. In passing from one stage of development to another, or from one subperiod to another, the natural price will vary as a result not only of technological changes but also of variations in wages, profits, and rents:

> The natural price itself varies with the natural rate of . . . its component parts, of wages, profit, and rent; and in every society this rate varies according to their circumstances, according to their riches or poverty, to their advancing, stationary, or declining condition. (*WN* I., vii., 33)

In chapter vii of the first book Smith discusses systematically the behavior of prices in the short and long run. In chapters viii, ix, and x of the same book he discusses the behavior of the "natural rate" of wages, profits, and rent in the different periods and subperiods of the "progress of improvement."

In analyzing the variations of the natural rate of the "three original sources of all revenue," Smith apparently uses the criterion of supply and demand, but it should be clear that his criterion has very little to do with the one followed by economists of the marginalist tradition, a criterion epitomized by two curves, one independent of the other. To clarify this point, let us consider very briefly some of the views set forth by Smith.

In the progressive stage of society, the demand for labor rises, while "the production of men" can only be increased under conditions of increasing cost, because each laborer has "to bring up a greater number of children." Therefore

If [the] demand [for labor] is continuously increasing, the reward of labor must necessarily encourage in such a manner the marriage and multiplication of laborers, as may enable them to supply that continually increasing demand by a continually increasing population. (*WN* I., viii., 40)

The demand for labor, according as it happens to be increasing, stationary, or declining, or to require an increasing, stationary, or declining population, determines the quantity of the necessaries and conveniences of life which must be given to the laborer; and the money price of labor is determined by what is requisite for purchasing this quantity. (*WN* I., viii., 52)

The increase in the demand for labor can, for a time, raise wages to the level needed for a greater expansion of population, but once this higher level is reached, it will remain there, even if demand continues to increase, so long as population, and hence the supply of labor, increases at the same rate. However, when demand increases persistently faster than population, wages can continue to rise. One could say that the expansion of demand affects the cost of production of men, and it is this cost—the cost required by the general conditions of society—that regulates wages in a given stage of development. The increasing or declining state of the wealth of society also determines variations in profits, but in a direction often opposite to that of wages. As for rents, in the "progress of improvement" they tend to increase, first, because the expansion of the demand for the produce of land comes up against the general scarcity of land itself (Smith speaks of the rent of land as a monopoly price only in this broad sense) and, second, because that expansion meets with particular scarcities (unimproved wilds to raise cattle, certain types of land fitted to some particular produce, mines). The said scarcities give rise to an increase in price and this makes it possible to increase production albeit at higher costs. However, once the particular levels of rent for different types of land have stabilized at some stage of development, they become elements of costs (though in the course of historical time they are the result of increasing prices).

Although wages, profits, and rent are regulated by the variations of demand during the different stages of economic development, variations of this kind in fact seem to depend on the general conditions of society rather than on strictly economic forces. It is from this standpoint that in each historical period either the levels or the rates of change of wages, profits, and rent are given. In this sense Marx is right in observing that these three elements "determine autonomously"[2] the natural price, or, better, as Sraffa says, the natural price is arrived at by a process of *adding up* the wages, profits, and rent.[3] There is no doubt that, apart from a number of general remarks, Smith does not *analyze* the relations between wages, profits, and rent, and in particular we find in his work only hints as to the inverse relation between the wage rate and the rate of profit. Neither does he analyze the relations between these three elements and variations in the system of prices. Still, Smith's theory of prices would seem to be indeterminate rather than wrong. In any case, if we make use of Smith's analysis, we have to take into account his peculiar procedure (based on the tripartite division that I have mentioned, i.e., stage of development, long and short run); such a procedure, in Smith, seems to perform a role similar to that of the method of successive approximations adopted by later economists.

1.3 The Conditions of Production and the Measure of Price Changes

The great difference between the marginalist and the classical conception of competition indeed entails more than only the role assigned to free entry or the obstacles to entry of actual or potential entrants ("new rivals")—a concept only recently rediscovered and put at the basis of the analysis of market structure—there are deeper arguments.[4] Marginalist economists view economic life as an "arc," whereas classical economists as a "circle" or a "spiral." The former give to the psychological aspects of the behavior of consumers no less importance—in fact even a greater importance—than to the conditions of production. The classical economists, on the other hand, consider the habits of consumers as the result of the general conditions of society. Besides, they do not conceive of consumption *in abstracto*; they distinguish between necessary and unnecessary, or between productive and unproductive consumption. The former, which is made possible by saving, is the consumption of "productive laborers," and it represents one set of the requirements for the repetition, or for the enlargement, of the social process of production. The other set of requirements is given by technology which, by determining the quantity of productive labor to be employed, also helps to determine the amount of necessary consumption. The analysis of natural and market prices, then, should be conducted not with reference to supply and demand as such but to the technological methods of production and to the conditions of necessary consumption.

Here we can discuss particularly the changes in price that take place in the long run. In this context effectual demand determines the amount to be produced: price is determined by the cost of production. If, in the course of time, effectual demand tends to increase (i.e., if the extent of the market tends to expand), new and more efficient methods of production can be introduced, thanks to progress in the division of labor, and the "natural price" thus decreases. But the effectual demand affects price only indirectly, that is, by determining changes in the methods of production. In Smith's words

The increase of demand . . . , though in the beginning it may sometimes raise
the price of goods, never fails to lower it in the long run. It encourages
production, and thereby increases the competition of the producers, who, in
order to undersell one another, have recourse to new divisions of labour and
new improvements of art, which might never otherwise have been thought
of.[5]

Cost and price reductions then are determined by an increase in the division
of labor which is generated by a persistent expansion of the market. In other
words, Smith's increasing returns are the result of irreversible changes,
occurring in the course of time. The increase in the division of labor implies an
increasing number of operations to produce the same products or new products. Such operations can be performed, on the one hand, by an increasing
number of firms or, on the other, by a decreasing number of firms of ever
larger size. As a rule the latter phenomenon is the consequence of the
economies of scale, which were of little importance in Smith's time but in
several branches have become important in the last hundred years or so.
(Viewed in a dynamic or, more precisely, in a historical perspective, such
economies have a destructive power with respect to competition both in the
classical and in the neoclassical sense, as Alfred Marshall and several economists after him have correctly recognized.)

Increasing returns, however, do not prevail everywhere; they prevail in
manufactures and in certain agricultural productions. In other types of production the tendency toward diminishing returns (also of a dynamic character) prevails. The increase in production, which in this case takes place under
conditions of increasing costs and price, is caused by the progressive expansion of demand. But again, demand affects output directly, and price only
indirectly, by determining changes in the methods of production.

Since Smith intended to study the consequences of technological progress
on relative prices, he needed a standard to use in intertemporal comparisons.
Having discarded money as the unit, since the very conditions of production
of the precious metals used as money undergo changes in the course of time,
Smith adopted labor commanded, that is, he decided to take the wage rate of
common labor as the unit. The idea, that this standard corresponds to labor
embodied if the distributive shares are constant, is not new, but it is well to
reflect on it.

Since for Smith "the whole price . . . resolves itself either immediately or
ultimately into the . . . three parts of rent, labor and profit" (*WN* I., vi., 11), P,
the price of a given commodity, can be seen as the sum of all revenues per unit
of output.[6] If we call H the number of hours of labor directly or indirectly
embodied in that commodity, W the wage rate per unit of time (per hour), and

δ the ratio of total wages per unit of output and price, we have (measuring both P and W in terms of an abstract paper money or in terms of a given commodity)

$$WH = \delta P.$$

If we compare the value of the commodity we are considering in two different periods, indexes 1 and 2, and assume that owing to technical progress H_2 is smaller than H_1, then the ratio expressing labor embodied (H_1/H_2) is equal to the ratio representing labor commanded $(P_1/W_1)/(P_2/W_2)$ if $\delta_1 = \delta_2$, that is, if the share going to wages does not vary.

Ricardo and Marx maintain that Smith oscillates between the two standards (labor commanded and labor embodied) and that his theory of value is ambiguous and even inconsistent. In fact, on the one hand, Smith says that labor embodied regulates exchangeable values only "in that early and rude state of society which precedes both the accumulation of stock and the appropriation of land" (*WN* I., vi., 1); on the other hand, Smith argues several times as if the two expressions were equivalent.

Now, there is no contradiction between the first point of view and the assumption that the two standards can be, and as a rule are, equivalent. The former implies $\delta = 1$ for all commodities; the latter implies a δ less than one and constant in the course of time for each commodity but not necessarily equal for all the different commodities. The former refers to exchangeable value among commodities, the latter refers to intertemporal comparisons of the value of the same commodity. Although Smith does not explicitly make the assumption of a stable wage share, that assumption seems to be consistent with his views as to what happens in the "progressive" state of a country's development. Indeed Smith, differently from Ricardo and Marx, maintains that wages too tend to increase with the increase in income, so that the wage share can well remain stable. If, then, the specific shares going to profit and rent vary, this does alter our argument. After all, that assumption does not seem so farfetched if one thinks of the large literature intended to explain the relative stability of the wage share in modern times—say, in the hundred years preceding the second world war.

Ricardo denies, at least as a rule, the equivalence between the two standards (labor commanded and labor embodied) mainly on the basis of the tendency toward diminishing returns from land, a tendency that Smith is far from considering universal in agriculture. In particular, Smith thinks that corn is generally produced under conditions of constant costs.

Let us consider Ricardo's argument. If the quantity of labor required to produce a given quantity of food and necessaries increases—says Ricardo—

Table 1.1

Ricardo						Smith					
H	W	HW	δ	P = HW/δ	P/W	H	W	HW	δ	P = HW/δ	P/W
1	5	5	0.25	20	4	1	5	5	0.25	20	4
2	10	20	0.50	40	4	1	10	10	0.25	40	4

the money wage should increase in proportion to preserve the purchasing power of laborer, but

food and necessaries in this case will have risen, if estimated by the *quantity* of labour necessary to their production, while they will scarcely have increased in value, if measured by the quantity of labour for which they will exchange. (*Works* I., i., 14)

A numerical example may clarify the question. I refer to the conditions of production of corn in two situations and consider the consequences of both Ricardo's and Smith's assumptions. In both cases wages increase. In the case of Ricardo such an increase is made necessary by the increasing costs of corn in terms of labor (in terms of purchasing power the wage rate does not increase), whereas in the case of Smith the increase of wages does not depend on this (the unit again is in terms of paper money or, if δ is taken as constant also in the case of the commodity used as money, in terms of a commodity produced with quantities of labor varying in inverse proportion to wages). See table 1.1.

Following Ricardo's assumptions of diminishing returns, constant purchasing power of wages in terms of corn (W/P), it is true then that the value of corn would rise if estimated by labor embodied (H); it would not rise at all—according to his second assumption—if measured by labor commanded (P/W). (The rise in δ is the necessary consequence of the said two assumptions. For Ricardo, a rise in δ would imply a decline in the share accruing to profits.) But it is also true that, on the basis of Smith's assumptions, labor embodied and labor commanded are equivalent, provided δ remains constant even if the wage rate increases.

The assumption that corn is produced at constant costs plays an important role in Smith's analysis in that it allows him to use the price of corn as a standard measure instead of the price of labor to make intertemporal comparisons. Smith uses the former instead of the latter for practical reasons, because "the price of labor can scarce ever be known with any degree of exactness," whereas the prices of corn "are in general better known" (*WN* I., v., 22). Such a substitution is possible precisely because corn, which represents "the principal part of the subsistence of the laborer," is produced at approximately constant costs.

This is the consequence of two contrasting forces: on the one hand, the real price of corn would tend to decrease owing to the increase of the productive powers of labor; on the other, the real price of corn would tend to increase because the real price of cattle, "the principal instruments of agriculture," tends to increase. In early times cattle were almost free goods, because there were large areas of "unimproved wilds"; later the "unimproved wilds" became insufficient and cattle had to be raised, to an increasing extent, by labor.[7] Moreover the relatively high costs of transportation of corn, considerably higher than gold and silver, to some extent isolate the different nations,[8] a consideration that allows Smith to maintain that the forces affecting the cost of corn tend to compensate each other in every "stage of development.' (Ricardo is very critical of Smith's corn standard, but nowhere does he discuss the arguments concerning the two contrasting forces or the comparative costs of transportation.)

Smith was aware that a precise balance between those two contrasting forces was out of the question, but he thought—correctly in my opinion—that silver or gold would have been a much worse standard when considering long historical periods because in time the value of these metals is bound to vary considerably owing to the discovery of new, abundant mines or to the gradual exhaustion of the existing mines. Silver or gold could be used only for relatively short periods; for long or very long periods corn was to be preferred. To be sure, after the revolution in the means of transportation, which took place in the last quarter of the nineteenth century, and after the gradual substitution of cattle as an instrument of agriculture by tractors and other machines, Smith's arguments no longer hold. But in Smith's time these arguments were reasonable; moreover he related his analysis to the distant past.[9] This is not simply an instance of Adam Smith's method of casting all his arguments in a historical perspective; in my view his approach is principally due to the fact that he was conscious of living in a period of great actual and potential economic and social change, so that long-run comparisons were important as a precondition for understanding the direction and the velocity of these changes. This appears clearly in chapter xi of Book I, where the corn standard is used to distinguish movements of prices due to the relative scarcity or abundance of silver from those determined by changes in the conditions of production. The point is that the "progress of improvement" causes the "real price" of certain commodities to rise and that of other commodities to fall (the "real price" being the price in terms of labor or corn). The behavior of the real prices of the different sorts of commodities can therefore be taken as an indication of the stage of development reached by a country: as I said, for Smith the theory of prices and the theory of economic growth intertwine.

More particularly one of the main purposes of the long "Digression"—where the corn standard is used precisely to isolate the price changes due to the relative scarcity or abundance of silver—was to eradicate the mercantilist opinion that the increase in the quantity of gold and silver in Europe had in some way promoted economic growth:

> The increase of the quantity of gold and silver in Europe, and the increase of its manufactures and agriculture, are two events which, though they have happened nearly about the same time, yet have arisen from very different causes, and have scarcely any natural connection with one another. The one has arisen from a mere accident, in which neither prudence nor policy either had or could have any share: The other from the fall of the feudal system, and from the establishment of a government which afforded to industry the only encouragement which it requires, some tolerable security that it shall enjoy the fruits of its own labour. Poland, where the feudal system still continues to take place, is at this day as beggarly a country as it was before the discovery of America . . . . Spain and Portugal, the countries which possess the mines, are, after Poland, perhaps, the two most beggarly countries in Europe . . . . Though the feudal system has been abolished in Spain and Portugal, it has not been succeeded by a much better.[10]

In any case it is clear that the corn standard works better than the silver standard, considering the purposes Smith had in mind. It is equally clear that the emphasis Ricardo laid on diminishing returns from land is in some way connected with the conditions of his times, though Ricardo does not seem to be aware of this: the price of corn fluctuated on a very high level and, presumably also because the much higher costs and risks of transportation originated by the Napoleonic Wars, the cultivation of corn underwent, in England, a considerable expansion, with the consequences envisaged by Ricardo.[11]

All things considered then, even if the corn standard lost much of its meaning after the transport revolution and the increased use of machinery in agriculture, it remains useful for the comparison of values "at distant times and places" in the historical period studied by Smith and even until the middle of the past century. As a matter of fact that standard is still used today by economic historians, when they study the economy of relatively ancient periods. In any case beginning with the second half of the nineteenth century, data concerning the price of labor were more complete and less unreliable than had been the case before and during Smith's time. And we should not forget that the corn standard was used by Smith only as a substitute for the labor standard.

1.4 Different Standards of Value

Smith was mainly interested in analyzing the impact of changes in technology on the values of different commodities in different times and places, whereas, as Sraffa has pointed out, "the problem of value that interested Ricardo was how to find a measure of value which would be invariant to changes in the division of the product".[12] In dealing with this problem, Ricardo started with labor embodied but then modified his position by introducing, as a measure of value, an abstract money "produced with such proportions of the two kinds of capital as approach nearest to the average quantity employed in the production of most commodities" (*Works* I., i., VI. 3). The final step, along this route, has been Sraffa's standard commodity, which is in fact rigorously "invariant to changes in the division of the product" in terms of its own means of production.

From the point of view of accumulation the best standard is "value" conceived as the property of a commodity to command labor: since for Smith, the accumulation of capital consists in the progressive increase in the number of productive laborers, and since this increase (owing to progress in the division of labor) is necessarily accompanied by an increase in the efficiency of productive laborers, technical progress reduces the command of commodities over labor. It follows that the rate of increase in total output, or the "annual produce," is higher, at least as a rule, than the rate of increase in the number of productive laborers (the possibility of making the assumption of an unchanged technology when total output increases is alien to Smith).

The distinction between "labor commanded" and "annual produce" corresponds to the distinction between "value in exchange" and "value in use," or else between "value" and "riches".[13] In modern language the best measure of this type of "value" is the wage deflator, whereas the best measure of "riches" is the price deflator, both measures being necessarily approximate but the former less than the latter. Smith started his great work with the consideration of "riches" but then concentrated on "values"; therefore he was justified in using almost exclusively the wage deflator.[14]

In his introduction and then in several other places, but always incidentally, Smith considered the behavior of the "annual produce" as such or in relation to the great body of consumers (i.e., to the whole population, or what we call today per capita income), the level of which depends, according to Smith, on the efficiency of the productive workers and on the proportion represented by such laborers of the total population. In modern language, if we call Y the "annual produce" in money terms, P_y a price index, π_y overall productivity, and E employment of productive workers, we have the following identity:

$$\frac{Y}{P_y} \equiv \pi_y E. \tag{1.1}$$

Dividing both terms by total population, we have

$$Y_c \equiv \pi_y E_s, \tag{1.1}$$

where Y_c is the real per capita income (real in the modern sense) and E_s the share of productive employment. By multiplying both terms of (1.1) by P_y/W_y, we have

$$\frac{Y}{W_y} = \frac{\pi_y E P_y}{W_y}, \tag{1.1a}$$

where W_y is wage per productive worker.

If we consider a price equation of the type

$$P = \frac{\alpha W_y}{\pi_y}, \tag{1.1b}$$

where $\alpha = 1 + r$, with r being the rate of profit, we have, applying (1.1b) to the whole economy and substituting (1.1b) in (1.1),

$$\frac{Y}{W_y} = \alpha E. \tag{1.2}$$

Assuming as constant the distribution of income between profits and wages, this shows that variations of demand for productive labor correspond to the variations of the "annual produce" measured in wage units.

If we take into account imported raw materials, the price equation becomes

$$P = \alpha \left(\frac{W_y}{\pi_y} + M_y \right), \tag{1.3}$$

where M_y is the money value of raw materials per unit of output, and for the whole economy we have

$$\frac{P_y}{W_y} = \frac{\alpha}{\pi_y} \cdot \frac{P_y}{P_y - \alpha M_y}. \tag{1.4}$$

Substituting (1.4) in (1.1a), we have

$$\frac{Y}{W_y} = E\alpha \frac{1}{1 - \alpha M_y/P_y}. \tag{1.5}$$

This shows that if we allow for imported raw materials, two conditions regulate the correspondence between demand for productive labor and "annual produce" measured in wage units: (1) stability of distributive shares and (2) the constant ratio between the prices of raw materials and those of finished products.

If we consider the amount of commodities commanded by labor (i.e., real wages in the modern sense), we have

$$\frac{W_y}{P_y} = \frac{\pi_y}{\alpha},$$
(1.6)

or if we use equation (1.3),

$$\frac{W_y}{P_y} = \pi_y\left(\frac{1}{\alpha} - \frac{M_y}{P_y}\right).$$
(1.7)

This equation shows that in an open economy the variations of "real wages" correspond to those of productivity, given α and the ratio M_y/P_y (this ratio is relevant when considering the question of the terms of trade); it also shows that given α and M_y/P_y, the behavior of P_y can coincide with that of W_y if productivity does not vary. In such a case the variations of prices and wages go together, so the deflator used is a matter of indifference.

As is well known, Keynes prefers to use the wage unit rather than a price index on the grounds that the "general price level" is uncertain and "undetermined" and "more suitable in the field of historical and statistical description".[15] Moreover Keynes, like Smith, was interested in analyzing the forces that regulate the volume of employment. Keynes, however, considers technology as given, so that in his theory, apart from its lesser uncertainty, the wage unit does not play, the role it plays in Smith, for whom technological changes and the consequent increase in the "productive powers" of labor were essential characteristics of modern economies. In addition to allowing for technological changes, new goods make any price deflator very ambiguous, especially in the long run; likewise the appearance of new skills in the labor force gives rise to ambiguity, but this is much less serious. All things considered, then, the view that the wage unit in Keynes can be substituted by a price index is well founded, whereas it would not be the case in Smith. In principle, then, the wage unit is a much better standard than the price deflator, but it does not satisfy that "perfect precision—such as our causal analysis requires, whether or not our knowledge of the actual values of the relevant quantities is complete or exact" (Keynes, *General Theory* 40). Such precision can, and must, be the prerogative of a standard to be used in measuring the changes in relative prices arising from changes in the distribution of income, given the technology.

In brief, we probably need three standards of value. We may use a price index as a deflator when we intend to consider the variations of the "annual produce" or of "riches." We may use a wage unit (labor commanded) when we intend to consider the variations of the demand for labor or, more properly, the consequences of technological progress. (These two standards are necessarily approximate.) We must use a different, rigorous, standard when we intend to consider Ricardo's problem.

A final observation: "Labor commanded," as a standard, is not only an analytical tool, whose use is to be recommended in the theory of economic development, it also has certain practical uses. As a matter of fact, we encounter it when we visit another country, where we cannot rely on the exchange rate to compare the prices of goods with those in the country we live in. To make meaningful comparisons, we are bound to use the rule of labor commanded, which we do use even if we are not fully aware of that fact. This becomes an even more stringent necessity if we visit a country in an entirely different stage of development or with radically different institutions.

1.5 The Competitive Mechanism and the Process of Economic Growth

According to Smith, "as art and industry advance," the prices of different commodities behave in different ways: certain commodities become dearer and dearer, whereas others tend to fall (when I say "prices," I mean "real prices" or prices in terms of labor). Several sorts of rude produce belong to the first category: for example, "cattle, poultry, game of all kinds, the useful fossils and minerals of the earth." As a rule vegetable food and manufactured products belong to the second category. The animal products grow dearer because "during a long period in the progress of improvement," the quantity of such commodities can increase only at increasing costs. (In this context we are referring to stages of development, and therefore we have to allow for both technological changes and variations in the three component parts of the natural price.)

It is worth noticing that, apart from corn which is a special case, agricultural products are not concentrated in the "increasing cost" category but can be found in both categories. Thus division of labor, a process that works everywhere, tends to prevail in most vegetable products, because the improvement in the methods of cultivation affects such commodities no less than corn and because they require less land (and presumably less use of cattle) than corn (WN I., xi., n. "Conclution of the Digression"). "As art and industry advance," however, the price of vegetable products would tend to fall less than the price of manufactures, since the scope for the division of labor in agriculture is naturally more restricted than in manufactures.[16]

The price of manufactures tends to fall, thanks to the increase in the "productive powers" of labor, that is, to the decrease in the labor input. The decrease as a rule is such as to more than compensate both the increase in the price of labor and the increase in the price of raw materials (WN I., viii., 56; I., xi., III, "Effects of the Progress," 1–2).

In the short run it remains true that the market price of manufactures depends on supply (i.e., on the quantity brought to market), and demand. In the long run the market price tends to coincide with the natural price which depends on costs, that is, referring to the price equation (1.3), on the cost of labor (W_m/π_m) and on the cost of materials (M_m). (since we are considering the manufacturing sector, here M_m is the money value of raw materials both imported and produced at home in other sectors.) If W_m increases but π_m rises more than in proportion, the cost of labor decreases, and this decrease may be such as to more than compensate the increase (if any) in M_m.[17] The falling trend of prices of manufactures, then, depends on the fall in the labor input, that is, on the rise in the "productive powers" of labor. In the opinion of Smith, this rise is more rapid than that of the wage rate.

The wage rate in the short run depends on the demand for labor; it depends also on the price of provisions, but paradoxically, in the short run the wage rate and the price of provisions frequently vary in opposite directions.[18] In the long run the level of wages depends on the "trend" of the demand for labor and on the price of provisions, so as a rule the supply of labor will adapt itself to demand. In each stage of development the purchasing power of wages in terms of provisions tends to be constant. The real price of labor tends to increase "in the progressive state of the society," which implies an increasing accumulation of capital, that is, an increasing demand for productive laborers. In its turn the accumulation of capital depends on profit, in the sense that profit is the precondition for accumulation. It is enough that profit be "something more than what is sufficient to compensate the occasional losses to which every employment of stock is exposed": this is the lowest—the minimum acceptable or "tolerable"—rate of profit (WN I., ix., 10, 18). For several reasons too high a profit may represent a brake and not a stimulus to accumulation, and the fall in the rate of profits, up to a point, can even speed up accumulation. It is true that an "extraordinary profit" may stimulate accumulation but only if it is temporary, and it is temporary only if the entry is free and competition can work, though not immediately:

The establishment of any new manufacture, of any new branch of commerce, or of any new practice in agriculture, is always a speculation, from which the projector promises himself extraordinary profits. These profits sometimes are very great, and sometimes, more frequently, perhaps, they are quite otherwise; but in general they bear no regular proportion to those of other old trades in the neighbourhood. If the project succeeds, they are commonly at first very high. When the trade or practice becomes thoroughly established and well known, the competition reduces them to the level of other trades. (WN I., x., I, 43)[19]

High *and* stable profits are always the consequence of monopoly, that is, of obstacles to entry. For several reasons which often coexist, monopoly—except in very special cases[20]—is damaging for economic growth:

1. High price. "The monopolists, by keeping the market constantly understocked, by never fully supplying the effectual demand, sell their commodities much above the natural price, and raise their emoluments, whether they consist in wages or profit, greatly above their natural rate." (*WN* I., vii., 26)

2. Bad management. "Monopoly . . . is a great enemy to good management, which can never be universally established but in consequence of that free and universal competition which forces everybody to have recourse to it for the sake of self-defense." (*WN* I., xi., I, 5)

3. Extraordinary waste. "Since the establishment of the English East India Company, for example, the other inhabitants of England, over and above being excluded from the trade, must have paid in the price of the East India goods which they have consumed, not only for all the extraordinary profits which the company may have made upon those goods in consequence of their monopoly, but for all the extraordinary waste which the fraud and abuse, inseparable from the management of the affairs of so great a company, must necessarily have occasioned." (*WN* IV., vii., III, 91)

4. Reduction in revenue and therefore savings. ". . . as capital can be increased only by savings from revenue, the monopoly, by hindering it from affording so great a revenue as it would otherwise afford, necessarily hinders it from increasing so fast as it would otherwise increase, and consequently from maintaining a still greater quantity of productive labor, and affording a still greater revenue to the industrious of that country [the country that has established the monopoly of the colonial trade]." (Ibid., 57)

In Smith's conception, then, the fall in the rate of profit was a positive phenomenon *if* it reflected the gradual elimination of monopolistic barriers, especially those determined by laws and institutions, that is, provided it reflected increasing competition and did not fall to the minimum acceptable level. When the rate of profit is approaching this level, however, stagnation is not the necessary outcome: with very low profits, capital would go in the direction of foreign trade or would "disgorge itself" into the carrying trade, both at home and abroad (*WN* I., ix., 9–10; II., v., 35). For Smith, then, the tendency of profits to fall has both a different cause and a different effect than for Ricardo. For Ricardo, in the long run, the fall in the rate of profit would simply bring accumulation to a halt (*Works* I., vi., 28). Smith, however, indicates two more possibilities: one is given by "the acquisition of new territory, or of new branches of trade," which may check and, for a time, even reverse the tendency of profits to fall; the other is given by the export of capital (WN I., ix., 12, 10), which (we can infer) would increase the revenue of the investors or of the lenders but certainly not contribute to the accumulation of capital in the home market. In any case, if it is true that very low profits are a consequence of the great prosperity of a country, it is also true that very low profits discourage further accumulation.[21] The rate of profit, then, would approach the minimum level and accumulation would tend to stagnate "in a country which had acquired its full complement of riches" which "is consistent with the nature of its laws and institutions" (WN I., ix., 15). In modern language this peculiar type of stationary state would be described as economic maturity.

Competition, then, is seen by Smith as an almost uninterrupted process of economic growth at the end of which there is a kind of stationary state.

All events, spontaneous and political, that reduce monopolistic barriers, and thus increase competition, contribute to sustain economic growth. In this connection the restoration of free importation by gradually reducing import duties, the abolition of the exclusive privileges of the great companies in the colonial trade, and the repeal of the statute of apprenticeship (i.e., the elimination of what are "real encroachments upon natural liberty") are all measures that, though extremely difficult to introduce, will promote economic growth. In a different sense,

Good roads, canals, and navigable rivers, by diminishing the expence of carriage, put the remote parts of the country more nearly upon a level with those in the neighbourhood of the town. They are upon that account the greatest of all improvements. They encourage the cultivation of the remote, which must always be the most extensive circle of the country. They are advantageous to the town, by breaking down the monopoly of the country in its neighbourhood. They are advantageous even to that part of the country. Though they introduce some rival commodities into the old market, they open many new markets to its produce. (WN I., xi., I, 5)

Falling prices of those productions where the effects of the division of labor can prevail over the effects of natural scarcity, rising wages, and falling profits are, for Smith, the main aspects of a process of growth characterized by the competitive mechanism.

The statistical picture of the nineteenth century seems to bear out Smith's expectations. During two periods, 1800–1815 and 1850 to 1870, prices tended to rise as a consequence of external events such as the Napoleonic Wars and the American Civil War and also fluctuations in the rate of increase of the

Table 1.2

	1820–1870	1870–1897
1. Agricultural prices		
1a—Vegetable products	Declining	Declining
1b—Wheat	Stationary	Declining
1c—Animal products	First stationary, then slowly rising	Declining
2. Prices of exports (mostly manufactured products) (A)	Falling	Falling
3. Prices of imports (mostly primary products) (B)	First slowly falling, then stationary	Falling
4. Terms of trade (A/B)	Falling	Stationary
5. Wages in manufacturing	First stationary, then slowly rising	Rising

monetary stock. But the fundamental trend of most prices was downward. To make appropriate comments, it is advisable to exclude the first two decades, which were strongly influenced by the Napoleonic Wars, and to divide the next 80 years into two periods, 1820 to 1870 and 1870 to 1900, or more precisely, 1897, when the long-term fall of prices came to an end. The reason for this subdivision is that in the seventies the transportation revolution (railways and steamships) occurred in the most advanced countries of the world, with consequences that were particularly marked in the agricultural markets. Table 1.2 shows the main trends in the two subperiods[22]

The behavior of prices and wages during the first subperiod corresponds almost exactly to Smith's expectations; even the expectation of a fall in the price of vegetable products, which was slower than the fall in the prices of manufactures, seems to be borne out by the facts. In the second period there are certain exceptions; the prices of wheat and of animal products are falling. In Smith's conception, such behavior would be possible, assuming an increasing relative scarcity of the metal used as money—gold in that period. I think that, at most, this can be accepted as a subsidiary hypothesis. The main explanation is the rapid fall in costs due to the transportation revolution which opened world markets both to the vegetable products of North America and to the animal products of South America. A third exception may be given by the behavior of the terms of trade. Since most of the exports of the United Kingdom were, and still are, manufactures and most of the imports were, and still are, primary products, the terms of trade should have been falling, as had happened in the first subperiod; instead they were stationary. Such behavior can be explained only in part by the transportation revolution, and I will reconsider this question later on.

Apart from these three exceptions the behavior of other prices and of wages corresponds to Smith's expectations also in the second subperiod. In this subperiod even the rate of interest—which was gradually falling—seems to behave in the way that Smith would have expected in a mature economy. Another indication of such Smithian maturity was the notable increase of investment abroad.

On the whole in the nineteenth century the competitive mechanism seems to prevail. The structure within which such a mechanism works is characterized by relatively small firms and easy entry, by the absence, or irrelevance, of trade unions, by the relatively modest size of government revenue and expenditure, and, of course, by extremely limited government intervention in the economy.

1.6 A Comparison between the Past and the Present Century

The modern picture has changed radically: small firms can be found in great numbers in agriculture and the retail trade, but agriculture, in countries like the United Kingdom, represents a tiny fraction of total income and employment. The retail trade, apart from great imperfections since the time of Smith (and not ignored by him), is not and has never been a leading sector in economic growth. Not only banking and insurance but also several branches of industry are dominated by large firms that as a rule are organized in the form of joint stock companies, though their legal framework is different from the one existing in Smith's time.[23] Trade unions, which were prohibited in those times, have been organized and are today very powerful.[24] In several branches of industry production has been carried out by a decreasing number of firms of an increasing size, that is, a process of concentration has taken place. Certain companies that have acquired, for technical reasons, one form or another of monopolistic power have been nationalized; several prices are administered by public bodies, especially in public utilities. More generally, the intervention of government has acquired a very large and continuously growing importance. Large corporations, powerful trade unions, and growing government intervention are all variously linked together and, fundamentally, are all the result of the same objective process, that is, of the process of concentration.

At the origin of this process we do not find changes in "utility" or in the tastes of the consumers; we find changes in the conditions of production, namely, technological progress which has influenced the whole of economic life, including directly or indirectly changes in the habits of consumers. In the final analysis, at the root of the process of concentration we find a particular kind of division of labor: an increasing specialization of operations coordinated within organizational units of increasing size. This kind of division of labor, as I have already observed, has given rise to various types of "economies of scale." Thus today we have besides the strictly technological and organizational economies of scale, what we may call commercial, financial, and even "scientific" economies of scale (since only very large companies can afford to organize costly laboratories for applied scientific research). The process of concentration has given rise first to large joint stock companies and then also to cartels and, mainly through mergers, to trusts and conglomerates. In certain activities the process of concentration has surpassed national boundaries and acquired world dimensions, giving rise to multinational corporations and accelerating the changes in the structure of world trade and the international division of labor.[25]

In such a situation the market form prevailing in industry, and particularly in manufacturing industry, is certainly no more Smith's competition, though it would be misleading to say that it is similar in character to Smith's monopoly. In a great number of activities, particularly in industry which is the most dynamic sector of the economy, a novel market form has emerged, oligopoly, that partakes of some of the characteristics of monopoly and some of those of competition, as several contemporary economists have pointed out. We find oligopoly not only in highly concentrated industries producing homogeneous commodities but also in industries producing highly differentiated commodities.

In the industrial markets where oligopoly prevails, entry is not free: the main obstacle to entry is given by the relatively large size of output to produce or to sell economically, a size large in relation to the extent of the market. (In differentiated industries costly and risky advertising campaigns need first to be launched and then to be repeated in order to break into the market; therefore large sales are necessary to recoup these costs, which represent a variety of overhead costs.)

If the main obstacle to entry is given by the size of the output the individual firm must produce in relation to the extent of the market, then that obstacle shifts, so to speak, if the market expands. Under the said conditions we cannot assume, not even as the result of a long-run tendency, a unique level of cost of production for all the firms; we have to allow for different cost levels in different firms. The larger the size of output, the lower the cost; but given the extension of the market, the larger the size, the more difficult is the entry of a new firm. On these contradictory elements the industry finds a sort of dynamic equilibrium, that is, a situation acceptable to all firms. Such a situation changes either because the market expands or because costs vary, or both (the market expansion necessarily implies cost changes, whereas the opposite is not true). In any case costs represent the logical basis of two concepts—the entry-preventing price and the elimination price—which are essential in order to analyze both price determination and price variations.

In competition the expansion of production can take place *either* because demand expands, which in time promotes cost and price reductions, *or* because costs are reduced and these reductions, which generate an "extraordinary profit," attract competition and promote an expansion of production. In both cases the result is a greater production and a lower price. Owing to the obstacles to entry in oligopoly, the first route to growth—demand— becomes ever more important relative to the second one. The demand can increase not only "naturally" (due to an expansion originating in private firms or in foreign demand) but also "artificially" (e.g., public expenditure and public orders to firms). The cost reductions are transformed into price reductions only when they depend on innovations accessible to all firms or on the reductions in the prices of the means of production, especially labor and raw materials. As for the cost of labor, it falls when money wages increase less than productivity—or, as Smith puts it, when the reduction in the quantity of labor per unit of output more than compensates the increase in wages. But this behavior, which Smith considered to be the rule in a rapidly expanding economy, is today less and less frequent, owing to the great power acquired by the unions.

In oligopoly, as well as in competition, prices depend on costs, but unlike competition, prices depend on costs not only in the long run but also in the short run. The difference is very important indeed, because it is this dependence that largely explains why technological progress does not give rise any more to a downward trend of prices, at least in industry. As a matter of fact, with constant prices of raw materials, technical progress reduces costs only if wages do not rise or if, as Smith assumes, wages rise less than in proportion to the reduction of labor input. The Smithian case still occurs today, but more and more seldom; as a rule, owing to the market power of the trade unions, the cost of labor either remains constant or increases, and consequently prices, or more precisely wholesale prices, either remain constant or, much more often, increase. Retail prices increase even when wholesale prices remain constant, because wages increase at similar rates all over the economy, but the efficiency of labor in retail trade often increases less than the general average; moreover services increase in proportion to wages. Today as in the past, the Smithian ratio P/W tends to fall due to technical progress while both prices and wages tend to rise (the latter more than the former). In modern conditions inflation is a tendency arising from the very structure of the product markets as well as of the labor market.

Under the new conditions demand—in the sense of market size—has not only a strategic role in economic growth, it has an essential role also in short-run changes of income and employment. The fact is that in competition, when demand falls, price falls, since firms cannot do anything to prevent that fall. In oligopoly, firms, and particularly the leading firms, which control sizable shares of the market and must be concerned with the behavior of total demand, can avoid a price fall by reducing their output; they can also avoid a price rise when demand increases. As a matter of fact the leading firms normally command a certain amount of unused capacity to face seasonal fluctuations and the long-run increase in demand, if such an increase is expected; the unused capacity can also serve as a deterrent against potential entrants. Therefore an increase of demand normally determines an increase of output and not of prices; if prices increase, this occurs because costs increase.

The outcome of all this is that, under contemporary conditions, in industry a considerable price fall can take place only during a severe slump in output and employment, mainly as a consequence of a fall in costs, whereas in the past century a price fall was a normal occurrence and only exceptionally accompanied by an interruption of the process of economic growth. Money wages, which in the past century were fluctuating with the business cycle, although on a rising trend, have in our century shown an increasing downward rigidity. After the second world war absolute decreases in money wages are practically absent in all advanced countries; what is left to be explained is the change in the rate of increase.

Technological progress and product differentiation, then, have progressively increased the obstacles to entry in a growing number of markets. Moreover, though such a trend has been to some extent counterbalanced by decreasing transport costs, all things considered, the market power of many firms has increased. This, however, has only in certain periods and in certain countries given rise to a general increase in profit margins, since especially in the postwar period the market power of the unions has increased not less but more than the market power of the firms. The consequence has been an increase both in the wage rate and the share of wages in the national income and, correspondingly, a reduction in the profit share, at least in the industrial sector of several countries. In any case the market power of the unions depends on that of the firms.

Since the market power of the modern oligopolistic firms is not as a rule the result of legal or institutional obstacles to entry, but of obstacles determined by the very process of economic growth, it cannot be progressively reduced in the way Smith suggested for the monopolies of his own times. Yet that power is often enhanced by laws and agreements of various kinds, which can be attacked on the legal and political plane. Besides, the reduction of protectionist barriers between countries—a typically Smithian prescription—can to some extent reduce that power. On the whole, however, the structure of contemporary advanced economies, characterized by giant corporations, powerful trade unions, and a large government apparatus, poses problems of economic policy completely different from those envisaged by Adam Smith. In truth we can learn not so much from his prescriptions as from the nature of his approach, which is at once theoretical and historical and points to the necessity of studying economies in their global movements.

1.7 The Terms of Trade and Underdeveloped Countries

I have already noted that, whereas during the first sixty or seventy years of the last century the terms of trade of the United Kingdom had a tendency to fall (i.e., they moved "against" British exports, mostly manufactured goods, and in favor of imports, mostly primary goods), in the last thirty years of the century the terms of trade remained about stationary. I also noted that the falling trend corresponded to Smith's expectations, whereas the stationary trend did not, because, according to him, the rate of increase in the "productive powers" of labor tends to be higher in the case of manufactures than in the cases of agricultural and mineral products. In other words, in agricultural and mineral products the increase in productivity is unable to compensate, or more than compensate, the effects of natural scarcity.

In this century it appears that the terms of trade of those industrialized countries that import most of the raw materials they use have until very recently remained stationary or, more probably, have risen; that is, they have moved in favor of manufacturers and against primary products.

As is well known, the question of the terms of trade is a very controversial one, especially if we consider, on the one extreme, the industrialized countries and, on the other, the countries that base their economy on the production and export of a limited number of primary commodities. Here it is enough to observe that, if it is true that the rate of increase in productivity has been higher in industrialized than in underdeveloped countries, then stationary terms of trade will increase the gap between the two categories of country. It is an indication that the fruits of technological progress have been largely "captured" by laborers and the other income earners of industrialized countries. (The different behavior of productivity depends not only or not so much on the nature of agriculture or on grounds of natural scarcity as on the much slower technological progress of the poorer countries.)

All in all the present-day relations between advanced countries and underdeveloped countries resemble those between "towns corporate" and the country as described by Smith:

> The government of towns corporate was altogether in the hands of traders and artificers; and it was the manifest interest of every particular class of them, to prevent the market from being overstocked, as they commonly express it, with their own particular species of industry; which is in reality to keep it always understocked. Each class was eager to establish regulations proper for this purpose, and provided it was allowed to do so, was willing to consent that every other class should do the same. In consequence of such regulations, indeed, each class was obliged to buy the goods they had occasion for from every other within the town, somewhat dearer than they otherwise might have done. But in recompence, they were enabled to sell their own just as much dearer; so that so far it was as broad as long, as they say; and in the dealings of the different classes within the town with one another, none of them were losers by these regulations. But in their dealings with the country, they were all great gainers; and in these latter dealings consists the whole trade which supports and enriches every town. (WN I., x., II, 18)

Certainly the direction of the trend in the terms of trade is not, in itself, a decisive factor for the development of underdeveloped countries; Kindleberger's "capacity to transform," the capacity of an economy to adapt itself and to exploit the changing conditions of the internal and international markets, is even more important. It is also true, however, that an adverse or even a stationary trend in the terms of trade is an additional brake on the development of underdeveloped countries. Moreover their high and relatively rigid specialization is itself a consequence of the domination of certain advanced countries, so that the behavior of the terms of trade *and* the rigidity of the specialization are to be analyzed together.

It seems that in recent years the movements of the terms of trade have often been against the advanced countries and in favor of underdeveloped countries. The most striking change of this kind has been that of the price of oil. Owing to the greater political strength of several underdeveloped countries worldwide, a political strength that has been enhanced by the rivalry among the great powers; to certain natural scarcities that are beginning to appear despite technological progress in agriculture, in mining, and in the invention of substitutes; and further to the instability of the "dollar standard" and the consequent higher "propensity to speculate" in raw materials— considering all these forces and changes, it is possible that the terms of trade between manufactures and primary products will tend to move more and more often in favor of the latter products. Such a tendency, if it asserted itself, would create new economic hardships for the advanced countries.[26] But it is to be feared that any process through which countries now underdeveloped will move toward equality with respect to the advanced countries will be long, difficult, and painful for all. And since most underdeveloped countries in olden or in recent times were colonies, it is well to enlarge the scope of our thoughts and reflect on the following important observations of Adam Smith:

> The discovery of America, and that of a passage to the East Indies by the Cape of Good Hope, are the two greatest and most important events recorded in the history of mankind. Their consequences have already been very great; but, in the short period of between two and three centuries which has elapsed since these discoveries were made, it is impossible that the whole extent of their consequences can have been seen. What benefits, or what misfortunes to mankind may hereafter result from those great events, no human wisdom can foresee. By uniting, in some measure, the most distant parts of the world, by enabling them to relieve one another's wants, to increase one another's enjoyments, and to encourage one another's industry, their general tendency would seem to be beneficial. To the natives, however, both of the East and West Indies, all the commercial benefits which can have resulted from those events have been sunk and lost in the dreadful misfortunes which they have occasioned. These misfortunes, however, seem to have arisen rather from accident than from any thing in the nature of those events themselves. At the particular time when these discoveries were made, the superiority of force happened to be so great on the side of the Europeans, that they were enabled to commit with impunity every sort of injustice in those remote countries. Hereafter, perhaps, the natives of those countries may grow stronger, or those of Europe may grow weaker, and the inhabitants of all the different quarters of the world may arrive at that equality of courage and force which, by inspiring mutual fear, can alone overawe the injustice of independent nations into some sort of respect for the rights of one another. But nothing seems more likely to establish this equality of force than that mutual communication of knowledge and of all sorts of improvements which an extensive commerce from all countries to all countries naturally, or rather necessarily, carries along with it. (*WN* IV., vii., III, 80)

Smith's conception of social life, I have already noted, is by no means idyllic and contrasts quite decidedly with the conventional optimism that would prevail later on. Yet his conclusions, as well as his recommendations, are never pessimistic. In this particular but extremely important case we can accept Smith's conclusion provided we recognize that, under modern conditions, "an extensive commerce" as such is not enough to promote equality, even if we take into account all the qualifications accompanying that conclusion. Smith himself, in another respect, points out that that "liberty and independency" which were arrived at by the inhabitants of the towns "much earlier than the occupiers of land in the country," were the prerequisite of the rise and progress of the towns in Europe, after the fall of the Roman Empire (*WN* III., iii., 3). After the second world war several colonies or quasi colonies have in fact acquired some sort of "liberty and independency." But this is only a prerequisite of a process of development that under modern conditions will necessarily be very different from all the processes analyzed in *The Wealth of Nations*. Even the processes of development taking place in our time in advanced countries are very different from those studied by Smith. All this, however, does not mean that today *The Wealth of Nations* can interest only historians of economic thought or students of economic history. Because, to try to understand the societies in which we live, we have to try to understand on the theoretical plane the logic of their movements in long or very long periods. And in this direction the approach developed by Adam Smith in his great work can still give us invaluable help today.

Notes

I am is grateful to W. A. Eltis, P. Garegnani, L. Meldolesi, and A. Roncaglia for their very helpful critical comments and suggestions, and to A. Skinner for help in improving the English expression.

1. References are to the Cannan edition (Methuen, 1930).

2. Marx, *Theorien über den Mehrwert*, Vol. 2 (Berlin, Dietz Verlag, 1959), X., B., 1.

3. *The Works and Correspondence of David Ricardo*, edited by Piero Sraffa with the assistance of Maurice Dobb (Cambridge University Press, 1951), I., xxxv.

4. At present an increasing number of economists use the concept of entry in the analysis of market forms, but more than forty years ago Alberto Breglia was already making a systematic use of this concept ["Cenni di teoria della politica economica," *Giornale degli economisti* (February 1934)].

5. *WN* V., i., e. 26: "Of the Public Works and Institutions which are necessary for facilitating particular Branches of Commerce."

6. This conception of Smith has been repeatedly criticized on the grounds that "a commodity residue" cannot be eliminated. This is true. But, as Sraffa has shown in his *Production of Commodities by means of Commodities* (Cambridge University Press, 1960), ch. vi, this "commodity residue" can be made as small as we like by applying the method which he calls "reduction to dated quantities of labor" which permits us to "resolve" prices into wages and profits (for simplicity rents are neglected).

7. *WN* I., xi., e. 27: "Digression concerning the Variations in the Value of Silver during the Course of the Four Last Centuries."

8. See especially I., xi., c. 21 (part II); I., xi., e. 38; IV., i., 12.

9. In the long "Digression concerning the Variations in the Value of Silver" included in chapter xi of the first book, Smith considers the price of corn in the four centuries preceding his time and distinguishes three periods, the second of which (1560–1640) is dominated by the so-called price revolution. On the basis of his assumptions, Smith

attributes the variations in the price of corn mainly to variations in the value of silver, the former being the measure of the latter. Smith's interpretation, which has an important bearing on the study of price history, has never, so far as I know, been challenged by economic historians.

10. *WN* I., xi., n. 1; "Conclusion of the Digression." (These observations imply a sharp criticism of the view, maintained by some economists and economic historians in our times that the price revolution strongly stimulated economic growth.)

11. According to Smith, in the period 1700 to 1770, the average price of a quarter of wheat fluctuated around the level of 40 to 50 shillings. From 1770 to 1790, according to Tooke and Newmark, the average price did not vary very much; that price jumped to much higher levels from 1790 to 1820, oscillating, first, around 60 to 70 shillings and, then, around 80 to 90 shillings per quarter, with peaks exceeding 100 shillings. In the following three or four decades the average price of wheat fell to its old level, oscillating around 55 shillings, without showing either a tendency to rise or to fall. T. Tooke and W. Newmark, *History of Prices* (6 vols., 1838–57; reprint ed. by T. E. Gregory, London, P. S. King and Son, 1928). See figure 1.1 in the appendix.

12. *Works* I., xlviii.

13. The distinction between value and riches, which played an important role in classical economic theory, has become blurred in modern economic theory, which lays a much greater emphasis of utility (value in use) at the expense of the conditions of production and changes in these conditions in the course of time. J. B. Say can be rightly considered as the forerunner of such theoretical development; see Ricardo's forceful criticism of his views in *Works* (I., xx., 14–16).

14. If it is so, then Schumpeter's criticism of the concept of labor commanded is not well founded. Schumpeter thought that the choice made by Smith of this standard was due "to his ignorance of the method of the index number, already invented in that time." J. A. Schumpeter, *History of Economic Analysis* (Oxford University Press, 1954), ch. iii, sec. 4. (It is only true that the price deflator necessarily implies an index number, whereas this is not the case for the wage deflator if the wage rate of common labor is taken as the unit.)

15. J. M. Keynes, *The General Theory of Employment, Interest and Money* (London, Macmillan, 1946), ch. iv. There are several points in common between Keynes and Smith. One is the wage unit; another is the very limited interest in the distribution of income and the great interest in the demand for labor; still another is the question of the relations between wages and prices. It must be said, however, that the similarities in the two theoretical constructions, though very interesting and to some extent significant, do not go very far. To mention only one important difference, Keynes, unlike Smith, was not interested in the economic consequences of technical progress.

16. *WN* I., i., 4. Smith refers this observation to agriculture in general; I refer it to the fall in the real price of vegetable products compared to that of the price of manufactures, since it is quite clear that, in the case of animal products, the effects of the division of labor are more than counterbalanced by the adverse effects of natural scarcity and of increasing costs.

17. Ricardo considers particularly this later possibility; for the rest, he repeats almost literally Smith's concepts: "The natural price of all commodities, excepting raw produce and labour, has a tendency to fall, in the progress of wealth and population; for though, on the one hand, they are enhanced in real value, from the rise in the natural price of the raw materials of which they are made, this is more than counterbalanced by the improvements in machinery, by the better division and distribution of labour, and by the increasing skill, both in science and art, of the producers." (*Works* I., v., 4)

18. The reason is that "in years of plenty, servants frequently leave their masters, and trust their subsistence to what they can make by their own industry. But the same cheapness of provisions, by increasing the fund which is destined for the maintenance of servants, encourages masters, farmers especially, to employ a greater number." The opposite is the case in years of scarcity. (*WN* I., viii., 45–46)

19. This view, which was accepted in full first by Ricardo and then by Marx, anticipates quite clearly, though in a very embryonic way, the main thesis on innovations worked out by Joseph Schumpeter: Schumpeter's innovator is nothing else but Smith's projector. However, see *WN* II., iii., 26, II., iv., 15.

20. As, for instance, in the case of a temporary monopoly, granted by law by means of a patent, of a new machine. (*WN* V., i., III, art I., 48)

21. Compare this interpretation with that proposed by G. S. L. Tucker in his book *Progress and Profits in British Economic Thought, 1650–1850* (Cambridge University Press, 1960), ch. 4.

22. Sources: B. R. Mitchell (with the collaboration of P. Deane), *Abstract of British Historical Statistics* (Cambridge University Press, 1962); A. Imlah, "The Terms of Trade of the United Kingdom 1793–1913," *Journal of Economic History* (1950), n. 2; K. Martin and F. G. Thackeray, "The Terms of Trade in Selected Countries, 1870–1938," *Bulletin of the Oxford Institute of Statistics* (November 1948).

23. It is well known that Smith was very critical of joint stock companies, as he knew them. It is perhaps less known that Smith was in favor of joint stock companies in the case of four activities, the operations of which were "capable of being reduced to what is called routine," that is, banking, insurance, canal and aqueduct construction, and management. Apart from these activities Smith was utterly skeptical as to the capacity of joint stock companies to prosper or even to survive for long, at least in foreign trade, without exclusive privileges granted by law: "Without a monopoly, however, a joint stock company, it would appear from experience, cannot long carry on any branch of foreign trade. To buy in one market, in order to sell, with profit, in another, when there are many competitors in both; to watch over, not only the occasional variations in the demand, but the much greater and more frequent variations in the competition, or in the supply which that demand is likely to get from other people, and to suit with dexterity and judgement both the quantity and quality of each assortment of goods to all these circumstances, is a species of warfare of which the operations are continually changing, and which can scarce ever be conducted successfully, without such an unremitting exertion of vigilance and attention, as cannot long be expected from the directors of a joint stock company." (*WN* V., i., e. 30, "Of the Public Works and

Institutions which are necessary for facilitating particular Branches of Commerce.")
This passage shows very well that Smith's conception of competition is neither idyllic
nor aseptic, like the conception of most contemporary economists—with the exception of Schumpeter, Rothschild, and a few others. Not even the division of labor, so
much praised for its positive effects on economic growth, is seen by Smith as an idyllic
process. (*WN* V., i., III, art. II., 50)

24. "The masters, being fewer in number, can combine much more easily; and the law,
besides, authorises, or at least does not prohibit their combinations, while it prohibits
those of the workmen." The combinations of the masters, however, "are frequently
resisted by a contrary defensive combination of the workmen; who sometimes too,
without any provocation of this kind, combine of their own accord to raise the price of
their labour. Their usual pretences are, sometimes the high price of provisions;
sometimes the great profit which their master makes by their work. But whether their
combinations be offensive or defensive ... They are desperate, and act with the folly
and extravagance of desperate men, who must either starve, or frighten their masters
into an immediate compliance with their demands ... those tumultuous combinations
... generally end in nothing, but the punishment or ruin of the ringleaders." (*WN* I.,
viii., 12, 13) The labor market: *quantum hodie mutatus ab illo*!

25. The multinational corporations operating in "new manufactures" and in "old
established manufactures" base their dominating position mainly on one kind or
another of economies of scale, which are the outcome of a long process of division of
labor. A third category of multinational corporations operating in agriculture and
mining in certain underdeveloped countries base their dominating position on conces-
sions backed by political power for the exploitation of natural resources; such corporations enjoy advantages very similar to those "exclusive privileges" granted to the
joint stock companies operating in the colonial trade in the time of Adam Smith. On the
other hand, certain multinational corporations operating in manufactures enter into
dealings with governments either to sell a part of their products to them or to influence
their behavior; it seems that in such dealings "fraud and abuse" are not exceptional at
all.

26. It is worth reflecting on what equation (1.7) shows concerning real wages (real in
the modern sense): if we consider M_y as the price of imported raw materials and P_y as
the price of finished products, it appears that an increase in the ratio M_y/P_y brings
about, *ceteris paribus*, a diminution either of real wages or of the rate of profit.

Appendix: Ricardo on Diminishing Returns

Adam Smith is mainly concerned with economic development, whereas David
Ricardo is interested almost exclusively in the analysis of the relations between income distribution and the changes in relative prices, with practically
no interest in the problem of economic development. This view is rather
common, but it is not really correct. Ricardo studies the factors affecting the
changes in the distribution of income because he believes that such a study is
essential to understanding the conditions of accumulation, that is, economic

development. As a rule a stable share of profits will imply a stable rate of profit, and until the rate of profit is above a certain minimum, accumulation will take care of itself and will proceed. If the rate of profits falls and approaches the said minimum, then accumulation will tend to come to an end. In fact the share and the rate of profits tend to fall as a consequence of diminishing returns from land. This is regarded by Ricardo primarily as a tendency due to the natural characteristics of land; Ricardo, however, repeatedly emphasizes that this tendency can be counterbalanced either by improvements in agriculture or by a policy of unrestricted corn imports, or by both these forces. Yet he believes that the tendency toward diminishing returns is so powerful that in the long run the algebraic sum is likely to be negative: the problem is then to slow it down as much as possible.

Why did Ricardo insist so much on the diminishing returns from land?

The theoretical tradition does not justify such insistence. Contrary to a rather widespread belief, Adam Smith—who was Ricardo's Virgil in his visit to the Inferno and the Purgatory of the economy—does not support the so-called law of diminishing returns from land. According to Smith, the division of labor in agriculture has a more limited scope than in manufacturing, so the increase in productivity tends to increase at a lower speed than in the other great sector of the economy; but this is very different from saying that in the course of time productivity in agriculture tends gradually to fall when the cultivated area is extended—which is what Ricardo says. More precisely Smith maintains that two categories of agricultural products should be distinguished—vegetable products and cattle; only this second category is subject to a sort of tendency toward diminishing returns which differs, however, from the one described by Ricardo. Corn, which is produced with the help of cattle, is on the border line; its real costs are constant, as a result of two contrasting tendencies, one toward increasing and the other toward diminishing returns.

As indicated in this chapter, the main reasons for Ricardo's insistence are historical and are to be related to the very peculiar conditions during his lifetime determined, first, by the French Revolution and then by the Napoleonic Wars. In that period British trade suffered from serious hindrances and even blockades. As a consequence for a period England had to provide for the growing population with her own resources much more than in the past. As a further consequence the prices of agricultural products, especially of wheat, underwent unusual increases; cultivation was extended to not very fertile lands, and rents increased considerably. Soon after the end of the Napoleonic Wars the situation changed, and the price of wheat went

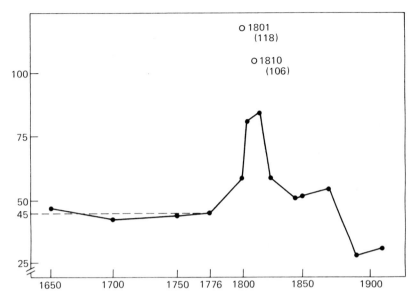

Figure 1.1
Price of wheat in Great Britain (shillings per bushel). Sources: For 1650 to 1770, Smith (*WN* I, xi, III); for 1770 to 1850, Tooke and Newmark (*A History of Prices* [1837–57] 1928); for 1850 to 1910, Mitchell (*Abstract of British Historical Statistics* 1962); for 1801 to 1810, Ricardo (*Works* V, 213). The points on the curve represent three-year averages; the two circles outside the curve give annual prices.

back to a level only a little higher than that prevailing in the time preceding those great military and social upheavals. But Ricardo did not live long enough to observe adequately the behavior in the price of wheat after the Napoleonic Wars. If today we reconsider the behavior in the price of wheat in the last two or three centuries, we have to conclude that Smith was nearer to the truth than Ricardo, and Smith, as I have recalled, thought that the production of wheat can be expanded at constant labor costs. In fact, if we except the hump of the mentioned period—we could call it "the Ricardian hump,"—the prices of wheat vary within relatively narrow limits from 1650 to 1870. After 1870 these prices fall considerably because of the large influx of North American wheat into the European markets; the price of wheat becomes highly competitive through the development of railroads and the steamship, two technological innovations of historical significance.

Figure 1.1 shows the behavior of the price of wheat from 1650 to 1910; 1776—one of the years singled out in the graph—is the year when *The Wealth of Nations* was published; in 1817 the first edition of Ricardo's *Principles* appeared (the third edition was published in 1821); Ricardo died in 1823.

Ricardo, then, was looking at the increasing prices of corn not because of temporary historical circumstances but as a natural tendency; hence the importance of a "policy of leaving unrestricted the importation of foreign corn" (*Principles—Advertisement to the Third Edition*) if not to offset, at least to reduce and postpone the evil effects on accumulation of diminishing returns.

On this prescription two observations are to the point:

First, in Ricardo's time a social and political struggle was under way between the landed aristocracy and the emerging industrial bourgeoisie. Ricardo was clearly in favor of the latter (he considered the former an "unproductive class"), and with this analysis he was preparing logical ammunition for that struggle, which had its climax in 1842 with the repeal of the corn laws.

Second, at first sight Ricardo's prescription appears as an instance of Smith's recommendation of free trade. It is not exactly so. To be sure, that prescription fits very well into the tradition inaugurated by Smith. But Ricardo's free trade is completely concentrated on the importation of foreign corn, whereas Smith's recommendation concerns the imports and exports of all commodities as well as internal trade.

According to Ricardo, in the long run wages depend on the price of necessaries, of which food constitutes the principal part. If the price of food increases, money wages must increase in proportion; in its turn an increase of wages determines a decline of profits. This is the way through which diminishing returns from land determine the tendency of profits to fall and accumulation to slow down.

Here we find an additional important difference with Smith, for whom wages depend primarily on the demand for labor and not on the price of food. In Smith's conception, if the state of society is progressive, demand can systematically exceed supply, so wages—both nominal and real—tend to rise.

The analytical differences between Smith and Ricardo appear clearly when the two great economists consider the evolution in the American colonies. For Smith institutions and policies which are favorable to private initiative (including the very limited intervention of government in economic affairs), as well as free land and abundant resources, stimulate the process of economic development, and hence the increase in the demand for wage labor. At the same time free land contributes to determine a systematic gap between demand for and supply of wage labor, since wage earners can easily become independent producers. (*WN* I., 77–79, 89, 95; II., 76–83).

For Ricardo, on the contrary, the abundance of cultivable land causes the price of food to remain persistently low. Therefore money wages tend to be persistently low and profits persistently high. This state of affairs is favorable to accumulation—and on this specific point Ricardo reaches the same conclusion as Smith, though by way of a completely different route. The difference refers to the behavior of wages and to the consequences of this behavior. Ricardo, differently from Smith, concludes that, in the said circumstances wages would have remained at a low level; hence, he says, "in America and many other countries where the food of man is easily provided, there is not nearly such great temptation to employ machinery as in England, where food is high, and costs much labour for its production" (*Principles* 395).

This statement by Ricardo presupposes two propositions: (1) in the long run wages depend primarily on the price of food; (2) "machinery and labour are in constant competition, and the former can frequently not be employed until the labour rises." The first proposition, which in principle is plausible, has proved to be wrong; the second proposition is valid and important, and analytically useful even now.

As for the first proposition, if one would justify Ricardo by saying that in his time his idea that in the long run money wages vary with the price of food did correspond to reality, it would be necessary to note that in the American colonies of that time the behavior assumed by Ricardo did not correspond to reality, and even at that time this fact was not too difficult to ascertain. Moreover, in principle, such behavior could not be taken for granted: after all, half a century earlier Adam Smith was suggesting more correct hypotheses. The same critical remark applies to Marx, who envisages a behavior of wages similar to the one hypothesized by Ricardo, though for different reasons. It is true that Marx criticizes Ricardo because, he says, it is perfectly possible in certain circumstances for labor to be scarce with respect to demand and wages to be high relatively to the price of food—as in fact they are in the American colonies. (Marx is well aware of this.) But Marx considers this as an exceptional situation that cannot last indefinitely: in the course of time wages would fall to the "normal European level," that is, to the minimum level, even though, for Marx, such a mininum is to be conceived as social and historical and not biological.[1]

As final remark, Ricardo's views on the behavior of productivity in agriculture differ from those of Smith primarily for methodological reasons. In general, Ricardo, who does not care at all for historical factors, works out his analyses on a very abstract plane, whereas Smith's arguments are always put into a historical perspective. Ricardo's method, however, with its drastic simplifications, has opened the doors to the static analysis of our time: the Ricardian thesis on diminishing returns can illustrate this point very well. The ideal future development of economic analysis, in my judgment, would be a combination of the Ricardian rigor with the Smithian conception, in which history is not a field to be left to specialists but the necessary background of the theoretical economist.

Note

1. See K. Marx, *Capital*, Vol. 1 (1867; reprint Progress Publishers, Moscow, 1977), XXV; *Theories of Surplus Value* (Progress Publishers, Moscow, 1968–69), XVIII, B.1.

2   The Problem of Economic Growth in Marx and Schumpeter

2.1 Introduction

The problem of economic development cannot be studied in isolation, since it presupposes a global view of the economy. This comes out very clearly in the theoretical framework of Marx and Schumpeter: in the final analysis the whole of Marx's and Schumpeter's work deals exclusively with the different aspects of the problem, in its specific and complex dimensions. Yet among these various observations some are more closely linked to the problem of economic development. Consequently it is possible to isolate some of the propositions put forward by Marx and Schumpeter, provided we bear in mind that these are to be treated only as an expository device and that the comprehension of these propositions presupposes the study, difficult but worthwhile, of the works of these two great thinkers.

Our task remains difficult even though the procedure is fairly straightforward. This is so not only because the two conceptions are extraordinarily complex but also because mistaken or unilateral interpretations are not uncommon, especially in the case of Marx. In this chapter we consider some propositions that are pertinent to the analysis of development but open to possible misunderstandings.

2.2 Marx

Net income and Surplus Value in the Classics and Marx: Simple and Expanded Reproduction

The concept of surplus value takes a central position in Marxian theory. Marx uses this concept in both his analysis of the single capitalist and society as a whole. Unless otherwise stated, this chapter refers only to the second type of analysis. Many of the criticisms and confusions raised by this concept may be avoided if it is recognized that (1) the notion of surplus value is largely the same as the notion of net income in Quesnay, Smith, and Ricardo and (2) the usefulness of the notion of surplus value in the analysis of the process of production does not necessarily depend on the acceptance of the Marxian theory of the source of value.

There are of course differences between the *produit net* of Quesnay, *net income* of Smith and Ricardo, and *surplus value* of Marx. The *produit net* of the physiocrats consists only in ground rent (*rente foncière*), whereas Marx's surplus value is formed by rent, profit, and interest (nonlabor income). Smith's and Ricardo's notions of net (social) income coincide with Marx's concept of surplus value, although the notions of total output or gross revenue have a different meaning in Smith and Ricardo, from that in Marx. In Smith and Ricardo gross revenue exhausts itself ultimately in wages, rent profit, and interest; in Marx, who criticizes this notion, gross revenue includes not only variable capital (i.e., the wage bill) and surplus value but also the flow of goods that reproduces and expands the "constant capital" (machines and raw materials).[1] (Modern economists call a part of constant capital, "investment"—the output of machines—and include as consumption both wages and the unearned incomes spent on consumption.)

It is important to note that for Smith and Ricardo, as well as for Marx, growth in total income can come about only through "accumulation," that is, through productive employment which generates surplus value and thus investment of net income.

In order to study the accumulation process, Marx develops two schemes: one for simple reproduction and another for expanded reproduction, or accumulation. A large part of Marx's work is devoted to the analysis of these two schemes.[2] Under simple reproduction all net income is consumed by the income recipients; hence the process repeats itself at the same level (modern economists would say that net investment is zero). Under expanded reproduction either a part or the whole of net income is accumulated, that is, transformed into additions to constant and variable capital (in modern parlance, net investment is positive and the wage bill increases). The two schemes are developed in Volume 2 of *Capital*, where Marx introduces the famous distinction between two basic sectors—the sector producing means of production and the sector producing consumption goods—and indicates also their mutual equilibrium condition for simple and expanded reproduction. It is in the case of expanded reproduction that Marx sets down the ideal conditions for the process called "balanced growth" by modern economists.[3]

The scheme of simple reproduction, which structurally derives directly from Quesnay's *Tableau économique* and which in essence describes the economic process of a stationary society, is a mere tool of analysis, a pure abstraction.[4] The truly relevant hypothesis for the study of the production process is the second one, the hypothesis concerning expanded reproduction, or accumulation. For Marx *the capitalist economy is not and cannot be a stationary economy.*

This is the first Marxist thesis on economic growth which is discussed in what follows.

The Necessity of Accumulation: Technical Innovatuons and Competition; Wage Increases and the Introduction of Machinery

Where does the *necessity* for accumulation and hence for development originate? Essentially it comes from the impulse of capitalists to get richer and from their desire to dominate. The capitalists are always on the look out for opportunities conducive to the expansion of the level of their income, which consists of surplus value.[5] These opportunities are continually served by the utilization of material resources (e.g., energy) and even more by the application of technological advances to the production process, often in the form of new and better machines. For Marx the process of accumulation is typically set in motion by the introduction of new machines by one or more firms. As long as the remaining firms keep producing with the prevailing methods of production, the individual value diverges from the social value of the product. The innovating firms thus obtain, in addition to the absolute surplus value (which according to Marx exists also under simple reproduction independent of accumulation), an extra profit, or in other words, an "extra surplus value." The social value is determined by the socially necessary labor time, which is, in Marx's words, "the labor time necessary to produce . . . under the normal conditions of production and with the average degree of skill and intensity prevalent at the time" ([1867] 1977, 47). It therefore corresponds to the notion of the "normal" cost of production or to the cost of the representative firm. Marx assumes that the new method, which will lower production costs, will involve not only an increase in the "productive power of labor" but also an increase in total output. In order to find on outlet for the increased production, the innovating capitalist will sell at prices below the social value of output (social value corresponding to the prevailing price) but above its individual value (above its own cost of production). As a result the other firms are progressively compelled to introduce the new method, lest they be eliminated from the market.[6] "[Competition] compels [the individual capitalist] to constantly extend his capital in order to preserve it, but extend it he cannot except by means of progressive accumulation" (Marx [1867] 1977, 555).

Hence the first impulse initiating the entire process of accumulation arises from the adoption of new methods of production, and in this connection we could say that accumulation stems from an autonomous innovation (Hicks 1932). The innovation spreads itself out because of competition and a decline in prices.

As the accumulation process expands, the demand for workers increases as well. The latter expands in proportion to accumulation (i.e., in proportion to the mass of constant and variable capital) in those branches where the innovation process does not take place and where expansion occurs on an unchanged technical basis. By contrast, the demand for labor grows less than proportionately in those branches where the process does take place, which is where the technical basis of production is altered by innovations that augment the "productive power of labor."

Yet as accumulation continues and the demand for labor grows, wages tend to rise, thereby squeezing profits. To offset this tendency, capitalists progressively introduce machines of a labor-saving type (this is a case of induced innovation theorized by Hicks).

It is at this point that the classical discussion on the effect of machines on the demand for labor becomes relevant to the analysis.

The original proposition that the introduction of machinery could generate unemployment was put forward by John Barton in an essay published in 1817 (Barton 1817), but it was developed in a unique way by Ricardo. In his chapter "On Machinery," added to the third edition of *Principles*, Ricardo recanted his former views by showing that for any *given level of total capital advanced*, the introduction of machines can create a "redundant population" (unemployment) and thus worsen the "living conditions of the worker." This thesis was in opposition to the one prevailing among economists, who held that the "wage fund," which they regarded as the physical quantity of the means of subsistence, is not reduced by the introduction of machinery, so *even without additional capital* the workers eliminated from a given branch can be quickly reabsorbed by the same or other branches. Ricardo, by presenting a numerical example based on the single firm, rejects that view and maintains that the "wage fund," which he regards in monetary terms, is permanently cut after the installation of machines. He fundamentally states that the unemployed workers can be reabsorbed into other branches *provided* additional capital comes into existence (Ricardo [1821] 1951, 388–390). Marx, who in part criticizes and develops Ricardo's argument, attacks the compensation thesis.

Even the supporters of the thesis, says Marx, admit the *monetary* fund of wages will diminish. Although the physical mass of means of subsistence will consequently not diminish, it is incorrect that the physical fund will be used in the same way as before, to employ the workers expelled from their jobs. The fact is that with the decline of the (monetary) wage fund and the employed workers, effective demand will decline as well and with it the price of subsistence goods. Hence the production of these goods will be discouraged; the capital invested in their production will tend to move to other branches of production so that during the process of readjustment a part of the workers employed in the production of means of subsistence will also lose their jobs.

Marx, like Ricardo, does not at all deny that if *additional (variable) capital* is created, workers can be reabsorbed. He acknowledges that "machinery . . . *may bring about an increase of employment in other industries*," especially in the industries supplying means of production to the industries that adopt them and expand the quantity produced (Marx [1867] 1977, 1:417). He admits, as does Ricardo, that additional capital formation could be stimulated by the reduction in the prices of commodities produced by machines, a reduction that will free part of capitalists' income. He points out, however, that this is an altogether different question compared to the one put forward by the advocates of compensation.

By assuming the existence of an accumulation process, Marx, like Ricardo, concludes that the introduction of machinery slows down the increase in the demand for labor relative to the accumulation of capital, in particular constant capital. As accumulation occurs, the "organic composition of capital" (the ratio of constant to variable capital) tends to rise. The demand for labor, which is reflected in variable capital, can certainly increase; thus employment can expand, notwithstanding the growing adoption of machinery. But the longer accumulation goes on and the more wages increase, the stronger will become the tendency to substitute machines for workers. At a certain point the demand for labor will decline, both in a relative and an *absolute* sense. Unemployment, which up to that point was declining, will start to rise. In the long period unemployment ("reserve army" or "redundant population") tends to be periodically renewed.[7] Unemployment does shrink during the phases of "hectic prosperity," but it never disappears. It is necessary to dwell on this point at some length for two reasons. The first is that Marx's argument on the relation of machinery to the issue of compensation has been often misunderstood or misinterpreted.[8] The second is that this argument is at the roots of his thesis on the rise of the organic composition of capital, which plays a fundamental role in the whole of Marxian theory. This thesis combines specific propositions about economic growth, wIth the forms in which it specifically manifests itself. This thesis is, in Marx, of great relevance in explaining why growth takes place through *alternating periodical episodes*, or *cycles*. We now turn to this question.

Accumulation, Unemployment, and the Business Cycle

For accumulation to take place, material means of production as well as additional workers are required. Additional means of production can come from development, that is, from previous accumulation. Where do additional workers come from? The answer of the economists who preceded Marx was: From the natural increase of population. Marx maintained that this increment is absolutely insufficient. Capital accumulation on an invariant technical basis, with a given organic composition of capital and a given "productive power of labor," would pretty soon lead to a rise in wages. Profits would fall, and accumulation would cease. A rather long period of time would have to elapse before the growth of population could sequeeze wages and thereby recreate favorable conditions for accumulation. Hence "capitalist production can by no means content itself with the quantity of disposable labor power which the material increase of population yields. For its free play it requires an industrial reserve army independent of these natural limits" (Marx [1867] 1977, 593). Unemployment is therefore a necessary condition for accumulation, and it is created by accumulation itself, as long as it takes place on a changing technical basis. The introduction of labor-saving machines causes unemployment, slows down wage increases, and by expanding labor's productive power, prevents possible wage rises from lowering profits. Yet once in motion, accumulation can proceed at such a pace that the number of workers absorbed in production exceeds those expelled from it. Unemployment declines, and wages rise. This happens during the phase of prosperity but cannot continue indefinitely, its limit being given by the exhaustion of the availability of labor.[9] At this point accumulation is temporarily stopped, to be resumed when a sufficient quantity of spare labor has been created (not by natural increase in population but by the introduction of machinery). The alternating changes in the level of unemployment are a crucial factor for the business cycle.[10]

Given the importance of the issue, it seems worthwhile to give three relatively long quotations from Marx:[11]

[1] The mass of social wealth, overflowing with the advance of accumulation, and transformable into additional capital, thrusts itself frantically into old branches of production, whose market suddenly expands, or into newly formed branches, such as railways, etc., the need for which grows out of the

development of the old ones. In all such cases, there must be the possibility of throwing great masses of men suddenly on the decisive points without injury to the scale of production in other spheres. Overpopulation supplies these masses. The course characteristic of modern industry, viz., a decennial cycle (interrupted by smaller oscillations), of periods of average activity, production at high pressure, crisis and stagnation, depends on the constant formation, the greater or less absorption, and the re-formation of the industrial reserve army or surplus-population. In their turn, the varying phases of the industrial cycle recruit the surplus-population, and become one of the most energetic agents of its reproduction. This peculiar course of modern industry, which occurs in no earlier period of human history, was also impossible in the childhood of capitalist production.

[2] It is only since the time when mechanical industry has taken roots so deep as to exercise a dominating influence over all of social production; when, thanks to mechanical industry, foreign trade has begun to prevail over internal trade; when the world market has annexed one after the other vast territories of the New World, Asia, and Australia; when, finally, industrialized countries competing among themselves have become sufficiently numerous—it is only since that time that business cycles appear, whose phases following one another stretch over years and years and always terminate with a general crisis, which is the conclusion of a cycle and the starting point of a new one.

[3] The expansion by fits and starts of the scale of production is the preliminary to its equally sudden contraction; the latter again evokes the former, but the former is impossible without disposable human material, without an increase in the number of laborers independently of the absolute growth of the population. This increase is effected by the simple process that constantly "sets free" a part of the laborers, by methods which lessen the number of laborers employed in proportion to the increased production. The whole form of the movement of modern industry depends, therefore, upon the constant transformation of a part of the laboring population into unemployed or half-employed hands. (Marx [1894] 1977, 3:592–593)

Marx is therefore clearly observant of the existence of a business cycle. In fact, as Schumpeter correctly pointed out, Marx was probably the first economist to develop a theory of the cycle and not just a theory of crises (Schumpeter 1942, 41). Moreover he was also clearly observant of the relationship between cycles and growth. The cycle, for Marx, is the particular form that accumulation or growth takes in a capitalist society, and the cycle itself first and foremost reflects the employment cycle of workers.

Any attempt to give a global appraisal of the Marxian theory of the cycle is bound to run into complex problems of interpretation. In the final analysis, precisely because for Marx the cycle is nothing but the evolutionary form of capitalism, his entire work, which has as its object the study of that evolution, is concerned with the question of the cycle.[12] However, it is possible to find in Marx's work several observations concerning specific aspects of the cycle as well as of crises.[13] The basic phenomenon that gives unity to Marx's conception, is always represented by the changes in the "technical basis" of production, by the variations in the composition of capital and the resulting variations in the phases of the industrial reserve army.[14] This is the criterion to remember if one wishes to understand, and thus criticize the Marxian theory of cycles and crises. To make the point clearer, let us consider one of the two most common interpretations of the theory—the "contradiction" between the productive capacity and the consumption capacity of the masses. The former, according to the comment couched by Engels in a Malthusian style, tends to grow in a geometric progression, whereas the latter tends to expand only in an arithmetic progression.[15]

Taken by itself, the foregoing proposition exposes itself to possible objections, the first being that of superficiality. Yet it is possible to present it in a more satisfactory form, by taking into account the interpretative criterion mentioned at the start of this chapter, and by coordinating Marx's scattered observations.

If with accumulation unemployment tends to dwindle, the limit given by the capacity to consume is, so to speak, relaxed. This limit is stretched further if, in addition to a continuing fall of unemployment, unit wages begin to rise. It is precisely at this point that another limit—costs—comes into being; this is the limit that depends on the relations of production. To slow the rise in costs, the industrial capitalists will increasingly need to substitute machines for workers. By so doing, they mitigate the difficulties arising from the costs side but worsen the complications arising from selling growing quantities of commodities. This is because, by substituting machines for workers, they freeze a part of the wages into fixed capital, which therefore depresses the absolute amount, or the rate of increase, of workers' incomes. In other words, the industrialists struggle between a Scylla and Charybdis; wages are at the same time costs as well as incomes. In the last phase of prosperity the industrialists, in order to escape from Scylla, land themselves into the laps of Charybdis.

Evidently, at the root of this process lie the variations in the organic composition of capital and in unemployment.

The Financial and Monetary Aspects of the Cycle

From what was said earlier, it already appears, albeit implicitly, that the part Marx assigned to credit and money in the cycle is of a secondary and subordinate nature. He attacks the theories that pretend to explain the varying phases of the industrial cycle by means of the expansion and contraction of credit, labeling them as superficial. For Marx these are only "mere symptoms" of the cycle's phases. Yet Marx points out more than once that the most violent and immediate manifestation of the crises is to be found in the sphere of money and credit. Furthermore he warns that the monetary and financial developments that follow the crisis also contribute to its worsening.

Producers and merchants operating in the different stages of each chain of production do not, as a rule, settle reciprocal payments in cash. They regularly use instruments of credit. Payments take place when the last agent in the chain, the merchant, sells the final good to the consumer against cash. The entire chain breaks up if the sale does not take place, or if it is carried out at a price lower than that used as a reference in the preceding obligations, since "the same sum of money acts for a whole series of reciprocal transactions and obligations" (Marx [1905] 1968 2:514). during the crisis this phenomenon occurs in many branches. To avoid bankruptcy, producers try to honor financial obligations; they are ready to sell their products against cash, and not against credit instruments, even at a loss: "a person may *sell* in order to *pay* and . . . these forced sales play a very significant role in the crisis. . . . During the crisis a man may be very pleased if he has sold his commodities without immediately thinking of a purchase" (Marx [1905] 1968, 2:503).

In short, everybody tries to take cover behind ready cash, which is desired as such not to buy goods to be invested in productive activities. As a consequence the rate of interest rises: "The rate of interest reaches its peak during crises, when money is wanted at any cost to meet payment" (Marx, [1894] 1977, 3:361).[16] The explanation given by Marx for the increase of what today is called "liquidity preference" seems to me more adequate than that advanced by Keynes. In a nutshell, for Marx the increase in the liquidity preference is typically an *effect* of the crisis, which in its initial phase takes precisely the form of a monetary crisis.[17] (This is mostly true of the cyclical crises that preceded the first world war, whose downturns were normally accompanied by financial panic. After the war the phases of financial panic, or liquidity crises, either disappeared or they manifested themselves in some irregular way or new form.)[18]

The Thesis of the Immiserization of the Working Class

The basic unity between cycle and trend (to use contemporary terminology) appears characteristically from the following remark: "For the rest, the same vicious circle would occur once more under expanded conditions of production, with an expanded market and increased productive forces" (Marx [1885] 1977, 2:253). Marx never stopped stressing the powerful productive development generated, as a part of its own logic, by industrial capitalism. Take, for example, the following passage: "Development of the productive forces of social labor is the historical task and justification of capital. This is just the way in which it unconsciously creates the material requirements of a higher mode of production" (Marx [1894] 1977, 3:255).

Then, we might ask, how is it possible to reconcile this thesis with the much better known "immiserization" of the working class? Who benefits from that enormous productive development? Is it possible that Marx really believed that no such benefits would accrue to the working class?

Marx is far more complex on this issue than what might have appeared to many of his critics and also to his large number of followers. There are several reasons for the ambiguities arising from Marx's position. There are passages where it seems that Marx believed that all the benefits of productive development will accrue to the "capitalist class." In other passages he seems to lean toward the thesis of a relative rather than absolute immiserization of the "working class."[19] Furthermore in his short work, *Wages, Price and Profits*, Marx rejects the classical view that wages necessarily and inevitably tend to the minimum physical level of subsistence. He maintains that such a minimum constitutes only an "ultimate limit" of the wage rate, whereas in fact the wage is determined by a social minimum, that is, by the "traditional standard of life." The social limit is higher and can also be increased by trade unions whose actions, according to Marx, are more successful in preventing a reduction of real wages than in obtaining sizeable increases (Marx [1898] 1950, 362–71).

To resolve these ambiguities, it is necessary to bear in mind that the thesis of immiserization is based on the notion of increasing organic composition of capital, which refers to the progressive mechanization of productive processes. Immiserization would then arise from the long-run increase in unemployment, which likewise is subject to cyclical fluctuations, and from the growing intensity and oppressiveness of working conditions caused, according to Marx, by the utilization of machines in a profit-motivated economy. In such an economy the introduction of machinery is essentially a means to reduce labor costs rather than to lower the physical hardship of the worker.

The same causes which develop the expansive power of capital, develop also the labor power at its disposal. The relative mass of the industrial reserve army increases therefore with the potential energy of wealth. (Marx [1867] 1977, 1:603)

And:

Within the capitalist system all methods for raising the social productiveness of labor . . . mutilate the laborer into a fragment of a man, degrade him to the level of an appendage of a machine, destroy every remnant of charm in his work and turn it into a hated toil. . . . It follows therefore that in proportion as capital accumulates, the lot of the laborer be his payment high or low, must grow worse. (Marx [1867] 1977, 1:604)

The thesis of immiserization therefore cannot be judged by changes in real wages alone. It is necessary to take into account variations in total unemployment, and as far as the employed workers are concerned, changes in remuneration ought to be weighed against effort and toil.

Examined from this angle, the thesis appears more complex than it had at first. Although both politically and theoretically the *problem* of unemployment is relatively recent, the *phenomenon* of unemployment, which is typically cyclical, is evident in the entire course of development of major capitalist countries. In order to assess the unrealistic character of the hypothesis of full employment, often advanced by classical and neoclassical economists, it is sufficient to give a glance to statistical data, or estimates, of unemployment in England and the United States.[20]

In Marx the assessment of the hardship of work appears vague, nay, elusive. Even if hardship is observed to be on the increase, it does not seem possible to maintain that it has outpaced the benefits arising from the reduction in working hours and from the more than considerable increases in real wages that have taken place in the most advanced capitalist countries. It is true that when Marx was writing, the tendency toward a rapid growth of real wages had not manifested itself in England.[21] It is equally true that this tendency manifested itself only in some and not in all countries that can be considered capitalist. Yet even when such qualifications are accepted, it is evident that the thesis of a progressive deterioration of the condition of the working class does not tally with the facts. Paul Sweezy, a serious Marx scholar, has pointed out that the tendency toward immiserization, whether absolute or relative, is only a tendency or an abstract "law"; in no way can it be considered as an actual prediction (Sweezy 1968, 19). Marx himself has warned that this law "like all other laws is modified in its working by many circumstances, the analysis of which does not concern us here" (Marx [1867] 1977, 1:603). But the following objection can therefore be made: if the tendency has been, at least in some countries, more than offset by the countertendencies, it means that the countertendencies were stronger. Hence they demand the attention of the scholar more than immiserization. Among such countertendencies built on the fundamental phenomenon of productive development, we can include the action of the trade unions which over time have augmented the bargaining power of the workers. It is true that in Marx's times the trade unions were still rather weak. But from Marx's own analysis it is also possible to deduce that the evolution of capitalism *had* to generate over time a strengthening of the trade unions.

The advance of industry, whose involuntary promoter is the bourgeoisie, replaces the isolation of the laborers, due to competition, by their revolutionary combination, due to association. (Marx and Engels, 1959, 19)

And:

... with this too grows the revolt of the working class, a class always increasing in numbers, and disciplined, united, organized by the very mechanism of the process of capitalist production itself. (Marx [1867] 1977, 1:714)

For Marx it would have been more reasonable to expect, as a result of the growth of trade unions and of the sustained growth of production, an improvement—not a deterioration—in the conditions of the workers, even though such an improvement would be achieved through struggle.

Why was Marx, we may ask, not aware of the hidden contradiction in his statements? It is likely that his position was influenced by political and ideological motives. In fact Marx looked with a critical eye at the purely reformistic tendencies of the trade unions. For Marx to insist on the possibility to obtain increasing real wages solely by means of trade union action meant the slowing down or the weakening of the revolutionary tendencies aimed at the "ultimate abolition of the wages system" (Marx [1867] 1977, 1:79).

The contradiction in the view that the capitalist economy is bound to grow while real wages remain stationary is a serious one. It must be pointed out that well before the beginning of the sustained process of growth that asserted itself with modern industrial capitalism, Adam Smith, not being misled like Ricardo by a wrong evaluation of the tendency of diminishing returns from land, or like Marx by ideological reasons, considers the tendency of wages to increase to be as a normal phenomenon in an expanding economy.

Progressive Concentration of Firms: The Tendency toward Monopoly

Of Marx's many views on long-run tendencies in capitalist countries, his most vital argument is undoubtedly that concerning the progressive concentration of firms, or as he puts it, "of capitals". Some economists, among them Alfred Marshall, even consider it the underlying theme of the whole of Marxian thought:

Marx and his followers resolved to be practical, and argued that history showed a steadily hastening growth of large business and of mechanical administration by vast joint-stock companies, and they deduced the fatalistic conclusion that this tendency is irresistable; and must fulfill its destiny by making the whole state into one large joint-stock company in which everyone would be a shareholder. (Marshall 1923, 176–177)

Whether it is valid or not to make the analogy between a socialist state and a large joint-stock company, it is certain that Marshall here captures the essence of Marx's economic conception. Marx often referred to the tendency toward concentration, but the issue is discussed at some length only in two passages (Marx [1867] 1977, 1: c.23; [1894], 3: c.27). There are several factors at the roots of this problem. The first among them is competition. Marx acknowledges that because of competition, only the most efficient firms survive. At the same time he sees that the need for productive efficiency arising from competition will cause an increase in "the minimum amount of individual capital" necessary to undertake a business activity. Furthermore the development of credit

which in its first stages furtively creeps in as a humble assistant in accumulation . . . soon becomes a new and terrible weapon in the battle of competition and is finally transformed into an enormous social mechanism for the centralization of capitals.
At the same time the progress of accumulation increases the material amenable to centralization, i.e., the individual capitals while the expansion of capitalist production creates, on the one hand, the social want, and, on the other, the technical means necessary for those immense industrial undertakings which require a previous centralization of capital for their accomplishment. (Marx [1867] 1977, 58)

The expansion of credit leads in time to the formation of joint-stock companies which have the following effects:

[1] An enormous expansion of the scale of production and of enterprises, that was impossible for individual capitals.

[2] The capital, which in itself rests on a social mode of production and presupposes a social concentration of means of production and labor power, is here directly endowed with the form of social capital (capital of directly associated individuals) as distinct from private capital, and its undertakings assume the form of social undertakings as distinct from private undertakings. It is the abolition of capital as private property within the framework of capitalist production itself.

[3] Transformation of the actually functioning capitalist into a mere manager, administrator of other people's capital, and of the owner of capital into a mere owner, a mere money-capitalist. Even if the dividends which they receive include the interest and the profit of enterprise, i.e., the total profit (for the salary of the manager is, or should be, simply the wage of a specific type of skilled labor, whose price is regulated in the labor market like that of any other labor), this total profit is henceforth received only in the form of interest, i.e., as mere compensation for owning capital that now is entirely divorced from

the function in the actual process of reproduction, just as this function in the person of the manager is divorced from ownership of capital. . . .

This result of the ultimate development of capitalist production is a necessary transitional phase toward the reconversion of capital into the property of producers, although no longer as the private property of the individual producers, but rather as the property of associated producers, as outright social property. . . .
This is the abolition of the capitalist mode of production within the capitalist mode of production itself, and hence a self-dissolving contradiction, which *prima facie* represents a mere phase of transition to a new form of production. It manifests itself as such a contradiction in its effects. It establishes a monopoly in certain spheres and thereby requires state interference. It reproduces a new financial aristocracy, a new variety of parisites in the shape of promoters, speculators and simply nominal directors; a whole system of swindling and cheating by means of corporation promotion, stock issuance, and stock speculation. It is private production without the control of private property. . . .
(Marx [1894] 1977, 3:436, 437, 438)

What Marx has outlined in so vividly are not strictly economic consequences of the process of concentration. He did not elaborate on the pure economic aspects. Furthermore, although he clearly referred to a trend that in the course of time would have brought about the diffusion of monopolistic situations, his analysis of monopoly is very unsatisfactory. His entire theoretical construct presupposes, as in the classics, competition. On monopoly, Marx limited himself to repeating almost literally the brief comments made by Ricardo.[22] Marx does not ask himself what the tendency of accumulation will be when a large segment of the economy is dominated by large corporations with monopolistic power: this problem has been dealt with by some of the followers of Marx, such as Rudolf Hilferding and Lenin, although they approached it more in relation to the political and sociological implications than to the economic ones.

All the same, as Schumpeter rightly noted, "to predict the advent of big business was, considering the conditions of Marx's day, an achievement in itself" (Schumpeter 1941, 34). It is worth reminding the reader that big businesses and coalitions, such as the trusts and cartels in the most developed capitalist countries, began to be formed only in the last decade of the nineteenth century.

Marx's thesis of concentration, despite its sketchy formulation, turned out to be his most fertile concept. When today we discuss the "necessity" or the "inevitability" of the process of concentration of firms, we are in fact discussing something that originated with Marx.

Some economists—Friedrich von Hayek, Lionel Robbins, and before them

Luigi Einaudi—have denied that the process of concentration is "inevitable." Other economists have stressed that if growth leads to concentration, it also gives rise to a multitude of small firms. This is true but it is also true that often small firms are satellites of large firms and that, in any case, the process of concentration has asserted itself in several important branches of economic activity—not only industry, but also finance and certain services—so as to change radically the organization and the functioning of the advanced economies.

Concentration is not an "inevitable" process in the sense that it happens outside the activity of individuals, businessmen, and politicians. It is basically a process prompted by the search for greater technical efficiency, by the desire to produce at reduced costs. Crises are, in the final analysis, a consequence of that tendency (see Breglia 1942). This process is taking, and has taken, different forms in different countries. True, concentration has not always been the outcome of a search for greater efficiency: political pressures, especially protectionist policies, have likewise favored or determined monopolistic positions. Regardless of any formal distinction between "economic forces" and "political forces," the very fact that concentration gained a hold on the economics of many disparate countries with different political institutions, even in countries with strong free trade (laissey faire) traditions, can show that it was not the case of pure destiny, but true process. The outcome may or may not be that predicted by Marx (this is not of importance at this point). It cannot, however, be doubted that the phenomenon of concentration takes the form of a process that has changed and is still changing the economic world in which we live.

2.3 Schumpeter

The strict interconnection between the Schumpeterian and the Marxian theories of growth cannot be better expressed than by quoting the following passage from Schumpeter's introduction to the Japanese edition of his *Theory of Economic Development*:

It was not clear to me at the outset what to the reader will perhaps be obvious at once, namely, that this idea and this aim [Schumpeter's own] are exactly the same as the idea and the aim which underlies the economic teaching of Karl Marx. In fact, what distinguishes him from the economists of his own time and those who preceded him, was precisely a vision of economic evolution as a distinct process generated by the economic system itself. In every other respect he only used and adapted the concepts and propositions of Ricardian economics, but the concept of economic evolution, which he put into an unessential Hegelian setting, is quite his own. It is probably due to this fact that one generation of economists after another turns back to him again, although they may find plenty to criticize in him. (Clemence, ed., 1951, 166).

In the posthumously published monumental work, *History of Economic Analysis*, Schumpeter writes:

On the other hand, we now see Marxist economics in its true light. Its individual features, or some of them, will come in for notice and appraisal in their places. Here I wish only to insist on the greatness of the conception and on the fact that Marxist analysis is the only genuinely evolutionary economic theory that the period produced. Neither its assumptions nor its techniques are above serious objections—though, partly, because it has been left unfinished. But the grand vision of an immanent evolution of the economic process—that, working somehow through accumulation, somehow destroys the economy as well as the society of competitive capitalism and somehow produces an untenable social situation that will somehow give birth to another type of social organization—remains after the most vigorous criticism has done its worst. It is this fact, and this fact alone, that constitutes Marx's claim to greatness as an economic analyst. (Schumpeter 1954, 441)

The differences in the theoretical construct of Schumpeter and Marx are large. But much more significant than the differences are the commonalities. It could appear strange to call Schumpeter a conservative Marxist. But if by this definition one means to imply the basic affinity, beyond the analytical schemes, of the two conceptions, then it would no longer appear contradictory.[23] However, as far as the analytical structure is concerned there are important points of convergence. These will emerge from the following sketch of some specific characteristics of Schumpeter's thought.

"Simple Reproduction" in Marx and the "Circular Flow" of Schumpeter

The starting point of the Schumpeterian analysis of growth is the scheme of circular flow, that is, of the economic process as self-reproducing. In essence this scheme, which is one of a stationary economy, corresponds to Marx's simple reproduction (as by the same token the analysis of growth corresponds to Marx's schemes of expanded reproduction). There are naturally several differences. In Marx's simple reproduction, besides wages, we have all the forms of capitalist incomes called by Marx surplus value. Under these circumstances surplus value exists independent of accumulation and of changes in technical methods. In Schumpeter's circular flow there are, besides wages, rent and monopolistic incomes; neither profit nor interest (which is a share of profit) appears in Schumpeter's circular flow. For Marx as well as for Schumpeter, the scheme of simple reproduction is an abstract one. For both, the capitalist economy is inconceivable without growth. These schemes can, however, have a certain correspondence with reality. As we have already seen in Marx, a part of total output is reproduced under unchanged conditions. Schumpeter considers separately the innovating firms and those that do not change the way in which factors are combined but react only to economic changes caused by the other firms or by "exogenous factors." Moreover for Schumpeter the scheme of circular flows approximates reality only between the end of an old and the beginning of a new cycle. After having analyzed the scheme of circular flows, Schumpeter raises the question, "What is it that makes that process change in historic time?" (Schumpeter 1939, 72).

Schumpeter makes the distinction between changes that are "endogenous" and those that are "exogenous" to the economic system. Among the "exogenous" factors are wars, earthquakes, and the actions of public authorities. These factors, although important, are of an irregular character and are not susceptible to systematic treatment. Rather, it is the similarity in the main traits of the economic evolution in several capitalist countries that makes plausible the hypothesis that economic change is propelled by regular factors endogenous to the economic system, and thus susceptible to systematic treatment:

Factors of change internal to the economic system are changes in tastes, changes in quantity (or quality) of factors of production, changes in methods of supplying commodities. (Schumpeter 1939, 73)

Schumpeter, however, attaches only secondary importance to changes in tastes:

We will, throughout, act on the assumption that consumers' initiative in changing their tastes—*i.e.*, in changing that set of our data which general theory comprises in the concepts of "utility functions" or "indifference varieties," is negligible and that all change in consumer tastes is incident to, and brought about by, producers' action. (Schumpeter 1939, 73)

(He continues by explaining the reasons for this assumption). Nor does he attach great importance to changes in the factors of production as far as economic growth is concerned:

Increase in productive resources might at first sight appear to be the obvious prime mover in the process of internal economic change. Physical environment being taken as constant (opening up of new countries enters as we have seen into a different category). That increase resolves itself into increase of population and the increase of the stock of producers' goods. (Schumpeter 1939, 74)

Yet he acknowledges that changes in population have to be accounted for among the external factors because "there is no unique relation between them and variations in the flow of commodities" (Ibid.). By itself the increase in population leads only to a diminution of real per capita increase. By further stressing these points and combining them with his observations about tastes, Schumpeter, who on these issues is rather close to the classics, in particular to Ricardo, notes that

"needs," whatever they may be, are never more than conditioning factors, and in many cases mere products of entrepreneurial action; it is not they that set the capitalist engine into motion, as the old household examples (China and so on) show; and economic development (capital consumption included) has *never* been conspicuous in the countries which to the observer seem to be most lavishly supplied with needs. (Schumpeter 1939, 1035)

Schumpeter does acknowledge the relevance for development of the increase in the stock of productive resources, such that depends not on changes in the methods of production but on the mere expansion of aggregate savings. Yet he maintained that savings become important only insofar as they are the outcome of a previous process of development. Hence to explain development, it is necessary to start from a stationary society without taking into account savings, where savings are defined as the additional flow of savings and not just the flow of goods and money sums used for the replacement of capital stock. This can be done only in subsequent approximation. (As is well known, Schumpeter ascribes to the creation of credit the same role that aggregate savings have in many growth theories.)

Changes in population (the external factor) and in aggregate savings (the endogenous factor) tend to occur, if they occur, at a rate that changes only but slowly, to use Schumpeter's own words. Hence by themselves these two factors cannot give rise to particular disturbances or imbalances but can only generate a smooth growth of the economic system. These types of changes can be theoretically accounted for by the scheme of circular flow once small modifications are introduced in it.

The internal changes that Schumpeter deems crucial for a comprehension of the process of development (as distinct from mere growth) are those he calls "innovations":

Of course, in reality, all three factors—changes in tastes, growth, and innovation—interact and mutually condition each other, and observed historic changes are the result of them all. But we can satisfy ourselves of their logical independence by visualizing societies in which internal change is merely caused by autonomous change in consumers' tastes or merely by growth or merely by innovation.

If we do this, we immediately realize that innovation is the outstanding fact in the economic history of capitalist society or in what is purely economic in that history, and also that it is largely responsible for most of what we would at first sight attribute to other factors. . . .

The changes in the economic process brought about by innovation, to-gether with all their effects, and the response to them by the economic system, we shall designate by the term Economic Evolution. (Schumpeter 1939, 86)

Recall that for Schumpeter growth is a gradual and slow process whereas the "process" of development is discontinuous and vigorous and that economic evolution and economic development are similar concepts (though evolution is considered broader than development). This distinction between evolution and growth is interesting but debatable. For Schumpeter growth would occur with the mere addition of people and goods (which are saved and used productively) without changes in the methods of production. But, we may ask, will growth proceed indefinitely under such circumstances? The answer is in the negative. In the long run diminishing returns in agriculture and the exhaustion of mines would make their effects felt, so growth must slow down and eventually cease altogether. In the long run growth cannot continue at a constant pace without changes in technical methods to offset at least the effect of diminishing returns. In this connection it may be better to distinguish between changes in techniques that take place continuously and are absorbed by the system—the Marshallian notion of internal and external economies would belong to this type of change—and technical changes that take place in a discontinuous form generating disequilibria. On closer examination Schumpeter seems to deal only with the latter type.

In his *Theory of Economic Development* Schumpeter considers the following set of innovations: (1) the introduction of a new good, (2) the introduction of a new method of production, (3) the opening of a new market, (4) the conquest of a new source of supply of raw materials, and (5) the new organization of any industry into something a monopoly, as, for example, through trustifi-cation, or the dissolution of a monopoly (Schumpeter 1961, 66).

In *Business Cycles* he puts forward a similar list, but at the same time he defines an innovation by using the production function concept. "As we know, this function describes the way in which quantity of product varies if quantities of factors vary. If, instead of quantities of factors, we vary the form of the function, we have an innovation" (Schumpeter 1939, 87).

It must be noted that, strictly speaking, this definition does not apply to the opening of new markets nor to the formation or elimination of a monopolistic position. In such cases there may be an increase in production but *not necessarily* a different production function in the mathematical sense ex-pressed by Schumpeter. If anything, either event can be a *condition* for the implementation of an innovation. Only the introduction of new methods of production and the discovery of new sources of raw materials (as long as, naturally, such a discovery reduces the coefficients of production for each unit of raw material produced) are to be strictly considered as innovations.

The person who actually brings about innovations in the economy is the entrepreneur, whom Schumpeter neatly distinguished from the simple administrator or manager. This is one of the most suggestive concepts put forward by Schumpeter. It has especially drawn attention from economists, although it was often viewed in its superficial aspects:

Everyone knows of course, that to do something new is very much more difficult than to do something that belongs to the realm of routine, and that the two tasks differ qualitatively and not only in degree.... (Schumpeter 1939, 99)

Carrying out a new plan and acting according to a customary one are things as different as making a road and walking along it. (Schumpeter 1961, 85)

Lastly, one must consider "the reaction of the social environment against one who wishes to do something new" (Schumpeter 1961, 86).[24]

However, in Schumpeter's theory those who are capable of introducing new combinations between factors of production usually obtain above-normal gains and thus carry with them a crowd of imitators. The resistance to the new and the tendency to imitate those who succeed in breaking through that resistance play an important role. In this way he explains why:

... First, that innovations do not remain isolated events, and are not evenly distributed in time, but that on the contrary they tend to cluster, to come about in bunches. ... innovations are not at any time distributed over the whole economic system at random, but tend to concentrate in certain sectors and their surroundings. (Schumpeter 1939, 100–101)

As a consequence

Industrial change is never a harmonious advance with all elements of the system actually moving, or tending to move, in step. At any given time, some industries move on, others stay behind; and the discrepancies arising from this area are an essential element in the situations that develop. (Schumpeter 1939, 101–102)

In every span of historic time it is easy to locate the ignition of the process and to associate it with certain industries and, within these industries with certain firms, from which the disturbances then spread over the system. (Schumpeter 1939, 102)

Evolution cannot therefore proceed without jerks; on the contrary "evolution is lopsided, discontinuous, disharmonious by nature ... the disharmony is inherent in the very *modus operandi* of the factors of progress" (Schumpeter 1961, 102).[25] According to Schumpeter, traditional theory (Walrasian or Marshallian) is useful to explain the process of a stationary economy or of an economy in steady-state growth. The theory is not suited to describe an economy in which innovations occur and which is undergoing a process of development. Nevertheless, traditional theory can be of use to describe "the responses to innovation by those firms which are not innovating themselves" (Schumpeter 1961, 99).

Along with the innovating entrepreneur, the protagonist of economic development, we find in Schumpeter the banker, the architect of the exchange economy who creates and puts at the disposal of the entrepreneur new purchasing power. The entrepreneur uses this buying power to extract a certain amount of factors from the circular flow, that is, from the previous uses in order to combine them in a new and more efficient way. In an economy different from an exchange economy, the diversion of factors from old to new uses takes place directly by means of an order from the ministry of production. According to Schumpeter, in an exchange economy such a creation of money is equivalent to an order.[26]

To highlight the role of the creation of monetary means in the process of development, Schumpeter makes a number of assumptions:

1. He assumes previous growth by beginning with a circular flow whereby firms finance themselves.

2. He assumes savings to be negligible (as indicated before).

3. He assumes that there are no unutilized factors.

From a logical standpoint these assumptions are justified in order to understand the role played by the creation of credit. However, Schumpeter admits that they are unrealistic, and he drops them in a subsequent approximation. Yet it does not seem that he clarified in a satisfactory way the consequences of having abandoned these assumptions, the first and the third in particular. In fact, to the extent that additional factors become available, either from a previous development or unused factors, the shift in factors and forced savings cease to be the necessary outcome of the creation of credit.[27] More specifically, if we take into account the existing process of growth and assume that output grows faster than population, the dilemma between consumption and investment (investment viewed as the production of nonconsumable goods) loses a good part of its harshness. The alternative is not between unchanged consumption and less consumption but rather between unchanged consumption (living standards) and increased consumption in the short run. Consumption would remain unaltered if all the increment in national income, in excess of population growth, were invested. In this case the increase in consumption is postponed. There is no dislocation of factors but a utilization of additional factors, even when new and more efficient combinations are implemented.[28] Obviously, these observations do not invalidate Schumpeter's analysis; they rather qualify it. They can acquire even greater significance when referring to the problems of growth facing the "ministry of production" in a collectivist economy. In a more limited way our observations can be applied to a growing private firm which invests its own profits: here it becomes clear that investing profits does not mean diminution of consumption but if anything an absence of an increase in consumption.[29] These observations may suggest a consequence worth considering.

For the community as well as for the private firms the most fundamental problem that constitutes a major obstacle is setting a process of growth into motion. Once this process is started, the investment of the increments of national income, or of profits, allows its perpetuation through decreasing sacrifices.

The Cycle Is the Form that Development Takes in the Era of Capitalism

In Schumpeter as in Marx, the problem of the business cycle is not independent of development: "alternating situations (*Wechsellagen*-Spiethoff) are the form economic development takes in the era of capitalism" (Schumpeter 1961, 215).[30]

The Schumpeterian analysis of the basic process of development has several other points in common with that of Marx, and these can be summarized as follows.

In the circular flow there are only two factors, labor and land, and all values can be imputed to these two factors. In the process of development the number of factors increases to three with the appearance of the entrepreneurs whose aim is to operate more efficient combinations of the first two factors. Values continue to be imputed to the two factors, albeit in different proportions because of the transfer of some factors from old to new uses. The additional value, surplus value or profit, coming out of the new combinations has to be imputed to the third factor, the entrepreneur. Where an innovation loses its novel character and becomes a part of the routine, with the entrepreneur replaced by an administrator, the value of the original factors, labor and land, increases up to the point of absorbing the entire profit. This process implies the action of competition. At first the attractiveness of extra gains gives rise to a cohort of imitators, provided there are no barriers to entry; hence the fear of losses induces various producers to adopt new methods, and those firms unable to change or to adjust are eliminated. The similarity of this process with the one put forward by Marx to explain the appearance and the subsequent disappearance of extra surplus value is quite

clear. Schumpeter's analysis of the cycle does not, however, find any counter-
part in that of Marx.

The innovating entrepreneurs disturb the initial equilibrium and are followed by those imitating them. The new purchasing power created by the
banks allows them to demand, or increase their demand for, capital goods. As
a result prices and output of these goods will increase more than prices and
output of all other goods. When the installation of new methods of production
comes gradually to completion as additional amounts of goods appear on the
market, entrepreneurs will then pay back to the banks their loans (autodeflation). Because of these two pushes, increase in output and deflation, prices
will fall, and prosperity is followed by a recession. In the process the system of
economic relations changes radically:

It is readily seen that, under our assumptions and with but minor qualifications, that sequence of phenomena leads up to a new neighborhood of
equilibrium, in which enterprise will start again. This new neighborhood of
equilibrium is characterized, as compared to the one that preceded it, by a
"greater" social product of a different pattern, new production functions,
equal sum total of money incomes, a minimum (strictly zero) rate of interest,
zero profits, zero loans, a different system of prices and a lower level of prices,
the fundamental expression of the fact that all the lasting achievements of the
particular spurt of innovation have been handed to consumers in the shape of
increased real incomes. (Schumpeter 1939, 137)

In this first approximation the cycle therefore displays two phases: prosperity
(a movement away from equilibrium) and recession (a movement toward a
new equilibrium).

In a second approximation Schumpeter takes into account the "secondary
wave," the process of diffusion of additional purchasing power, as well as the
reaction of firms that *do not* innovate in the wake of the innovations by some
others. The imitating firms will have new investment opportunities.
However, during prosperity speculative excesses as well as wrong calculations occur, so many firms stimulated by demand and by rising prices
expand production at an undiminished technical cost by borrowing from the
banks. Because of excesses and mistakes the liquidation of debts and the
decline in prices will involve significant losses. When size of debt liquidation
becomes abnormal, the downswing degenerates into a depression:

Indeed, the phenomena of this secondary wave may be and generally are
quantitatively more important than those of the primary wave. Covering as
they do a much wider surface, they are also much easier to observe; in fact they
are what strikes the eye first, while it may be difficult, especially if the
innovations are individually small, to find the torch responsible for the
conflagration. This is one reason why the element of innovation has been so
much neglected by the traditional analysis of the business cycle: it hides

behind, and is sometimes entirely overlaid by, the phenomena of what appears at first glance to be simply a general prosperity, which is conspicuous in many branches and strata and apparently unconnected with any activity that could in any way be called innovating, let alone "inventing." It seems only natural to think that for this general prosperity some equally general— e.g., monetary—explanation should be found that both it and the reaction to it should be looked upon, as they actually are by many fellow workers, as meaningless and functionless disturbances of economic life and of the march of progress. (Schumpeter 1939, 146)

Once the secondary wave is taken into account, the cycle has to be divided not in two but in four phases: prosperity, downswing, depression, and recovery. The first and the third phases correspond to movements away from equilibrium; the second and fourth phases, to movements toward equilibrium. The entire process consists of the disturbance of an initial equilibrium and the tendency toward a new equilibrium position. If in this context it can be said that the phases of prosperity, downswing, and recovery have a sound, healthful role in the process of development, a depression constitutes essentially the onset of disease. According to Schumpeter, government intervention is far more justified in this latter phase.

In his first approximation Schumpeter starts with a situation of perfect competition. In the second, however, he takes into account imperfections of competition. These imperfections can explain the existence of unemployed workers and other factors even before the beginning of the cycle during the phases approximating equilibrium conditions. It follows therefore that full employment ceases to be a property of equilibrium, and as much as it may appear paradoxical, it indicates a disequilibrium of a specific kind.[31]

Industries Leading the Cycle and Industries Towed By It: The Relevance of This Distinction for Theory and for Empirical Analysis of Development

For Schumpeter the cyclical process is not a movement around an equilibrium trend but a departure from equilibrium; it consists of a transformation of the whole economic system. One of the implications of this conception is a methodological one, which is worth emphasizing. The methodology of aggregates is, in principle, inadequate to explain the process of cyclical growth. Schumpeter criticized this methodology in *Business Cycles* (1939, 144, 1041), but it can be said that the criticism is inherent in his whole conception. It should be clear that in his view an empirical analysis of development would be very difficult if not impossible, since it would require a study of the variations in all the elements of the system and their mutual interaction. This, however, is not the case. Of crucial importance in this connection is the thesis that every historical cycle receives impulses from specifically determined innovating industries. These industries "lead" the cycle, while others are towed by it (see Burns and Mitchell 1946, 414–416). In his powerful analysis of the cyclical development of the British, German, and American economies, Schumpeter focused especially on the innovating industries in every single cycle, in an attempt to show the dominant role they played in the cycle. At the same time he also referred to those that are most subject to the impulses generated by the innovating ones. He also took into account the industries that play a significant role in the process because of external impulses. (Among the best analyses of single industries and their historical relation to the various phases of the cycle is that of the appearance and development of railways and the electric, automobile, and chemical industries; see Schumpeter 1939, ch. 7. In all these cases the Schumpeterian scheme is particularly convincing and illuminating.)

Yet, Schumpeter's inquiry on the industries leading the cycle is conducted in a descriptive manner. He did not develop any systematic method of analysis, and he exploited only in a limited way the distinction between innovating and "towed" industries. More specifically, Schumpeter fails to make fruitful use of an observation related to new products which could have been useful for an empirical analysis of development:

First, for a considerable time during which the new article is vigorously gaining ground, its price as well as its quantity may be very little sensitive to cyclical fluctuations. Demand may go on shifting upward through several consecutive depressions of the Kitchin, possibly even of the Juglar, and there may be no reason for the innovating firms to change their prices. . . .[32]

Needless to say, such behavior is for us anything but contrary to expectation, however much it may deviate from average behavior. (Schumpeter 1939, 541).

The context of this observation is Schumpeter's attempt to demonstrate that "price rigidity" is not necessarily a pathological phenomenon. The present writer is convinced that this observation can be generalized by detaching it from the specific issue of price rigidity. The idea that the behavior of prices and other quantities tends to differ significantly between the innovating and noninnovating industries can become a methodological criterion to be used in empirical studies of the process of development. In an unpublished paper on wages and prices I have examined several economic variables (quantities produced, prices, productivity per worker, wages) in relation to three types of industries in the United States: young industries in rapid growth, industries producing basic goods such as coal and steel, and mature industries producing consumption goods. It turned out that, on the average, changes in the mature industries are cyclical and coincide with the average variations of manufacturing industries (prices, manufacturing wages, average labor productivity, index of industrial production). By contrast, in the vast majority of cases variations in the young industries do not correspond to average industrywide changes. In other words, the fast growing industries, which presumably generate large cyclical impulses, are also those where irregular variations are more noticeable and where the overall business cycle is less apparent. This observation is of interest because it puts into proper perspective the contrast between the micro- and the macroeconomic, or aggregative, method of studying cyclical growth. Since at any one time the bulk of the industrial sector is formed by mature industries, the aggregate and averages can give us the picture of the general tendencies. Taken in this manner the aggregate method, and the use of averages, cannot be misleading but useful. In fact, in order to delve into the *origin* of cycles, and more generally to study the changes arising from firms and not from the action of government or external factors, it is necessary to analyze the industries that are growing more rapidly, that play therefore a central role in global process of growth, and, as has been already noted, that are characterized by a larger degree of cyclical irregularity. We can therefore conclude that Schumpeter's sharp condemnation of the aggregative method goes too far: to those who are aware of its limitations, the method can be helpful.

In his criticism of the aggregative model Schumpeter also gives some notice to a number of cyclical models that make use of global aggregates. But his criticism is concerned with other aspects of the models as well. He is particularly severe on those theories that treat the cycle as a self-perpetuating phenomenon, caused by a single initial shock:" some trouble, for instance, having occurred in the apple-growing industry at the time Adam and Eve dwelt in Paradise—but then might go on forever" (Schumpeter 1939, 187). The same critical attitude is taken toward the theories that assume an initial disturbance which is continually reproduced in a system where the data remain unchanged: "eventually" writes Schumpeter, "they would learn the lesson" (Schumpeter 1939, 531). (Schumpeter maintained that these kinds of disequilibria help explain particular fluctuations of the cycle but not the cycle itself.) It is worth studying the specific acute and instructive criticism put forward by Schumpeter in his argument against aggregative models, some of which are still in vogue (see Schumpeter 1939, ch. 6, n. 3, and ch. 10).

It is also necessary to emphasize another aspect of these models which, as we have already seen, can be criticized on the basis of Schumpeter's analysis of cyclical development. The thesis, which, strictly speaking, originates from Marx, that cycle and development are not separate phenomena but that one presupposes the other is becoming increasingly accepted. A few authors of "models" have attempted to relate the two phenomena. In most cases, however, the result is nothing but an artifical and mechanical grafting, achieved, for instance, by introducing the rather debatable concept of "autonomous investment." Development which is the rising trend, is then assumed, not explained.[33] This is not the case in the Schumpeterian and Marxist analyses where trend and cycle appear as two aspects of the same phenomenon. They are, so to speak, dialectically combined.

Consequences of the Progressive Concentration of Firms on the Business Cycle

How valid is Schumpeter's theory today?

The question is as complex as it is important and has to be given serious thought.

The essential ingredients of the Schumpeterian theory—innovating entrepreneurs followed by a host of imitators, elimination of firms incapable to adjust, appearance and disappearance of interest and profits—all presuppose competitive conditions. On this point Schumpeter is very explicit, although in a second approximation he tries to take into account the "imperfections" of competition. Yet the importance of a phenomenon, which Marx had already foreseen, could not have escaped an economist so aware of changes in economic life in historical time. That is the formation and growth of large and very large industrial enterprises capable of regulating to a greater and greater extent prices and even capable, by means of advertising, of influencing demand itself. Whether the Schumpeterian theory is still valid under the new conditions, though it undoubtedly has shed a great deal of light on economic growth under conditions approximating competition, is a problem, and it constantly preoccupied Schumpeter. To this problem he gave different solutions at different times. In the *Theory of Economic Development* he wrote:

And if the competitive economy is broken up by the growth of great combines, as is increasingly the case today in all countries, then this must become more and more true of real life, and the carrying out of new combinations must become in ever greater measure the internal concern of one and the same economic body. The difference so made is great enough to serve as the watershed between two epochs in the social history of capitalism. (Schumpeter 1961, 67)

In an article on the "Instability of Capitalism" which he wrote in 1928. Schumpeter maintains that under *Trustified Capitalism* some fundamental features of cyclical development either change and/or become less evident. Hence, given the importance (or rather the renewed importance as in the early stages of capitalism) of the self-financing of large industrial companies, the creation of credit takes up a secondary role. In the same article he even maintained that when under Trustified Capitalism some of the conditions leading to cycles are removed, the capitalist system will tend toward stability.[34] He seems to believe that that process was actually occurring.

The Great Depression obviously pushed Schumpeter to modify this judgment. In the *Business Cycles*, published in 1939, he almost reversed his position. This is not to say that he maintained that Trustified Capitalism tended to be more unstable and that prosperity and depression were more marked. He rather claimed that the *trustification* process was only in its infancy and therefore not yet relevant to the theory of the business cycle. He pointed out that as large companies acquire an increasing importance, it will be less likely that innovations will be introduced by new firms; hence some aspects of the cycle that he analyzed might disappear. In this context he wrote:

In order to take care of this case, which in future may steadily gain in importance, we introduce the concept Trustified Capitalism, in distinction from Competitive Capitalism. . . .

Giant concerns still have to react to each other's innovations, of course, but they do so in other and less predictable ways than firms which are drops in a competitive sea, and many details—in some points, more than details— would then have to be altered in our model. . . .

However, the sector of concerns which are "big" not only in the usual sense of the writers who figure out what percentage of the total national capital of the United States is controlled by the 200 biggest concerns but in the sense required by the present argument, is as yet not great enough to dominate the picture in any country. (Schumpeter 1939, 96–97)

The last statement is expressed in a manner that lays bare the uncertainty of the author. Such uncertainty comes out also from other statements which do not tally in full with the one just quoted:

. . . our model and its working is, of course, strongly institutional in character. . . . Our argument rests on (abstractions from) historical facts which may turn out to belong to an epoch that is rapidly passing." (Schumpeter 1939, 144)

Schumpeter's approach seems to be rather satisfactory for the period up to the first world war. After the war the structural changes in the capitalist economics as well as the characteristics of the *Konjunktur* changed so greatly from those of the prewar period that Schumpeter could not avoid qualifying his view:

It is obvious, however, that external factors in our sense continued to play a supernormally important role throughout the postwar period. That our second component of economic change, the cyclical process of evolution, was still present and asserted itself in the same manner as before is not obvious. Owing to the historical character of our subject—or the fact that it is "institutionally conditioned"—this question would arise in any case, even if there had been no war: whenever we wish to apply our analysis to an additional span of time, we must always ask whether our process still persists. (Schumpeter 1939, 693–694).

Nevertheless, he concluded that in the final analysis his process was still relevant.

In *Capitalism, Socialism and Democracy*, 1942 Schumpeter tackled the question of the meaning and consequences of the monopolistic power ascribed to the large industrial complexes. These complexes, he maintained, may have, and do have, monopoly powers in the short run. In the long run, however, they are subject to the competition arising from new goods, new techniques, and new organizational methods. This type of competition is quite different from the normal type of competition based on small and gradual changes, described by textbooks. In the short period, in a world dominated by competition and thus by uncertainty and risk, the gains derived from monopolistic practices can be considered as insurance premiums. In the long run these practices would not represent obstacles to development but necessary conditions for development to occur. Lastly, price rigidity connected with monopolistic practices does not have, in Schumpeter's view, the importance that many economists give it. Insofar as it effectively exists, price rigidity can have, in the short run and especially during a depression, a positive role by preventing, for instance, unnecessary bankruptcies and the ensuing chain reaction. (Schumpeter 1942, chs. 6–8).

In addition Schumpeter's position on this subject is significantly different from the one taken later in the *Theory of Economic Development*. There he neatly distinguishes between temporary monopolistic positions necessarily linked to innovations, which thus have a positive role to play in the process of development, and permanent monopolistic positions not connected to innovations. (Schumpeter 1961, 152, 208). In his more recent works that distinction seems to imply that most monopolistic positions are temporary and *as a rule* play directly or indirectly a positive role in the process of growth.

Now many serious doubts can be raised as to the ability of the Schumpeterian type of competition to neutralize the monopolistic power of the big industrial complexes. One thing is the consequences of Schumpeterian competition (new products, new techniques) that come on top of normal competition, and another the consequences of that competition when it comes to clash with the existence of large industrial undertakings. In this case it would be necessary to demonstrate that innovations in a world populated by giant enterprises with monopolistic powers are as easy as in a world where there are no barriers to entry of new firms. Those large enterprises can in fact successfully hinder the formation of new firms and can decide whether or not to carry out technical innovations. In short, it would have to be shown that all types of innovations can be indiscriminately introduced. A little thought demonstrated the following conclusion. No special considerations are required for monopolistic companies to carry out innovations that reduce unit costs without raising total costs. However, those innovations entailing an increase in total costs, which for technical reasons are far the most important,[35] will be carried out only if demand exhibits specific characteristics.[36] It is therefore doubtful that Schumpeterian competition can operate with unchanged intensity. The opposite is likely to be the case.

The Question of Economic Stagnation

In the years between the two world wars there was the Great Depression of the 1930s, which began in 1929 and was exceptionally grave. It was followed by an abnormally weak recovery.[37] How is it possible to explain the gravity of the depression and the weakness of the subsequent recovery?

Several economists have considered these two events as symptoms of a tendency toward stagnation in modern economics. This tendency has been ascribed to various factors: to the reduction in the growth rate of population, to the progressive decline in the propensity to consume as income grows, to the exhaustion of innovations and of territorial expansion. Yet the hypothesis that should appear as the most natural, that is, the tendency toward stagnation is to be linked to transformation in the economic structure and, in particular, to the growing "trustification" of modern economies, has never been systematically developed and discussed. Yet the economists who substantially accept this hypothesis, although not always in a clear and explicit manner, are not a small minority. Among them are economists who identify the seriousness of the Great Depression and the weakness of the subsequent recovery, with the growing "rigidity" of prices and more generally with the growing "rigidity" of the economic system. In turn such rigidity is seen as depending on a growing diffusion of monopolistic conditions, not only in the goods market but also in the labor market. (The tendency toward stagnation can be and has been reversed; but this is another mather.)

Schumpeter criticized the hypotheses previously mentioned (decline in population growth, lower propensity to consume, exhaustion of innovation and of territorial expansion). His criticism is sharp and on the whole effective (see Schumpeter 1939, 103–213; 1942, 111–120, 392–398). Although he did not systematically take into account the hypothesis that the tendency toward stagnation depends on the expansion of monopolistic structures, it can be seen from previous references, that he did bear it constantly in mind. His critique of the concept of price "rigidities" as well as of the effects of monopolistic practices are nothing but bits and pieces of a more or less explicit polemic against the economists who tend to explain stagnation in terms of "monopolization." Essentially, he excluded that the gravity of the Great Depression and the sluggish recovery following it are to be ascribed to changes in the economic structure. He viewed the Great Depression as a not altogether new phenomenon which he linked to the downswing of his debatable Kondratieff long cycle (Schumpeter 1939, 907–908). He ascribed the difficulties encountered by the recovery not to an internal malfunctioning of the system of business enterprises but to political measures hostile to capitalism. This last point introduced a well-known thesis he amply developed in *Capitalism, Socialism and Democracy*, according to which "capitalism produces by its mere working a social atmosphere—a moral code if the reader prefers—that is hostile to it, and this atmosphere produces policies which do not allow it to function" (Schumpeter 1939, 1038). This thesis goes beyond economics and enters into the wider field of sociology and politics. The outcome would still be a tendency toward stagnation but due to sociological reasons which would only indirectly have economic roots.

It should now become clear that both the depth of the Great Depression and the slowness of the recovery have great relevance to Schumpeter's theoretical construct. If it were possible to show that the two phenomena are linked to the growing trustification of the capitalist system, the Schumpeterian theory of the business cycle would have a limited explanatory power at least from World War I onward. Moreover the impacts of the "social atmosphere" and "hostile policies" could no longer be presented as a primary explanation. The "hostile atmosphere" would appear *essentially* as a consequence rather than as a cause of the economic malfunctioning of "trustified capitalism."

2.4 Concluding Remarks

Marx's central thesis was that an economic system based on private enterprises (the capitalist system) will tend to create, in the process of expansion, conditions that are incompatible with that very expansion, thus leading to a transformation of society into a "socialist" system.

Schumpeter basically accepted that thesis but attempted to prove it with arguments opposite to those used by Marx. Undoubtedly there is a remarkable difference in the two views. For Marx the capitalist system is undermined by *economic* factors: the general crisis of capitalism is mainly due to the "tendency of the rate of profit to fall" and only marginally to other factors. For Schumpeter, by contrast, the forces at work are mainly sociological factors. According to him capitalism is *economically* stable, and from this perspective its growth has no limits. If, however, the capitalist system shows growing frictions and tends to change over into a different system, this is due to institutional and sociological factors. In particular, reference is made to the "evaporation of the substance of property" and to the declining role of the entrepreneur in the process of growth. These institutional transformations depend on the process of concentration and "trustification." This process which is economic in character acquires significance for its sociological consequences. This is where Schumpeter gets close to Marx. It also seems worthwhile to mention Schumpeter's observations as they appear in *Capitalism Socialism and Democracy*.[38] The reader can easily compare them with those of Marx quoted in section 2.2 of this chapter. Schumpeter fundamentally accepts the Marxist thesis of concentration and only adds qualifications and comments worthy of consideration:

On the one hand, the capitalist process unavoidably attacks the economic standing ground of the small producer and trader. What it did to the precapitalist strata it also does—and by the same competitive mechanism—to the lower strata of capitalist industry. Here of course Marx scores. It is true that the facts of industrial concentration do not quite live up to the ideas the public is being taught to entertain about it (see Chapter XIX). The process has gone less far and is less free from setbacks and compensatory tendencies than one would gather from many a popular exposition. In particular, large-scale enterprise not only annihilates but also, to some extent, creates space for the small producing, and especially trading firm. Also, in the case of the peasants and farmers, the capitalist world has at last proved both willing and able to pursue an expensive but on the whole effective policy of conservation. In the long run, however, there can be little doubt about the fact that we are envisaging, or about its consequences. (Schumpeter, 1942, 140)

The consequences would in fact consist, as Schumpeter himself pointed out, of the elimination of a lot of small and medium enterprises and in the erosion of the foundations of property and free contracts. Here therefore Schumpeter has very little to add to what has been said by Marx.

The already mentioned thesis of the obsolescence of the innovating entrepreneur is presented in the following terms:

This social function is already losing importance and is bound to lose it at an accelerating rate in the future even if the economic process itself of which entrepreneurship was the prime mover went on unabated. For, on the one hand, it is much easier now than it has been in the past to do things that lie outside familiar routine—innovation itself is being reduced to routine.

Technological progress is increasingly becoming the business of teams of trained specialists who turn out what is required and make it work in predictable ways. The romance of earlier commercial adventure is rapidly wearing away, because so many more things can be strictly calculated that had of old to be visualized in a flash of genius. (Schumpeter 1942, 132)

As to the problem of the structural and institutional transformation of modern societies, which, strictly speaking, is of a metaeconomic nature, the foregoing observation is the most original of all Schumpeter's theses.

Postscript (1983)

This chapter was written 29 years ago. Since then *a lot of water has passed under the bridge*. During these years the present writer has developed new thoughts and has changed some of his views. It is therefore not surprising that the author feels the need to add a comment which in some respect is one of self criticism.

As appears from the discussion, I had then already some reservations about Marx's interpretative schemes as well as those of Schumpeter, who was my teacher at Harvard. My stronger reservations were about Schumpeter rather than Marx. Today I must say that in a sense my view has been reversed.

At the risk of some overgeneralization, it can be said that for Marxism the evolution of society depends on transformation of the relations of production. Cultural changes are "superstructural" and are determined by "structural" changes. According to the philosophy of idealism, and in contrast to Marxism, social evolution is determined by autonomous evolution of the mind (*spirito* in Italian; *Geist* in German). According to a view which can be ascribed, I believe, to intellectuals as different as Antonio Gramsci and Schumpeter, and which unfortunately has not been adequately further developed, what matters is the *interaction* between structural (or economic) changes and cultural (or super-structural) changes. In this type of interaction no prominence or even auto-nomy can be assigned to either of these forces. I now find myself close to the last view. I never fully accepted the materialistic or the idealistic conceptions, but in the past my views were less clearly defined, and I was inclined to give a certain priority to forces of a *materialistic* nature.

The unexpected students' revolts that took place in several developed capitalist countries in 1968 as well as other important events then and during the following years can be used to illustrate my current views.

These revolts can in no way be explained by Marxist criteria. Some of their important implications to the contrary can only be understood through the analysis developed by Schumpeter in *Capitalism, Socialism, and Democracy*.

The basic thesis of that book is that capitalism will end, after a very long process, not because of its failure but because of its economic achievements. The productive expansion brought about by capitalism creates a hostile atmosphere that makes its survival impossible. This atmosphere is in turn generated by the intellectuals whose number increases with the process of economic development. They become increasingly critical and dissatisfied.

Intellectuals are, for better or for worse, critics by nature. Critical rationalism gradually erodes all values, demolishing the noneconomic (i.e., cultural) walls of a precapitalistic nature which in essence protected the capitalist system. Moreover with economic growth the number of people holding degrees derived from higher education also increases. These people aspire to "intellectual"-type jobs, executive and directive positions which are positions of prestige and yield an income higher than the one society as a whole is capable of generating. This is an outcome of mass education, notably university education.

In mathematical terms the problem arises from the fact that the demand for and supply of intellectual labor are functions of altogether different variables. Demand for the intellectual labor force is a function of the speed and type of growth; supply is a function of average income. As the latter increases, the number of people with higher education and aspiring to an intellectual occupation also grows. Consequently in the intellectual labor market supply can exceed, and often does exceed, demand. The opposite takes place in the market for manual labor. Hence we get a growing number of frustrated people because they are employed in occupations that do not bear a relationship to their aspirations. This explains the growing anger of unemployed or ill-employed intellectuals which in turn contributes to the hostile atmosphere mentioned previously.

Schumpeter captured with precision the sense of emptiness and anguish that stems from the erosion of old values in a society which, because of the very logic of its functioning, has little to offer at the spiritual level. He also foresaw with equal precision the anguish and the dissatisfaction of youth as a contradiction deriving from the growth of mass education. In fact the student movements have, by and large, been formed and led by *petite bourgeoisie* intellectuals; the working class component was absent if not hostile. These movements were a typical product of the "superstructure." The importance assigned by Schumpeter to the superstructure might lead one to think that his approach was of an "idealistic" type. However, as we have seen in the preceding example, he always related the "superstructure" to economic transformations, not because the latter "determine" the former but because they always mutually interact. It is true that Marx too, differently from many of his followers, clearly recognizes such an interaction (e.g., see Marx [1939–1941] 1973, 109–111), but it is also true that he always tends to give preeminence to the economic structure.

In chapter 2 I was inclined to attribute the transformation of capitalism into a different system (i.e., through a long-run process with decreasing probabilities of a revolutionary break) to predominantly economic rather than cultural forces. I thought that the tendency toward stagnation in modern capitalism was inherent in its structure, which is becoming increasingly dominated by large and giant firms. I also added that the tendency could be counteracted by appropriate economic policies which would, however, lead to a radical transformation of the system. I gave a subordinate role to cultural forces.

Today any form of hierarchical ordering seems to me outdated. It is necessary to look at the global process. The tendency toward business concentration which characterizes the structure of modern capitalism is certainly very relevant to a discussion of the capitalist system. It was foreshadowed by Marx and amply analyzed by Schumpeter. Yet it must be said that the process asserted itself in many important sectors but not in others. Recent technological innovations largely stimulated by economic and social changes have created and are creating new room for small and vigorously dynamic firms. In any case the cultural forces singled out by Schumpeter play a very important role. In the long run the outcome of the whole evolution is the same: the transformation of the capitalist system into a different system, whose features, however, are not predetermined but depend on us. The roads leading to such an outcome cannot be found only or predominantly in the economic sphere. This is the point.[39]

Three final observations. First, I wish to point out that I have modified but not reversed my position on the comparative relevance of economic and cultural forces. Now I no longer consider the former as predominant, but rather neither appears to me to be subordinate to the other. In fact I am convinced—for reasons that I will discuss in chapter 5—that under contemporary conditions government action is essential to the process of growth to support and to prevent economic stagnation, though when this action is ill advised, it can contribute to inflation or that very serious new type of disease—stagflation. In any case, for better or for worse, under contemporary conditions government intervention is indispensable for economic growth.

Second, the comments presented in this Postscript refer almost exclusively to *Capitalism, Socialism, and Democracy*, a book that has been much more widely debated than the monumental treatise on business cycles. Among the works devoted to that book the short essay by Gottfried Haberler in "Schumpeter's *Capitalism, Socialism, and Democracy* after Forty Years" is worth mentioning.[40] Haberler equates public planning with socialism and is not enthusiastic at all that public planning is gaining ground in capitalist economics, though he agrees with those who maintain that there is a tendency for convergence of the two systems. Thus Haberler would substitute the Schumpeterian question "Can capitalism survive?" with the question "How far will the admixture of public planning go?" Such a question can move us to reflect on the numerous, changing meanings of capitalism, socialism, and public planning. To make my point clear, it is worth emphasizing that public planning in Japan or Austria is something thoroughly different not only from that of the Soviet Union—which is obvious—but also from that of France or Italy. Presumably it would be advisable to distinguish between conflicting and nonconflicting social situations—I mean conflicting in the Marxian sense. Another subject worth considering is the implications of the rising trend of the ratio between wages and salaries which is clearly visible in the major industrialized economies. Such a trend can imply a progressive reduction of class barriers and is relevant also with respect to the convergence Gottfried Haberler refers to.

Third, by placing pure economic forces at the same level as cultural forces, I naturally did not consider economic conflicts, which in Marx's conception are subsumed under the notion of class struggle, as uniquely or absolutely dominant. Other conflicts of a racial, religious, and ethnic character, or more generally cultural conflict, however, should become objects of study in their own right. The analysis becomes then much more difficult, and economists must comply with the interpretative powers of their discipline. Yet the social reality that we are attempting to understand is extremely complex, and a master key that can open all the doors does not exist.

Notes

1. See Marx (1977, vol. 1, ch. 12; vol. 2, ch. 19). For his critique of Smith, see Marx (1969, pt. 1, 97–103); for that of Richardo, see Marx (1968, pt. 2, 173–189, 547–550).

2. For Marx's discussion of simple reproduction, see Marx (1977, vol. 1, ch. 23; vol. 2, ch. 20); for expanded reproduction, see Marx vol. 1, ch. 19; vol. 2, ch. 21).

3. P. M. Sweezy (1968, chs. 5 and 10) gives a lucid summary of the two schemes and of the respective equilibrium conditions.

4. "Simple reproduction, reproduction on the same scale, appears as an abstraction, in as much as on the one hand the absence of all accumulation of reproduction on extended scale is a strange assumption in capitalist conditions, and on the other hand conditions of production do not remain exactly the same in different years." Marx

adds: "However, as far as accumulation does take place, simple reproduction is always part of it, and can therefore be studied by itself and is an actual factor of accumulation" (Marx [1867] 1977, 1: 398–399).

5. "To accumulate is to conquer the world of social wealth, to increase the mass of human beings exploited by him and thus to extend both the direct and indirect sway of the capitalist" (Marx [1867] 1977, 1: 555).

6. At the end of this process the price will be lower, individual and social values will coincide at this new reduced level, and the extra surplus value will disappear. Yet, if this process affects commodities that form part of "the necessary means of subsistence and are therefore elements of the value of labor power" (Marx [1867] 1977, 1: 303), then, according to Marx, this value as well as its monetary expression (the money wage) will diminish. As a consequence, given the number of hours each worker works, there will be a decline in the number of hours necessary to reproduce labor power, causing a rise in the rate of surplus value.

7. Neither Marx nor Ricardo employ the term "unemployment" but the expressions equivalent to those quoted in the text. Among economists the use of this term seems to be relatively recent. The word unemployment cannot be found in the first editions of *Palgrave's Dictionary*. In the appendix to the 1926 edition the term is presented in the following way: "until comparatively recently unemployment was regarded as a problem of character. The unemployed were mentally or physically unfit. All who truly wanted work could find it, was the common assumption. But this view was badly shaken at the beginning of the century. Unemployment was seen to be a normal feature—a problem arising out of the very nature of modern industrial organization."

8. Schumpeter himself did not provide a satisfactory interpretation in his *History of Economic Analysis*. He does not point out that for both Marx and Ricardo the argument is based on the assumption that total capital is given. He attributes to Ricardo, in contrast to Marx, a form of compensation which, as we have seen, Marx himself took into account (i.e., the formation of additional capital made possible by a fall in prices). Moreover Schumpeter claims that if Marx wanted to present his thesis in a less objectionable manner, he should have stressed that "displacement of labor by machines may be temporary so far as the effects of each distinct act of mechanization is concerned and yet explain permanent presence of unemployment on the assumption that such abstract acts occur often enough" (Schumpeter 1954, 681, n. 100). In fact Marx did take into account Schumpeter's way of looking at the problem:" since machinery is continually seizing upon new fields of production its temporary effect is really permanent" (Marx [1867] 1977, 1: 407).

9. See the notion of "full employment ceiling" developed by Hicks (1950).

10. Quite apart from the cyclical movement of unemployment due to the accumulation process, Marx distinguishes between three forms of unemployment: fluctuating unemployment, formed by workers who are no longer in productive age and are therefore fired but can be reemployed during the prosperity phase; latent unemployment especially in agriculture; and stagnant or chronic unemployment which is formed by workers employed in precarious activities. This type of unemployment is fed by the decline in precapitalistic industries—artisans and manufacturing—which succomb to the unequal struggle with mechanized industry.

11. First and third quotation from Marx ([1867] 1977, 1:592–593). The second quotation is a note added by Marx in section 3 of chapter 23; this note is translated from the Italian edition (Edizioni Rinascita 1953, 360), which takes it from the French edition of 1973.

12. See Schumpeter (1954, 1131). See also Dobb's introduction to the Italian edition of *Theories of Surplus Value* (Dobb 1954).

13. See Marx ([1867] 1977, vol. 1, ch. 25, sec. 3; vol. 3, chs. 15, 28, 30) and Marx ([1905] 1968, vol. 1, ch. 17).

14. Assuming that at the root of the cycle lies the process of progressive mechanization, Marx put forward an interesting hypothesis about the variation of the cycle. He criticized the view that the length of the cycle can be assumed to be relatively constant. He actually thought the duration of cycles will be gradually shortened by the laws of capitalistic production. This is because with the expansion of mechanization the economic life of plants is shortened, and so are the prosperity phases (in which competition is termporarily halted). At the same time the immediate power of expansion of capital increases. Accumulation will then proceed at a faster pace, but at the same time the limit of the available labor force will be reached more quickly.

15. Another interpretation can be found in the third volume of *Capital* ([1894], 1977, ch. 15) in which Marx advanced the proposition that the crisis is a temporary reaction against the tendency of the rate of profit to fall. This thesis has classical and pre-Marxian origins. The view that crises are linked to the tendency of the rate of profit to fall can be found in earlier writers such as J. S. Mill. (In Italy until the first world war several economists accepted this thesis, among them Camillo Supino and Augusto Graziani, Sr.) Marx restates it in original terms; the rate of profit tends to fall, he maintains, because as accumulation goes on, constant capital (especially machinery) tends to grow more rapidly than variable capital.

16. Similar observations are made by Supino (1892) to explain the divergence of discount and other interest rates.

17. In the second volume of *Capital* ([1885] 1977) Marx clearly stated that hoarding under capitalism is never an end in itself. Hoarding is the result of an interruption of the process of circulation. In the third volume ([1894] 1977) he maintained that the quantity of money does not affect the rate of interest. Yet he recognized the importance of what later became known as the Keynesian liquidity preference. Marx in fact acknowledged that the quantity of money affects the rate of interest during a depression when demand for money is determined by the desire to hoard, which is not to be seen as a primary impulse but as a result of the conditions determined by the depression.

18. Marx's analysis of money and business cycles is one of his most stimulating works and yet one of the most neglected both by friends and foes. One of the few exceptions is Pietro Manes who in his unprejudiced and original book on Marx gives due importance to that analysis (Manes 1981; note added in 1983).

19. "This does not, however, prevent revenue from constantly growing in value and in quantity. But it does not result in a proportionately larger part of the total product being laid out in wages" (Marx [1905] 1968, 2:562).

20. Since the first world war, unemployment fluctuated in England around 5 to 6 percent with a minimum of 1 to 2 percent at the peak of cyclical prosperity and a maximum of 12 to 13 percent. (It must be noted that these figures refer to the unionized nonagricultural labor force and not to total active population. According to Douglas, between 1890 and 1914 unemployment fluctuated in the United States around 7 percent with a minimum of 3 percent and a maximum of 16 to 17 percent. As it is well known, between the wars unemployment reached unheard levels of 20 percent and more in both countries. (Pigou 1929, 381–382; Douglas 1928, 445).

21. This tendency became clear in the last three decades of the nineteenth century. From 1850 to 1867, the period particularly studied by Marx, real wages fluctuated greatly but increased only very little.

22. Marx ([1894] 1977, vol. 3, ch. 46): "By 'monopoly price' we mean, generally speaking, a price that is determined only by the desire of the buyers and by their purchasing power, independently from the cost of production and from the value of the products." Ricardo ([1821] 1951, 385): "Commodities which are monopolized, either by an individual, or by a company, vary according to the law which Lord Lauderdale has laid down: they fall in proportion as the sellers augment their quantity and rise in proportion to the eagerness of the buyers to purchase them; their price has no necessary connection with their natural value: but the prices of commodities, which are subject to competition, and whose quantity may be increased in any moderate degree, will ultimately depend, not on the state of demand and supply, but on the increased or diminished cost of their production."

23. Schumpeter himself stated that "in order to be a socialist it is of course not necessary to be a Marxist; but neither is it sufficient to be a Marxist in order to be a socialist" (Schumpeter 1961, 58, n. 13). To this he added: "A man may accept Marx's analytic work entirely and yet be a conservative in practice" (Schumpeter 1954, 133, n. 18).

24. Schumpeter seems to give to the theory of the innovating entrepreneur a wider meaning than the purely economic one: "The writer believes although he cannot stay to show that the theory here expounded is but a special case, adapted to the economic sphere, of a much larger theory which applies to change in all spheres of social life, science and art included" (Schumpeter 1939, 97, n. 2).

25. Compare the point of view of Schumpeter with that of Marx who, by criticizing the concrete possibility of a balanced growth, stressed those factors that can be called objective factors: "Since, however, capitalist production can allow itself free rein only in certain spheres, under certain conditions, there could be no capitalist production at all if it had to develop *simultaneously* and *evenly* in all spheres." (Marx [1905] 1968, 2:352.)

26. Schumpeter analyzed more systematically than Marx the role of credit and banking in the growth and cyclical process. Yet Marx has treated this problem extensively and has developed observations worthy of further elaboration. (See Marx [1894] 1977, vol. 3, pt. 5). It must also be noted that Marx was aware of the phenomenon of the creation of money by banks. This is shown in its various forms in the second volume of *Capital*. He also saw the nature of bank-type means of payments, a rare fact in his days. His views are the following: "the bill of exchange form[s] the basis of money credit—

money proper, of bank notes, etc. These do not rest upon the circulation of money, be it metallic or government-issued paper money, but rather upon the circulation of bills of exchange" (Marx [1885] 1977, 401). This corresponds to the position expressed many years later by De Viti De Marco ([1898] 1935).

27. Marx, as we have seen, takes into account both conditions in his analysis of accumulation. The additional real factors stem from previous accumulation; additional workers come from the industrial reserve army which is constantly recreated.

28. In a footnote Schumpeter does allow for that possibility but he adds that one should speak about a notional shift and that such a shift does not differ very much from an actual one. (See Schumpeter 1939, 111, n. 1.)

29. Schumpeter explains in the following way why saving plays a secondary role in the process of growth: "By far the greater part of it does not come from thrift in the strict sense, that is, from abstaining from the consumption of part of one's regular income, but it consists of funds which are themselves the result of successful innovation and in which we shall later recognize entrepreneurial profit" (Schumpeter 1961, 72).

30. "Excluding as we do noncapitalist change, we have to define that word which good economists always try to avoid: capitalism is that form of private property economy in which innovations are carried out by means of borrowed money, which in general, though not by logical necessity, implies credit creation. A society, the economic life of which is characterized by private property and controlled by private initiative, is according to this definition not necessarily capitalist, even if there are, for instance, privately owned factories, salaried workers, and free exchange of goods and services, either in kind or through the medium of money. The entrepreneurial function itself is not confined to capitalist society, since such economic leadership as it implies would be present, though in other forms, even in a primitive tribe or in a socialist community" (Schumpeter 1939, 223). However, according to Schumpeter the capitalist structure has historically given to the entrepreneurs a large scope of action. Only in this framework which is at the very foundations of growth, the action of entrepreneurs gives rise to cyclical development. It follows that "the smaller the capitalist sector embedded in an otherwise precapitalist world, the less the fluctuations characteristic of the capitalist process will assert themselves and the more other causes of fluctuations, in our terminology external factors, will dominate" (Schumpeter 1939, 223). This observation which Schumpeter uses for the precapitalist phase can be of interest for the study of modern backward economies. This is in line with the view that sees the backward economies, where development is weak or nonexistent, as receiving cyclical impulses from the growing economies without contributing to those impulses.

31. Therefore in the second approximation Schumpeter is closer to Marx.

32. Schumpeter assumes that the Kitchin cycle lasts between 38 and 42 months and the Juglar cycle for a period of about 7 to 9 years.

33. Kaldor has observed that "the trend itself is not 'explained'; it is introduced as a datum. There can be no pretence, therefore, of these theories providing the basis for a theory of economic growth" (Kaldor 1954, 65).

34. There is a hint in that sense in Schumpeter (1961, 255).

35. It is precisely to this type of innovation that Schumpeter is referring (Schumpeter 1939, 93).

36. See Sylos-Labini (1954).

37. It is commonly acknowledged that recovery from the Great Depression was abnormally weak. Suffice it to look at the movement in unemployment in the more developed countries: it stayed high, with some oscillations till the outbreak of World War II. In Germany the absorption of unemployment started earlier, but it was due to rearmament and war preparations rather than to some spontaneous factors.

38. "Industrial property and management have become depersonalized—ownership having degenerated to stock and bond holding, the executives having acquired habits of mind similar to those of civil servants" (Schumpeter 1942, 219).

39. These points were developed by the author in the Eleventh R. C. Mills Memorial Lecture given at the University of Sydney, 21 October 1980 (chapter 3 of this volume).

40. In Arnold Weertje (ed.), *Schumpeter's Vision: Capitalism, Socialism and Democracy after Forty Years* (Praeger, New York, 1981; reprinted as Reprint No. 126 in the series of the American Enterprise Institute, Washington D.C., 1981).

References

Barton, John. 1817. *Observations on the Circumstances which Influence the Condition of the Labouring Classes of Society.* John and Arthur Arch, London.

Breglia, A. 1942. *Temi di economia e vita sociale.* Giuffrè, Milan.

Burns, A. F., and Mitchell, W. C. 1946. *Measuring Business Cycles.* National Bureau of Economic Research, New York.

Clemence R. V. ed. 1951. *J. A. Schumpeter.* Addison-Wesley: Reading, Mass.

De Viti de Marco, A. 1898. *La funzione della banca.* Reprint. Einaudi, Turin 1935.

Dobb, M. H. 1954. 'Introduzione' to K. Marx, *Storia delle teorie economiche,* Vol. 1. Einaudi, Turin.

Douglas, P. H. 1928. *Real Wages in the United States 1890–1925.* Houghton Mifflin, Boston.

Hicks, J. R. 1932. *The Theory of Wages.* Macmillan, London.

Hicks, J. R. 1950. *A Contribution to Theory of the Trade Cycle.* Clarendon Press, Oxford.

Kaldor, N. 1954. The Relation of Economic Growth and Cyclical Fluctuations. *Economic Journal* 64 (March): 53–71.

Manes, O. 1982. *Critica del pensiero economico di Marx—La basi teoriche del socialismo liberale.* Dedalo, Bari.

Marshall, A. 1923. *Industry and Trade.* Macmillan, London.

Marx, Karl H. 1898. *Wages, Price and Profit.* Reprint. *Karl Marx and Frederick Engels,*

Selected Works in Two Volumes. Foreign Languages Publishing House, Moscow, 1950, pp. 361–405.

Marx, Karl H.1905. *Theories of Surplus Value*, Pt. 2 Reprint. Progress Publishers, Moscow, 1968.

Marx, Karl H. 1905. *Theories of Surplus Value*, Pt. 1 Reprint. Progress Publishers, Moscow, 1969.

Marx, Karl H. 1939–41. *Grundrisse*. Reprint. *Foundations of the Critique of Political Economy*. Translated with a forward by M. Nicolaus. Allen Lane, London, 1973.

Marx, Karl H. 1867, 1885, 1894. *Capital*, Vols. 1, 2, 3. Reprint. Progress Publishers, Moscow, 1977.

Marx, K. H., and Engels F. 1848. *Manifesto of the Communist Party*. Reprint. L. S. Feuer, ed. *Marx and Engels*. Doubleday, New York, 1959.

Palgrave, R. H. Inglis. 1926. *Dictionary of Political Economy*. Macmillan, London.

Pigou, A. C. 1929. *Industrial Fluctuations*, Macmillan, London.

Ricardo, D. 1821. *On the Principles of Political Economy and Taxation*. Reprint. Piero Sraffa, ed., in collaboration with M. H. Dobb. Cambridge University Press, Cambridge.

Schumpeter, J. A. 1928. The Instability of Capitalism. *Economic Journal* 28 (September): 361–386.

Schumpeter, J. A. 1939. *Business Cycles*. McGraw-Hill, New York.

Schumpeter, J. A. 1942. *Capitalism, Socialism and Democracy*. Allen and Unwin, London.

Schumpeter, J. A. 1954. *History of Economic Analysis*. Allen and Unwin, London.

Schumpeter, J. A. 1961. *The Theory of Economic Development*. Trans. Redvers Opie. Oxford University Press, New York.

Supino, C. 1892. *Il saggio di sconto*. Bocca, Turin.

Sweezy, P. M. 1968. *The Theory of Capitalist Development*. Monthly Review Press, New York.

Sylos-Labini, P. 1954. Monopoli, ristagno economico e politica keynesiana. *Economia internazionale*, 4 (November): 758–779.

Sylos-Labini, P. 1981. Technological Change under Contemporary Conditions: An Economist's View. *Economic Papers* 66 (August): 1–17.

II

Innovations and Changes in Productivity

3   Technological Change under Contemporary Conditions: An Economist's View

3.1 Technological Change and Economic Theory

When considering economic growth, all economists agree technological change to be the main factor. However, many economists believe that technological change is important only to keep up the rate of economic growth, which in the long run would be smaller without it, but constant and greater than zero provided capital gradually accumulates and the labor force gradually increases. This view is untenable. If we take into account the tendency of diminishing returns from agriculture and mining, we are bound to recognize that, with unchanging methods of production, the rate of increase of the social product in the long run would necessarily tend to zero. This means that in the long run technological progress is not simply the main factor of economic growth: it is the necessary condition.

Despite the decisive role of technological change in the process of growth, the economic literature on technological change is relatively limited. The reason for this paradox lies in the fact that the still prevailing neoclassical theory is essentially static in character and offers little help if one wants to develop a dynamic analysis. It is true that in the last twenty years several important works on the subject have been published, beginning with the book *Productivity and Technological Change* by a very distinguished Australian economist, Wilfred Salter; but, at least until now, works of this kind remain largely separated from the main body of economic theory. This applies also to the models worked out by Nicholas Kaldor in the fifties.

This was not so in the time of the classical economists, particularly Smith, Ricardo, and Marx. Adam Smith, the founding father of modern economic theory, centered his inquiry into the causes of wealth of nations precisely on the division of labor, that is, the progressive specialization of productive operations—both among different productive units and within each unit. He considered the division of labor as the prerequisite of technological change and practically the only factor in the increase in the "productive powers" of labor, as he put it, or, in modern language, in the increase in productivity of labor. According to Smith, the division of labor is limited by the extent of the market: the more the market expands, the greater the possibility of the division of labor and therefore the greater the probability of technical change.

David Ricardo did not develop Smith's analysis of economic growth. However, he was the first major economist to analyze one of the most serious social costs of technological change, that is, what we now call technological unemployment. In a different framework Karl Marx used Ricardo's analysis as a starting point for his theory of capitalist accumulation which, in his view, was bound to proceed according to a wavelike movement and which had in technological change its propelling force. After Marx, economic theory turned toward problems of static equilibrium: technological change and economic progress were either neglected or treated in special chapters of descriptive character, completely separate from theoretical analyses. One of the few exceptions was Joseph Schumpeter, who in his main work *Theory of Economic Development*, published in 1912, presented a general model that had several important points in common with the models of the great classical economists and, in particular, of Marx, so much so that it is not paradoxical to call him a "conservative Marxist." But the dominance of the static neoclassical analysis was such that Schumpeter's work appeared more original than it was, and to some economists, it appeared as queer and eccentric. Since Schumpeter we have to go to the present day to find systematic works on technological change.

Most modern economists consider technological change as a process affecting economic life from the outside, that is, as an exogenous process. This is not correct. In some cases inventions can take place autonomously, following the logic of a certain scientific development or, as in the case of penicillin, as a result of chance; in other cases inventions have been stimulated by an impetus coming from war or, more generally, from the military sector. Often, however, invention is induced by economic stimuli. In any case the adaptation, application, as well as the speed of the diffusion of all inventions depend on economic conditions. First of all, they depend on the expansion of the "extent of the market"—to use Adam Smith's expression—which represent the general condition of technological change. The expansion of the market stimulates additional investment, and as a rule, the new capital goods are more advanced than the existing ones. At the same time the expansion of the market promotes the introduction of new goods that often satisfy needs of the higher order—in the sense of the German statistician Engel—and therefore presuppose an increase in the average per capita income. From both points of view—capital goods and consumption goods—economic growth appears as a self-propelling process.

If the expansion of the market represents the general condition of technological change, the increase of wages relative to the prices of capital goods, which give a systematic slant in favor of the mechanization of the productive operations, and the changes in the relative prices of certain goods represent specific conditions. In particular, the technological change due to increases in wages relative to the price of capital goods is itself self-propelling; in fact technological progress affecting machinery causes its price to fall relative to wages, and such a fall in its turn stimulates further technological progress of the same kind. It should be observed that the increase in trade union pressure has an effect similar to the relative increase in wages; indeed, to reduce the detrimental consequences of strikes, the industrialists tend to introduce innovations that increase the mechanization of production. The changes in relative prices of certain goods can stimulate the invention of new products or the development of substitutes; the case of oil is providing an important instance of this type of process, which we may call "dynamic substitution."

Technological change then consists of process and product innovations. In a direct way technological change is affected by the three economic conditions that I have mentioned; but in an indirect way it is conditioned by cultural, organizational, and even institutional innovations. Technological and institutional innovations are interrelated; one cannot develop without the other. Institutional innovations do not simply accommodate but stimulate technological innovations—if wrongly advised, they can act as a brake on technical progress.[1]

3.2 Technological Change and Economic Growth: The First Stage

Technological change takes place in historical time. The economist who studies this type of change is bound to become aware that economic analysis is historically conditioned even if it makes use of mathematical and econometric models—there is no contradiction between mathematics, economics, and history. This being so, we have to distinguish conceptually between different historical stages in technological change and economic growth, each stage needing a different theoretical model to explain it.

In modern times the first stage is the one analyzed by Adam Smith, and so it covers the sixteenth and seventeenth centuries. Agriculture is absolutely and relatively the most important economic activity; industry is in its manufacturing stage—it is manufacturing in the etymological sense, since the factory system and modern machinery are still to come. In agriculture the remnants of the feudal system are still relevant, and the precapitalist models of production are still prevalent so that technical change—and its source, the division of labor—meets with serious institutional obstacles. Obstacles of a similar kind, but comparatively less serious, were found in manufacturing industry, so free competition, that is, easy entry into the various markets, was not a reality but a target to be achieved. This in fact was the practical purpose of Smith's work. In his view the elimination of the institutional barriers hindering the expansion of the markets was the precondition of an acceleration of the division of labor and of technological change, the division of labor being limited by the extent of the market.

The process of the gradual enlargement of competitive conditions in manufacturing industry was characterzed by a fall in prices of manufactured products. As Smith emphatically pointed out, it occurred precisely because this process was bringing about a systematic fall in costs, particularly in the cost of labor per unit of output, due to technical change. Money wages, according to Smith, were either stationary or, more often, increasing, but productivity was increasing even more, thus causing a decrease of costs and prices. In agriculture too prices could fall, though more slowly, owing to the bigger institutional obstacles to the development of the division of labor. The fall of prices in agriculture, however, was to be expected only in the production of vegetable products rather than in the production of animal products, since in the former the obstacles to the division of labor were comparatively less serious than in the production of the latter. An increase of prices was to be expected also in mineral products, which come out of exhaustible resources.

In the first historical stage—the Smithian stage—technological change as a rule was due to the "common workmen," as Smith says, wage earners and artisans. When the production of machines had become the business of a particular trade improvements were introduced—again, according to Smith—also by the makers of machines, who were more skillful and ingenious than the "common workmen." (It must be noted that when Smith was writing the *Wealth of Nations*, the Industrial Revolution was still to happen, so for Smith "machines" meant sophisticated instruments such as the corn mill, rather than machines in the modern sense, put into motion by particular sources of energy like coal and oil.) As for the great inventions, these were the work of scholars and scientists or, as Smith said, of "philosophers"; but such inventions, and even more, their application, were extremely rare in those times.

3.3 Competitive Capitalism. The Second Stage.

During the nineteenth century the factory system and competitive conditions gradually asserted themselves in the majority of industrial markets. This is the second stage of technological change and economic growth, the stage that has been called competitive capitalism. In this stage the behavior of wages and prices was similar to that predicted by Smith. However, several important changes took place. The most important was the development of a sector producing plant and machinery, which in the modern sense is what we now call the investment sector—at the time of Smith a limited number of units were producing "machines" in the premodern sense, hardly forming a sector. When the development of the investment sector became socially relevant—in the United Kingdom probably well after the period of the Napoleonic Wars— economic growth became a cyclical process. This process was characterized by relatively regular fluctuations, though not strictly periodical, lasting as a rule seven or eight years—a striking regularity, considering the multitude of forces, economic and noneconomic, impinging on the economy. Since the investment sector is where the machines are produced, and since as a rule technological change is embodied in machines whose most recent models are also the most efficient, the investment sector became the principal source of technological change for the whole economy. Correspondingly, the machine makers became the most important innovators. At the same time, with the development of experimental sciences the inventions of the professional scientists became more and more frequent, and their application to productive activities was no more exceptional.

In this period the triad described by Joseph Schumpeter was probably to be found behind the most important innovations. These three constituted the inventor, the entrepreneur, and the banker—the inventor being a man of great intelligence, even of genius, but not necessarily a scientist; the entrepreneur being the innovator, that is, the man who understands the potentialities of an invention and implements it; the banker the person who finances the whole operation. At the time of competitive capitalism, entry was generally free, and the innovator, when successful and thus reaping high profits, was followed by a host of imitators, so that the investment expenditure of the innovating firms was directly or indirectly pushing up the level of economic activity in a phase of expansion, the prosperity phase. When the fruits of such investment were brought to the market in the form of rapidly increasing production, prices went down, resulting in a depression. This was followed by a recovery in which the conditions for a new cycle were prepared. This type of analysis, which is the one worked out by Schumpeter, is different but fundamentally not inconsistent with the analysis worked out by Marx half a century before. For Marx too innovations supply the main impulse for the cyclical accumulation of capital. For him, however, the key role is played by the movements of unemployment—in his analysis he speaks of the "industrial reserve army." During the prosperity phase the demand for labor increases, and unemployment decreases, thus pushing up wages and the demand for goods but, after a point, eroding profit margins. Capitalists then speed up the mechanization process to put a brake on wage increases. However, in so doing, they transform a part of "variable" capital (of the wage fund) into "constant," mainly fixed, capital and thereby indirectly put a brake on the expansion of demand as well. The decline in profit margin which is retarded but not halted by the introduction of new machinery, accompanied by a decline in the rate of expansion of demand, brings prosperity to an end. During the ensuing depression the conditions for a new wave of capital accumulation are created. Among such conditions an increase in unemployment is the most important. As for the timing of the cyclical process, Marx seems to refer to the average duration and to the replacement period of machinery; in his view replacement investment becomes a contributory factor of a new upswing.

It must be pointed out that, according to Marx, the industrial reserve army is fed by several sources, of which technological unemployment in the strict sense, that is, unemployment determined by the introduction of machinery displacing workers employed in modern factories, is only one. Another source is given by what we call today hidden unemployment in traditional agriculture. A further source is another kind of technological unemployment due to a structural decline of traditional manufacturing and handicraft caused by the competition of modern factories. This point is important because only when those two sources of unemployment started to disappear, owing to the shrinking employment in agriculture and in traditional handicraft, did wages begin to show a sustained increase and the modern labor movement to grow in strength.

During the past century, under conditions of competitive capitalism, prices were fluctuating, but their basic trend was downward for a substantial period. Money wages were also fluctuating, but their trend was more or less stationary during the first half of the century, then increasing, so that real wages were first increasing very slowly and then much more rapidly.

Marx and Schumpeter agree that capitalism is not, and cannot be, stationary. Their views, however, differ as to the beneficiaries of the process of growth. For Marx the benefits are reaped mainly by the capitalists; the workers, strictly speaking, the manual workers, could not obtain any substantial benefit, neither in terms of increasing real incomes nor in terms of the shortening of working hours. In this important respect Marx was wrong; it must be conceded, however, that he was writing at a time when a trend of rising real wages would not be easily perceived.

3.4 Oligopolistic Capitalism: The Third Stage.

In his view of modern economic history, Schumpeter emphasizes the fact that a few major innovations tend to dominate a period of several decades (about five). He refers to each such periods as a long cycle—the Kondratieff cycle. For Schumpeter each period is characterized by an industrial revolution, during which deep changes occur in the legal and institutional structure and in the structure of the product and labor markets. What I have called the stage of competitive capitalism, which spans the past century, would comprise two long cycles. However, even before the end of the century the structure of the product and the labor markets was undergoing very important changes, mainly due to the concentration process of firms.

In fact, as I hinted before, the increasing division of labor, that is, the increasing specialization of productive operations, in principle can take place either among different firms or within individual firms. If the former process had prevailed, one would have noticed in all trades a continuous increase in the number of firms, the size of which would not necessarily have increased. If the latter process had prevailed, one would have realized in each trade an increasing concentration, that is, a progressive diminution in the number of firms whose size was increasing.

Now it seems that both processes have taken place, but starting during the last two or three decades of the past century, the process of concentration has become dominant, so much so that certain new branches have been highly concentrated from their inception. On the other hand, in certain other branches the number of firms have been increasing systematically, but this did not imply an increasing competition in the classical sense. In fact product differentiation and quality competition were increasingly replacing price competition, also due to the development of advertising made possible by the extraordinary expansion of the so-called mass media, like the modern newspaper, radio, and television, all created or strongly stimulated by major technological innovations. The process of concentration itself is the consequence of technological change and, particularly, of what might be called "dynamic economies of scale": certain innovations necessarily imply in their implementation an increase in the size of output. Such a process has been characterized by the reappearance, in new forms, of the joint-stock company—in the seventeenth and eighteenth centuries to be found almost exclusively in colonial trade—then by trusts and cartels and, finally, by the large multinational or, as some prefer to call them, transnational corporations. It must be observed that among the propelling forces of this process, we have to include not only technological economies of scale in the strict sense but also organizational, commercial, and financial economies of scale.

Hand in hand with this process of concentration, a strengthening of the trade unions has taken place, partly originated by that very process. In fact trade unions are stronger in large firms, and they enjoy a certain market power over wages mainly as a result of market power over prices by the firms. That tendency, however, was partly influenced by political action and linked with the increasing influence of left-wing movements in the more industrialized countries. The strengthening of the trade unions has caused an increasing downward rigidity and an increasing upward flexibility of money wages. On the average, particularly after the second world war, the increase of money wages is no longer lower than the increase of productivity, as in the past century, but is equal or even higher. As a result prices are either stationary (but only at the wholesale level) or increasing; that is, in the new conditions structural inflationary pressures arose and were observable even before the oil and raw material price explosion of the 1970s. During the third stage of capitalism, then, the behavior of prices and money wages was characteristically different from that of the previous stage; the trend of prices was no more downward but clearly upward. The only important exception to this experience was the sharp fall of the thirties, but in that case the price fall—contrary to what was happening during the recessions of the past century—was accompanies by a slump and prolonged fall in output and employment.

Industrial fluctuations have also changed their character. They have become much more irregular than in the previous stage. The Great Depression of the thirties represents an extreme case of such irregularity. More recently industrial fluctuations have come primarily under the influence of public expenditure both for investment and for consumption, and not primarily of business expenditure as in the past. In fact public expenditure, which in the past century was negligible, except in war time, during the twentieth century has increased to a level where it represents a substantial share of total demand. Monetary policy itself, which in the past was regulated mainly in relation to business expenditure, is now increasingly regulated in relation to public expenditure.

The third stage in the development of capitalism has been defined by Marxists as the stage of "monopoly capital" and by Schumpeter as that of trustified capitalism. Personally, I prefer to call this the stage of oligopolistic capitalism. In this stage Schumpeter's triad loses its importance: more and more often the individual inventor is replaced by a scientist or by teams of scientists, working in research laboratories of large corporations as well as in public laboratories. The function of the banking system changes also under the impact of public expenditure and the great expansion of government bonds, and as a rule innovations no longer bring about a host of imitators. More and more often innovations are carried out by existing firms, especially large firms. Entry is more difficult, but the spread of technical knowledge is easier and quicker. Sometimes the relatively small firms are the innovating ones, but often the large firms buy up the inventions and even the innovations from the smaller firms, to develop them for the national and the international market.

In the third stage particularly after the second world war, public expenditure and public intervention in research becomes more and more important both for military and civilian purposes. (As is well known, military expenditure for research is particularly important in the United States, and the fallout of military research strongly affects the research organized directly for civilian economic purposes.) Public intervention does not take only the form of the creation and development of public research laboratories but also the form of financial support of various kinds to private laboratories and to the laboratories of the universities. Let us remember that at least three of the epoch-making inventions of our times—atomic energy, the electronic computer, and the numerically controlled machine tool—have had their decisive breakthrough in three universities—Chicago 1941, Pennsylvania 1942, and the Massachusetts Institute of Technology, 1951.

3.5 Technological and Keynesian Unemployment

Technological unemployment arises as a social problem already in the second stage of the development of capitalism; it reappears as a social problem also in the third stage, but as in the case of many other phenomena, it deeply changes its features.

In the past century, as I said, technological unemployment originated inside and outside the modern firms; it was created outside such firms by the decline of traditional industry, brought about by the competition of the modern firms. This second type of technological unemployment was withering away already before the end of the century. The first type has continued to occur up to the present day. It is different, however, from the old technological unemployment of the same type for several reasons. To some extent, in large firms technological unemployment is superseded by internal shifts of workers, since large firms have more scope than small firms to internally reorganize the labor force even when they introduce innovations that displace workers in certain operations. Moreover large firms, which have a long time horizon, do not find it convenient to dismiss all workers who become redundant in the short run: if they expected a sufficient increase in demand, they tend to keep part of the "redundant" workers, especially the skilled employees, even in bad times. Labor, even manual labor, has thus become to some extent, a quasi-fixed factor. However, another section of the workers in large firms, especially the unskilled ones, and those of the small firms who become "redundant" as a result of technological innovations, are likely to be expelled and become unemployed, particularly in bad times when demand shrinks or does not expand sufficiently. Indirectly, technological innovations can render more difficult the absorption of young persons who are looking for work for the first time. All in all the degree of absorption depends, on the one hand, on the rate of increase of productivity due to technological change, and on the other, on the rate of increase of effective demand.

The essential issue therefore is that of the relative speed of productivity growth on the one hand, and of the growth of demand and output, on the other. This is where one can introduce a dynamic version of the so-called Keynesian unemployment, that is, unemployment directly dependent on variations of effective demand.

In theory we can assert that *given output* every increase in productivity causes a proportional increase of unemployment; alternatively, *given productivity* every diminution of demand gives rise to an increase of unemployment (and this is Keynesian unemployment in the strict sense). In fact neither output nor productivity are constant over the course of time. At the aggregate level we have to see which of the two tendencies prevails. If effective demand increases more rapidly than average productivity, then unemployment falls; if, on the contrary, effective demand increases less rapidly than productivity, or diminishes, then unemployment increases. Thus we have two analytical problems: the first is to try to understand the forces determining the variations of effective demand; the second is to determine the forces causing the variations in productivity. Now, whereas the first problem has been amply debated, the analyses concerning the second problem are comparatively scarce. Here I only observe that productivity changes per unit of time—let us say, per year—can be seen as a function of changes in current total output and in the previous level of investment. Today, more than in the past, the expansion of output affects productivity mainly because in many firms labor is a quasi-fixed factor; investment affects productivity because as a rule investment embodies technical change, although it takes time to exert its effects on productivity.[2] We might say that in the fluctuating process of growth two sets of forces are at work—those promoting increases in total demand and those promoting technical change and productivity. The former acts as a labor-attracting force, the latter as a labor-repelling force. During the expanding phases of the business cycle the labor-attracting forces tend to prevail over the labor-repelling forces, and the opposite occurs during phases of contraction.

The propositions just mentioned are concerned with aggregate analysis. The more important and difficult problems arise when we attempt a disaggregate type of analysis. Yet such a second approximation is absolutely necessary in discussing technical change, since this change is by its very nature uneven, in the sense that it affects in a highly differentiated way the different branches of production and even different firms.

3.6 The Shortening of Working Hours

Technological change has not only the effect of promoting growth of output but also of a shortening of the working period during the life of each worker: less hours per week, fewer weeks per year (longer holidays), fewer years during the working life (later entrance into the labor market and earlier retirement). Here I limit myself to consider the shortening of the hours worked per week.

To put the matter in perspective, over the last hundred years or so in the United States total output has increased as a broad average by 3.5 percent per year, of which 1 percent has been due to increases in the labor force (natural increase plus net immigration); 2.5 percent can be attributed to the increase in productivity *per worker*. Productivity *per hour worked*, however, has increased more, about 3.0 percent per year; the difference between the increase in productivity per hour and that in productivity per worker, or about 0.5 percent per year, has been transformed into a shortening of the weekly hours of work, that is, into an increase of leisure. Broadly speaking, in 1850 the average length of the working week was 70 hours, today it is 40 hours or less. Or, to view the question from the standpoint of output and employment, today almost one-half of the labor force would be unemployed if, given the level of output reached today, each employed worker would work 70 hours instead of 40 or less per week; the difference would be even greater should we take into account the considerable increase in annual holidays. Of course this is a purely hypothetical case. It is interesting, however, because it appraises the extraordinary progress made in the last hundred years (the U.S. economy being fairly representative in this respect of other industrialized economies) and because it allows a critical reflection on the proposal often put forward by the trade unions to shorten the number of weekly hours of work as a means of reducing unemployment.

Basically, I am in sympathy with such a proposal. To avoid delusions, however, as an economist I feel it my duty to point out two kinds of difficulties.

The first difficulty lies in the fact that a shortening of hours not accompanied by a reduction of the wage rate causes an increase in the costs of firms. It is as if the wage rate had been raised but with the aggravating factor of a costly rearrangement of productive operations and, without further changes, a lower degree of capacity utilization. The ensuing financial difficulties of the firms could imply interruptions of production and even a spread of bankruptcies, with an increase of unemployment—an outcome opposite to the one intended.

In the second place the shortening of hours without a reduction in the wage rate is particularly difficult to implement at the time when it is most useful, such as during periods of recession or of relative stagnation when unemployment tends to increase. In periods of expansion, during which the firms are in better financial condition, it would be less difficult to introduce such a measure, but in such periods unemployment is declining and the trade unions are more interested in getting wage rises and less interested in reducing unemployment.

In the past the shortening of the working week has often taken place during periods of recession, during which both hours *and* wages were reduced. During the subsequent recoveries, however, the wage rate was raised to a higher level than that preceding the recession, while hours worked were raised only in part. More recently, the shortening of the working week has, on a number of occasions, been the result of the action of trade unions in particular firms or industries. Only after lags of different duration have the reduced hours been applied to other industries. But if the timing is not well chosen, lags can be too long, and disparities and tensions among firms and even among workers can arise, with serious negative effects on productivity, production, and employment. A long-run strategy seems to be necessary to deal adequately with these different aspects, including their international implications.

In taking the long-run view, one should consider carefully the very direction of technological change. Once we recognize that this process is largely endogenous rather than exogenous, we must try to influence it more consciously toward socially desirable targets, apart from the obvious objective of increasing productivity. One such objective is the further reduction in hours worked during the life of each person; another is to reduce the fragmentation and monotony of work without hindering efficiency. (Machines, not people, should become more specialized; an increasingly general and technical education should enable workers to become more flexible and hence more able to control different kinds of machines and more easily able to change their jobs.) Another socially desirable target is to reduce gradually the risk of accidents on the shopfloor and to make the workplace more healthy. Still another socially desirable objective is to reduce the hardships of technological change by aiming at transforming technological unemployment into a planned reorganization of jobs both within and among firms.

It must be said that in the past technological change has been regulated mainly to increase or at least to maintain profits. Some important steps in the direction of socially desirable objectives were taken either when such steps did not contradict the profit motive or when they were enforced by legislation. Due to the increasing influence of the trade unions and the labor movement in recent times, laws and other public interventions that direct technological progress toward socially desirable aims have been more and more frequent. To reinforce this process, prior consultation with the workers in decisions concerning technological progress and then participation of the workers themselves in such decision making are necessary. This road is long and difficult, particularly as conflicts will arise between economic and social objectives, but it is a road worth pursuing.

3.7 Technological Change and Economic Growth: A New Stage?

The technological and economic changes that we have experienced in recent years have become so profound and so rapid that they justify the hypothesis that we are entering into a new stage, the fourth one, in my opinion. The best way to evaluate the importance of such changes is to look at the recent evolution in the structure of employment.

In highly industrialized countries employment in agriculture is reduced to a very small fraction of total employment and is still declining. Employment in industry is either stationary or declining, if only in relative terms, despite the fact that industry, and particlarly manufacturing industry, remains the typical area of innovations which affect not only industry but the whole economy. Services, both private and public, have been expanding continuously and now employ the majority of the active population (between 60 and 70 percent). As regards employment in industry, we have noticed—at least in Italy during the last ten years—a peculiar phenomenon: a decrease in the employment in large firms (with more than 1,000 employees) and an increase in the employment in small firms with total employment remaining approximately constant.

What is the explanation of these trends?

Let us begin with the trend in industrial employment in Italy. The decline in employment in large firms could be the combined effect of the slowdown in the world economy following the explosion in the prices of oil and several raw materials and the acceleration of automation. We know that for various reasons the impact of the 1975 crisis and of the slowing down that has occurred since then has been more serious in large firms than in small firms. But why have the small firms been growing? Is this mainly because of the growth of relatively inefficient units in the so-called submerged economy, units capable of expansion because being small they are able to avoid the hardships created by frequent strikes and succeed in not paying the social costs? Again, with reference to Italy, I think that the recent development of small firms, which I suspect is a feature of many industrial countries, only in part can be explained in this way; to some extent it is due to other causes. To understand these causes, we have to start by considering the two types of division of labor described by Adam Smith.

The first type, the progressive specialization of productive operations among different firms, was for a long historical period eclipsed by the second, the one leading to concentration. At present, however, it seems to have acquired new vigor in certain branches of industry. Technologically, it seems that this new development has been opened up by certain innovations, such as microelectronics which originally were the product of defense and space research. There are several economic reasons aiding such development.

First, technological change is separating out an increasing share of those services formerly internal to the industrial firms and therefore included both in income and employment statistics, not among services, but in the industrial sector. In this area we find certain segments of research activity, repair services, and legal and technical services. Such a change, however, is not simply formal; it gives rise to an increasing number of highly specialized small firms which become more and more important also in terms of employment.[3]

Second, with increasing real incomes, an increasing number of persons become interested not so much in price but in the quality and design of consumer goods. This provides new opportunities to small firms, which can be successful if they use sophisticated means of production and adopt efficient methods of marketing, including exports.

Third, with rising real income, manual workers have shown an increasing resistance to accept repetitive and monotonous jobs, typically those required by the assembly line and other methods of mass production. As a consequence industrialists have speeded up automation and, for certain operations, have even introduced robots. But neither these decisions nor, in certain countries, the immigration of workers from less developed countries have substantially reduced the absolute and relative increase in real wages of repetitive jobs. As a further consequence the relative prices of goods produced with such methods have increased, thus contributing to a slowing down of the growth in the demand for such goods. All this, and especially the acceleration of automation, has contributed to determine the decline in the employment of large firms. At the same time skilled workers are increasingly preferring to accept less repetitive and tedious jobs in innovating *small* firms.

Last, but not least, the increasing pressure of the trade unions, which tends to be the more vigorous the larger the size of the firm, is a non-negligible factor both for the acceleration of automation and the decline in employment in large firms, and indirectly for the growth of small firms. It is true that small firms supplying only or mainly a given large firm cannot be considered as independent units; they are satellites of the large firm. But when small firms supply a variety of firms of different size, they can be considered as relatively autonomous in their development. I suspect that the second case is now becoming more frequent than in the past. (If the small firms supply the market directly, no doubts arise concerning their independence.) In any case the new possibilities of growth opened up by small firms does not imply both on the internal and the international level a diminution of the importance of large firms in terms of output and productivity—if not in terms of employment—and it is likely that in several branches the process of concentration will go on, becoming more and more international in character. On the other hand, under contemporary conditions the growth of small firms does not mean more competition in the classical sense, that is, price competition, because it means increasing product differentiation and diversification. The development of small firms, however, can have great importance in terms of growth of output and employment as well as in terms of technological change and productivity. Such a development is to be watched very carefully, especially by countries whose market is relatively small. Now a national market can be small because the per capita income of the population is very low or because the population is relatively small, or for both reasons. The small size of a market is a serious obstacle to industrial development because in several important branches economies of scale are relevant. The new possibilities opened to small firms imply a solution to such problems in certain industrial sectors. All this should be carefully considered by Australia, which for reasons of population can be considered a relatively small market. Thus the recommendation included in the recent "Report of the Committee of Inquiry into Technological Change in

Australia" to give special help to the innovating small firms should be fully approved. Probably, help should not be confined to extending financial facilities, as that report suggests, but include organizational and commercial aspects. In any case the development of modern technologies suitable for small firms could also have important international consequences; in this area Australia could become a center of reference for the Asian underdeveloped countries. On the other hand, since in several industries the economies of scale are likely to remain important, or even to grow in importance, another recommendation seems to the point: such industries should be encouraged to export a gradually increasing share of their production.

3.8 Manual and Intellectual Labor and Technological Change

The resistance shown by an increasing number of manual workers, including skilled ones, to accepting repetitive and montonous jobs is producing several improtant effects, which I should develop further. Both the increasing scarcity of workers willing to perform these jobs and the consequent increase in relative real wages have induced large firms, especially multinationals, to transfer the most repetitive and tedious operations to underdeveloped countries, where the workers, at least for the time being, are willing to accept such employment. At the same time this situation has stimulated either the immigration of workers from underdeveloped countries or the automation of the most repetitive operations, or both. (The introduction of new machines to fulfill certain operations as a result of a strong wage pressure or of a sheer scarcity of workers should not surprise us, since we have recognized the largely endogenous character of technological change. In this context I wish to give a paradoxical piece of information which I obtained from an industrial manager friend of mine, Mr. Corrado Santerimi, from the north of Italy, who told me that sophisticated robots, sold in Italy and abroad to very large corporations, are produced by small but highly specialized firms. In short, artisan skills have been adapted to modern conditions to meet the needs of mass production methods carried out by large and very large firms and to bring these methods to the highest possible level of automation.)

However, if in certain sections of the labor market we notice bottlenecks, in others we find high and even increasing unemployment, especially among the young with a relatively high level of education. These people look for jobs in industry and services, both private and public, but industry can absorb only a limited number of the young unemployed because the total employment in industry is now almost stationary, and the rate of absorption largely depends on the rate of retirement. Services, including technical services of the new type, can absorb and have absorbed a considerable number of young people. The record shows that most of the additional jobs in the last ten years have been provided by services, which, as we have seen, now represent about two-thirds or more of the labor force. Yet apparently the supply of persons willing to find a job in this sector in the last few years has increased more rapidly than demand, giving rise to a considerable amount of youth unemployment in all industrialized countries. If the pre-1973 rates of expansion of output and employment cannot be resumed, it is necessary to study special solutions to this problem, for instance, a kind of civil service for a limited period for works of public utility neglected by the market.

The increasing scarcity of persons willing to accept repetitive and mono-tonous jobs has not simply determined an increase in their real wages; it has determined an increase of these wages more rapid than the increase of compensations of other laborers, including the salary earners, that is, the so-called white-collar workers.

The reason for the increasing relative abundance of what I call intellectual labor is again to be attributed, in the final analysis, to the increasing real per capita income. Rising incomes, as well as expanding educational facilities offered by the public sector, having caused a rapid increase in the supply of young persons with secondary and university education in the labor market of the highly industrialized countries. This has brought about a gradual decline in the rate of increase in salaries. As a consequence the gap between the average wage and the average salary has been declining in the last twenty years or so. In Italy, for instance, and in the United States (and I presume that it is true in Australia too) certain jobs such as teaching in the elementary and secondary schools, which are performed by people with higher education, are paid even *less* than certain skilled manual workers. The average salary is still higher than the average wage, but the two types of compensation now-a-days overlap.[4] Given the trend, it is possible that the gap will go on declining and perhaps even reverse itself. This development, which is already provoking the protests of many persons, is welcomed by me because it means a reduction— or better, a further reduction of the class barriers at present determined more by the kind of labor, manual or intellectual, than by any other factor, including the ownership of the means of production.

Although it is necessary not to accelerate this process of reducing and eliminating the economic and social gap between manual and intellectual labor too quickly, to avoid dangerous countereffects, in the long run I see in this process many more advantages than disadvantages. Gradually, it can bring about the extinction of the manual worker, and this I consider a fully acceptable objective. I do not think that the so-called manual activities will disappear altogether from production, however. Rather they will not be, or will not necessarily be, the dismal privilege of a well-defined group of people—the class of manual workers. If the prevailing manual jobs were paid more, and even considerably more, than the intellectual jobs, and if higher education were widespread in the society, then there would be no real obstacle to mobility *in two directions* between manual and intellectual jobs. Moreover, given a general high standard of education, there would be no problem to the effectual and full participation of the workers—all types of workers—in the investment decisions (including the decisions concerning technological change) and to the management of the firms.

This vision could appear to some to be unduly optimistic, but this is not the case, for at least three reasons.

First, I think that the process I have referred to started only recently and will take considerable time to reach its zenith, because it will proceed, I believe, amid all sorts of social tensions and conflicts.

Second, this process is bringing, and will bring with it for a time, a painful phenomenon that we have to combat, that is, youth unemployment.

But there is a very important third reason why my vision could hardly be considered optimistic. It seems that the progressive lessening of economic hardships and the concomitant increasing leisure imply more and more serious moral and spiritual problems, as the debates among, and on, the present-day generation clearly show. No doubt these problems do not belong to the area of the economist. But the economist, like every civilized person, should be fully aware of such problems, even in theoretical speculations.

Notes

Eleventh R. C. Mills Memorial Lecture given at the University of Sydney, 21 October 1980.

1. See the author's *Progresso tecnico, società e diritto*, in "Studi in onore di Giuseppe Chiarelli," Vol. 4 (Milan: Giuffrè, 1974).

2. If we assume that productivity changes depend only on output, we have the following equation

$$\hat{\pi} = a + b\hat{Y},\tag{1}$$

where $a > 0$, $b < 1$, π is productivity per hour, and Y is total output; the cap over the variables indicates a rate of change over time. The employment equation is

$$\hat{N} = \hat{Y} - \hat{\pi}\tag{2}$$

or considering equation (1) and putting $b^* = 1 - b$,

$$\hat{N} = -a + b^*\hat{Y}.\tag{3}$$

If we take into account also the influence of past investment, the productivity equation becomes

$$\hat{\pi} = a + b\hat{Y} + c\hat{I}_{-n'} \tag{4}$$

where $\hat{I}_{-n}$ is the rate of change of investment in a previous period or in a given number of previous periods. The corresponding employment equation becomes

$$\hat{N} = -a + b^{*}\hat{Y} - c\hat{I}_{-n'} \tag{5}$$

Putting $\hat{Y} = \alpha\hat{C} + \beta\hat{I}$, where α and β are the weights in total output of total consumption, C, and total investment, I, we have

$$\hat{N} = -a + b^{*}\alpha\hat{C} + b^{*}\beta\hat{I} - c\hat{I}_{-n'} \tag{6}$$

where it appears that *current* investment has only a demand effect which contributes to push up employment, whereas *past* investment has a productivity effect which, taken by itself, pushes down employment.

3. See the article by F. Momigliano and D. Siniscalco published in *Economia e politica industriale*, March 1980.

4. In Italy the average salary/average wage ratio, at the beginning of the century was 4; twenty years ago it was 3.0, and at present it has fallen to 1.4. In the United States that ratio was 2.3 at the beginning of the century; then it fell and has fluctuated around 1.5 in the last twenty years.

4   Factors Affecting Changes in Productivity

Those economists who propose to explain the behavior of labor productivity are bound to realize very soon that there is a discontinuity between theoretical analyses and empirical research. This chapter is intended as a preliminary contribution toward bridging this gap.

Theoretical analysis is still to a large extent dominated by the traditional aggregate production function. However, whereas substitution is the main focus of the traditional theory, Keynesian theory is mainly preoccupied with the determinants of the level of activity. From this standpoint it appears to differ from though not necessarily opposed to, the traditional theory. A more directly antagonistic position appears to be that of the so-called "neo-Ricardians."

4.1 Keynes on Current Profits and the Marginal Efficiency of Capital

In Keynesian theory two strictly related distinctions are particularly relevant for our analysis: that between short- and long-term expectations and that between current profits (i.e., the excess of the value of output over the sum of input and user costs), on the one hand, and the marginal efficiency of capital (i.e., the sum of a series of expected receipts after deducting current expenses, including wages), on the other.[1] The second distinction refers to the two surpluses as if they were heterogeneous quantities. Indeed, Keynes treats the former surplus—current profits—as imputable to the productive process as a whole, whereas he sees the latter as deriving solely from capital goods as such. This is not correct. Both surpluses, and not only the former, derive from the productive process as a whole: the differences in the time horizon and risk do not justify the different treatment of the two surpluses. An important (and misleading) consequence of this conception is that the rate of interest is compared only with the marginal efficiency of capital—the expected rate of return from a capital asset—and not with the short-term profit.

To clarify this point, consider a firm that uses its plants at less than full capacity but has plentiful stocks of raw materials because it is expecting an expansion in demand for its products. To meet an initial demand expansion, the firm may need only to hire additional workers. But if it has no internal funds to finance the higher wage bill, it also must borrow in the short term. *The interest on this loan will be covered by the excess of receipts over costs, which in the case considered will appear to be imputable only to the expansion in labor employment. The same occurs when new machines are bought to meet higher demand: the excess of receipts over cost appears to be due to the capital goods, assuming that all other means of production are held in stock by the firm or by introducing the proviso "after deducting current expenses".*

Thus for the short run Keynes correctly assigns the excess of receipts over costs to the productive process as a whole, but when he turns to long-term expectations, his position is similar to that of traditional theory in treating the excess as imputable exclusively to the additional capital goods.

Yet the two general approaches are profoundly different: Keynes proceeds from the perspective of effective demand, whereas traditional theory is absorbed with the substitution potential between labor and "capital". But, having imputed the long-term surplus to durable capital goods only, Keynes opens the door to the ambiguous "neoclassical synthesis." The emphasis Keynes places on the "extreme precariousness" of long-term expectations, and on the instability that they can generate, is certainly valid, but it does not eliminate the ambiguity of his asymmetric treatment of the long and short run.

The differences among the three theoretical constructs can be spotted by considering the consequences each attributes to a reduction in the rate of interest:

1. The firm chooses more "capital"-intensive (less labor-intensive) techniques. This is the neoclassical point of view.

2. Investment is stimulated, and consequently employment increases. This is the Keynesian point of view.

3. Aggregate production is stimulated. This can be defined as the commonsense analysis.

Clearly there is a fundamental discrepancy between the neoclassical conception and the other two, for under normal circumstances an expansion in production requires an increase in investment and employment—an inference of both the Keynesian and the commonsense conceptions.

4.2 The Classical Conception of Profits

The "commonsense" view has become very controversial ever since the beginning of neoclassical theory. The "commonsense" position dovetails with the position of the classical economists. Yet the specific source, or "cause" of profit and, more generally, of the economic surplus, remains undetermined. Smith and Ricardo tended to see it in labor, naturally labor "assisted" by instruments of various kinds and combined with raw materials and inter-mediate products. The classical economists, however, did not probe deeply into this matter, since they considered it self-evident that the source of all value, including surplus value, was *labor*. They also considered as self-evident the fact that the surplus had to be shared among those who had advanced the means of subsistence to workers and furnished then with the other means of production.[2] Marx, as is well known, builds his whole theory on the assump-tion that labor is the source of profit and other capitalist incomes.

The classical conception of profit thus can be viewed from two standpoints: as generated by the productive process as a whole or specifically by labor— what Marx calls living or current labor. There is no contradiction between these two perspectives, nor does the position of Schumpeter conflict with the general classical conception. Schumpeter considers profit in each economic activity as the result of the productive process as a whole, but subject to the condition that the process is in time made more efficient through technological and organizational innovations. For Schumpeter and the classical economists, the rate of interest is a piece of the surplus, it is a tax on the profit of the entrepreneur. It follows that when the rate of interest drops, other conditions remaining unchanged, the whole productive process is stimulated.

Excepting Keynes's particular position, the fundamental contrast is be-tween the classical, including Marx and Schumpeter, and the neoclassical conceptions. According to the latter, profits and wages are equivalent factor rewards paid to capital, essentially or even exclusively fixed capital, and to labor. The equivalence of the nature of the two incomes derives from their correspondence to the marginal productivities of the two factors (i.e., the partial derivatives of total production after a very small factor variation).

Since it is impossible to produce an additional quantity, however small, of say, cotton yarn by means of an incremental application of labor, without an increase, however small, of raw cotton, the economic meaning of "the mar-ginal productivity" of a single factor is unclear. With characteristic caution Marshall (1949, 426–427, 432) qualified his analysis to the "net product" of a factor defined as the additional product obtained by an incremental appli-cation of that factor "after allowing for incidental expenses" (equivalent to Keynes's "running expenses"). This definition does not coincide with the mathematical concept of a partial derivative and is therefore not consistent with the marginalist theory of income distribution.[3]

Even if the concept could receive an unambiguous interpretation, it falters in explaining the distribution of income because it refers to an aggregate production function that emanates from a logically untenable concept: aggregate capital. It is important, however, to note that this criticism need not imply that the production function cannot be applied to the individual firm, nor that such a function cannot be used to analyze the (static) substitution among the individual factors of production.

4.3 Schumpeter's and Sraffa's Views on Profits

Schumpeter, in his *Theory of Economic Development* (1911) and later in his treatise on business cycles (1939), treats the classical conception of profits in a new guise. However, he makes certain propositions that appear to contradict that conception. Sraffa, on the other hand, who has made a signal contribution to a rigorous exposition of classical, in particular, Ricardian, theory, proposes two models. In the first, wages are *anticipated* and enter among the means of production, just as in the classical theory. In the second, wages are paid *post factum*; here Sraffa takes some leave of the classical conception.

In his *Theory of Economic Development* Schumpeter's analysis of profit and interest is close to, and certainly consistent with, the classical conception. In his *Business Cycles* Schumpeter reproposes this analysis in the theoreterical chapters, but in the empirical chapters there are statements more properly consistent with the neoclassical theory; for instance,

The prevailing cheapness of money will give them [the firms] a slant toward mechanization, which may be intensified by an increase and counteracted by the previous decrease in wage rates. (p. 954).

Coupled with a cheap money policy, a high-wage-rate policy was, under the circumstances of phase and country, the very recipe for the production of a maximum unemployment. (p. 995)

From the beginning Schumpeter had tried to present his theory as complementary, and not as alternative, to the traditional one: he was admittedly aiming at a synthesis, not a critique. However, on the "surplus" question a synthesis was not possible. True, Schumpeter refers only to the traditional view in his empirical analysis. But logical consistency precludes the conclusions of traditional theory.[4] The problem that surfaces in Sraffa's second model, where the wage is paid *post factum* is completely different. Here the abandonment of the classical assumption is by no means concerned with the nature of surplus generated by the productive process as a whole. If workers are not advanced their wages, they become "capitalists" to the extent they "advance" their wages to themselves. They have title to a share of surplus. (Such a hypothesis, which implies that saving stems not only from capitalists but also from workers, may be realistic today, but it was surely not representative of ruling conditions at the time of the classical economists, who could assume confidently that workers consumed the whole of their incomes.) Indeed, Sraffa warns the reader that, strictly speaking, it would be necessary to include that part of wages corresponding to "necessary" consumption among the means of production. On the other hand, in considering a process of development, firms lacking sufficient internal funds are compelled to apply to banks to finance their larger wage bills, and on these loans they must pay interest, in the strict sense.

The contraposition between the classical and the neoclassical conceptions, then, remains valid, and it is the earlier "commonsense point of view" that is correct. If a businessman is asked about the probable effects of a cut in the rate of interest, he will reach for the obvious answer: The reduction will stimulate the expansion of production, without affecting the choice of techniques. To be sure, if the long-term rate of interest is reduced, the short-term rate remaining unchanged, the purchase of durable capital goods will be stimulated. Yet this is not a necessary outcome. It is possible to finance—or at least to prefinance—the purchase of durable capital goods by short-term loans renewed at each maturity if such a procedure is more economical.[5]

The confusion that prevails in this field has been compounded by the fact that a fall in the rate of interest, in particular, the long-term rate, stimulates building activity which has a relatively long gestation period and gives rise to durable assets of longer duration than machines. All this, however, has nothing to do with the substitution between capital and labor. When the interest rate goes down, building and other activities are stimulated, but there is no reason to think that the techniques used in these activities have to be changed.

4.4 Wages, the Interest Rate, and the Choice of Techniques: The Relative Wage Effect

The capital-labor substitution, then, does not depend on a comparison between the interest and wage rates but between the price of machines and the wage rate. If the latter rises relative to the former, it will become profitable to save labor: in absolute terms, by making a more efficient use of labor, thus reducing its input per unit of output without changing the other inputs, or in relative terms by substituting machines for labor, or in both ways.[6] (Reduction in labor input and increase in labor productivity are equivalent expressions.) Such labor-saving measures need not imply a change in employment, which rather depends on whether output varies with respect to productivity. In particular, if output rises in the same proportion, then the labor saving is not actual but only potential, that is, total employment does not decline.

As for the substitution between machinery and labor, it is well to recall the following remark by Ricardo ([1817] 1951a, 395): "Machinery and labor are in constant competition, and the former can frequently not be employed until labor rises."

If we refer to the first model proposed by Sraffa, which considers production with a surplus and wages as necessary consumption, we can easily see that the choice between labor and fixed capital—plants and machinery—must depend not on a comparison between wages and interest but between wages and the price of machines. Naturally, Sraffa's first model, which is grounded in classical theory, must be construed so as to include the charges for fixed capital (Sraffa 1960, chs. 2 and 10). As is well known, under competitive conditions the rates of interest and profit tend to coincide. Thus if we start from a situation in which the two rates are equal and assume that the rate of interest is reduced, a net profit will appear, even though the entrepreneur has to pay interest to those who have lent the necessary funds. The lower rate of interest, then, will induce the firms not to introduce fixed capital to supplant workers but to expand production by employing greater quantities of *all* the means of production, including workers. The terms of the problem become more complex in Sraffa's second model in which production leaves a surplus and wages are paid out of the net product, but the substance of the analysis is not altered.

If wages vary with respect to the prices of capital goods, substitution will take place between labor and those goods, given technology and the organization of the productive process. However, if relative wages vary, technological and organizational changes will be stimulated. The first aspect entails the static substitution made central by the marginalist theory; the second one is a *dynamic* substitution, which is of much more relevance. Substitution—both static and dynamic—implies a relative saving of labor. The absolute saving of labor cannot be statical; it is bound to be dynamic, in the sense that it can only be the result of technological or organizational changes. (In this chapter, as should be clear by now, I am almost exclusively concerned with dynamic substitution and, more generally, with dynamic analysis, which allows for the changes that I have just mentioned and implies increases in productivity.)

4.5 Productivity Increases as Cause and Effect of Increases in Real Wages

We have to broaden our analysis to account for the fact that increases in productivity are both cause and effect of the long-run increase in wages relative not only to the prices of machines but to all, or almost all, prices. As cause, the increase in productivity induces trade unions to demand higher wages. (When productivity increases, firms themselves may decide without union pressures to grant higher wages to attract—and to keep—the most efficient workers and to ensure a peaceable atmosphere within the firm.) As effect, firms may offset wage increases by saving labor either in absolute terms, by rationalizing the productive process, or in relative terms, by introducing machines capable of increasing productivity. At this point, however, it is necessary to distinguish between industrial prices in general and the prices of machines. The behavior of the two price categories need not be the same, though it is reasonable to assume that the behavior of wages is the same in all industries.

What if wages increase more than productivity; that is, what if the cost of labor per unit of output rises, but firms do not succeed in passing the increase fully onto prices of finished products (the price of intermediate goods and of raw materials remaining unchanged)? Naturally their gross profit margin must fall. To counteract that firms will be spurred to speed up productivity, or in other words, to save labor both in absolute and in relative terms. In the case of wages outpacing the prices of machines, firms will find it profitable to save labor by substituting machines for labor.

We may recapitulate our argument by adopting a very simplified version of the industrial price, P, equation:[7]

$$P = a \; \frac{W}{\pi} \; ,$$

where W is the wage rate, π is the productivity of labor, and a is a constant. From this equation we get

$$a \; \frac{W}{P} = \pi,$$

or referring to the sector producing machines.

$$a' \; \frac{W}{P_{ma}} = \pi_{ma}$$

If the ratio W/P increases and shows a tendency to exceed π, there will be an incentive to save labor in absolute terms, that is, to speed up productivity increases without modifying other inputs. However, if the ratio W/P_{ma} is increasing, there will be an incentive for all firms to save labor in relative terms. It is quite possible to have a sequence going in the opposite direction, that is, from π to W/P or from π_{ma} to W/P_{ma}.

The easier it is for firms to shift cost increases onto prices, the weaker the incentive to raise productivity due to wage increases. In fact, if P or P_{ma} can be raised quickly in proportion to W, then the W/P and W/P_{ma} ratios will not vary, and the incentive under discussion does not operate. The said shift will be more or less difficult depending on the market structure, on the intensity of foreign competition, and on the economic policy (including the foreign exchange policy) adopted by the government.

To explain productivity variations, then, we have to include the ratios W/P and W/P_{ma} among the explanatory variables. They can be equivalent if we assume that the behavior of the two price categories is the same. We will make precisely this assumption and hypothesize that the shift of cost increases onto prices is partial.

An objection to including W/P_{ma} among the explanatory variables of productivity changes is that the entire price system varies with the distribution of income, as Sraffa has conclusively demonstrated; this implies that the numerator and the denominator of the W/P_{ma} ratio are interdependent.

However, it is not our task to discuss the relation between the changes in the distributive shares and in relative prices: for our analysis it is enough to recognize that if, for whatever reason, the ratio of wages to the price of capital goods increases, firms will find it profitable to save labor in relative terms. This point may be clarified further with the aid of Sraffa's models. Although these models assume *fixed* quantities of commodities, we could make use of them by assuming that, due to technological innovation, the production of a certain commodity employing the same means of production and the same labor is increased. This implies greater efficiency and also an increase in the productivity of labor. If we also assume that the (unique) rate of profit stays unchanged and that the industry considered is the one producing machines, we can easily see that the price of machines necessarily diminishes with respect to those of all other commodities and that the ratio W/P_{ma} necessarily increases. However, such assumptions are redundant, for W/P_{ma} may increase because of a change in distribution rather than from higher productivity in the machine-producing industry.

4.6 The Output Effect in the Short and the Long Run

Productivity then can be stimulated by the variations in W/P and W/P_{ma}, but productivity depends also on the size of the market and on new capital investment. We return to these ratios later; here we comment on the size of the market and productivity increases.

This relation was first considered by Adam Smith. For Smith, "the division of labour is limited by the extent of the market" (title of chapter iii, book I, of

The Wealth of Nations) and "the division of labour . . . occasions, in every art, a proportionable increase of the productive power of labour" (chapter i, book I). The modern version of this proposition, which takes the volume of output as an index of the size of the market, is called Verdoorn's law. Verdoorn's law relates productivity changes to changes in the volume of output (Verdoorn 1949);[8] in turn, the changes in output reflect those of effective demand.

Economists, discussing this law, however, seldom make the necessary distinction between long- and short-run effects of changes in output volume on productivity. In the short run an increase in output can determine a more efficient use of labor, often by exploiting earlier innovations ("learning by doing" takes time). This increase in production does not call for additional investment, so it can mean an absolute saving of labor. But as output grows, in the long run firms will introduce more efficient and additional machines to replace existing ones. Furthermore, if the market expands, certain plants and machines can be introduced that were not profitable in a more limited market. Productivity then increases by way of the reorganization process and by the introduction of new, more efficient machines. But in the short run say, up to one year, only the first type of adaptation is likely.

The impact on productivity of changes in output therefore comes at the end of a complex process. An increase in output stimulates a rationalization in the use of the labor force, especially when labor is a quasi-fixed factor. But this tendency can be accelerated or retarded by various economic factors, as, for instance, the changes in the W/P ratio.

4.7 Productivity and Investment: The Disturbance Effect of Investment

In principle, all economists agree that investment is a primary source of productivity increases, since most innovations are embodied in new plant and machinery. However, relevant econometric studies are rare. Perhaps the reason is that investment is supposed to affect productivity only in the long run and, in addition, after an unsystematic time lag.

If we take the view that there cannot be a rigidly determined time lag before the effects of investment are felt in productivity, shall we assume that such effects are necessarily irregular, or shall we assume that they are distributed according to some regular time sequence—of the form, for instance, of a Gaussian curve? An empirical test is the only way to settle this question. To this end, we consider productivity as a function of (1) total output, (2) the W/P_{ma} ratio, and (3) investment. Total output represents the short-run output effect, as reflected in available yearly data. The W/P_{ma} ratio can be assumed to represent an important incentive to save labor either absolutely or by introducing labor-saving machines. Since the effect takes time to manifest itself, it is reasonable also to lag this variable, and likewise, for analogous reasons, the investment variable.

As for investment, it is necessary to distinguish the determinants of its level from those of its composition (labor-saving and capacity-increasing investment). The *level* of investment depends primarily on demand pressure as expressed by the degree of utilized capacity; current profits, as the source of self-financing; the expected rate of profit; and the availability and the cost of external finance (Sylos-Labini 1974, ch. 1). The *composition* of investment depends primarily on the relative cost of labor. However, it is impossible to say to what extent a labor-saving investment is stimulated by an increase in the W/P_{ma} ratio, and to what extent it is independent of the increase. As it can be profitable to introduce labor-saving innovations even if that ratio holds firm, it would be wrong to assume that the changes in that ratio are the only reason for the labor-saving investment. Consequently we cannot exclude one of the two variables (investment and labor cost) on the ground that its influence is already fully contained in the other; it is advisable, instead, to include both variables. Conversely, the ratio W/P is not included inasmuch as I hypothesize that its behavior is similar to that of the W/P_{ma} ratio.

Thus we have the following productivity equation to test:

$$\hat{\pi} = a + b\hat{Y} + c\widehat{W/P}_{ma(t-n)} + dI_{t-n} \tag{1}$$

The cap over a variable indicates a rate of change.[9] I have used the rate of change for three of the variables, π, Y and W/P_{ma}; for the fourth variable, I, the investment level is used, since this variable represents the net addition to the stock of capital and therefore its behavior conforms generally to that of the rate of change of the capital stock. As for the lags of investment and of the relative cost of labor, from what we have said it follows that we have to test two hypotheses: one on distributed lags and the other on a single lag, which is to be interpreted as the modal value of a series of effects.

The estimates of Equation (1) seem to be reasonably satisfactory. However, in calculating the various lags, including zero lag, I also checked the belief that current investment has no effect on productivity (and on productive capacity). To my surprise, however, the tests showed that current investment does affect productivity, but *negatively* (see Sylos-Labini, 1980).

The reason behind this paradox emerges when one considers that year by year the majority of investment projects are carried out by existing firms, not by new firms, and that the installation of new plant and equipment generates various disturbances in the ordinary operations of current production. It even hinders physically some operations and absorbs the energies of managers and engineers, who thus devote less care to the ordinary business of their firms.[10]

It is important to point out that current investment is negative and statistically significant in both countries for which the tests were carried out, Italy and the United States. We will call the said negative effect of current investment on productivity "the disturbance effect."

4.8 Productivity and Research and Development Expenditure

A preplexing issue is whether it is necessary to include among the explanatory variables the expenditure on research and development. This idea is rejected for two reasons. First, the very meaning of that expenditure is ambiguous, since in certain industries "development" in the commercial sense is more important than "research" in the proper sense. In such industries the effects of the said expenditure can be more important for the volume of sales and production than for productivity; therefore only indirectly can that expenditure affect the increase of productivity. Second, as mentioned earlier, most innovations are embodied in investment, and innovations are very often the fruit of research and development expenditure. Thus it would be advisable to include this expenditure among the explanatory variables of investment, not productivity; investment in turn affects productivity.

One important warning. Although I have distinguished between short- and long-run output effects, in my productivity equation I use only the rate of change of current output, which but to a small extent includes the long-run output effect. More generally, in the productivity equation I present current variables as expressing short-run and lagged variables as expressing long-run influences of the various factors. This procedure can be justified by the limited purpose of my analysis. If we take a broader view of the long run and of the factors affecting productivity, we would have to take into account several other factors—to mention only one, the extent and the trend of the technical lag between the follower countries and the the lead country (in our time, the European countries and Japan, on the one side, the United States on the other). *Ceteris paribus* the productivity increases are easier and therefore higher in the follower countries than in the lead country (see Maddison 1982, ch. 5). However, these types of problems lie outside the scope of my analysis.

4.9 The Productivity Equation

The productivity equation to be considered is

$$\hat{\pi} = a + b\hat{Y} + cW/\widehat{P}_{\text{ma}(t-n)} + dI_{t-n} - eI, \tag{2}$$

where I_{t-n} is the long-run effect and I the short-run effect of investment. More generally, the equation incorporates factors that operate both in the short and the relatively long run, the latter, as I said, being represented by lagged variables.[11]

Although for the econometric estimates I examined both the whole economy and the manufacturing sector of Italy and the United States, I present here only the results concerning the manufacturing sector since productivity per hour is a more precise concept than productivity per person which is how productivity for the whole economy must be measured. Also, by focusing on the manufacturing industry, one can avoid the problem of accounting for the effects on productivity growth of shifts in employment shares.

For the manufacturing sector we tested both hypotheses concerning lags—distributed lags and a single dominant lag. The periods considered were 1962 to 1980 for Italy and 1950 to 1981 for the United States (the different time lengths used were determined by the availability of data). In the case of the United States an additional estimate was made for the period 1970 to 1981 because the behavior of productivity underwent important changes in the 1970s (case B').

The estimates which appear in table 4.1, refer to the two countries and the two hypotheses in this way: case A equations are for a single lag; case B for distributed lags. Following a suggestion of Gianni De Nicolò, who calculated all the equations, we tested an additional case A equation (case A') for Italy in which, instead of investment, we used in our estimate the first difference in the stock of capital, ΔK. As for the single lag hypothesis, in both countries the best results were obtained with a two-year lag. In Italy the distributed lags hypothesis has proved to be relevant only for investment, with the following weights attributed to this variable lagged 1, 2, and 3 years: 0.25, 0.50, and 0.25. A single two-year lag also proved to be the most convenient in obtaining the relative cost of labor, as seen in equations for cases A and A'. In the United States the most convenient lag structure of investment appears to be the same as that used for Italy. The lag structure of the relative cost of labor is 0.50, 0.25, and 0.25 for the variable lagged 2, 3, and 4 years. The distributed lag hypothesis was adopted for the entire 1950 to 1981 period and for the subperiod 1970 to 1981.

4.10 The Slowdown in Productivity Growth

The productivity equation can shed light on a phenomenon that has puzzled many economists—the slowdown in productivity growth. This slowdown has been particularly serious in the United States, and there still has been no good explanation for it.[12]

Among all the variables in the productivity equation that have contributed

Table 4.1

For Italy

Case A

$$\hat{\pi} = 0.53\hat{Y} + 0.30\widehat{W/P}_{ma-n} + 0.08I_{-n} - 0.06I_r$$
$$(6.63) \quad (1.77) \qquad\qquad (2.70) \qquad (2.43)$$

$R^2 = 0.796,$
$DW = 1.910.$

Case A'

$$\hat{\pi} = 0.54\hat{Y} + 0.35\widehat{W/P}_{ma-n} + 0.04\Delta K_{-n} - 0.03I_r$$
$$(6.45) \quad (2.08) \qquad\qquad (2.16) \qquad (1.95)$$

$R^2 = 0.783,$
$DW = 1.832.$

Case B

$$\hat{\pi} = 0.56\hat{Y} + 0.32\widehat{W/P}_{ma-n} + 0.09I_{(-n)} - 0.07I_r$$
$$(6.56) \quad (1.76) \qquad\qquad (2.21) \qquad (2.13)$$

$R^2 = 0.770,$
$DW = 1.857.$

For the United States

Case A

$$\hat{\pi} = 0.18\hat{Y} + 0.30\widehat{W/P}_{ma-n} + 0.13I_{-n} - 0.09I_r$$
$$(5.88) \quad (2.67) \qquad\qquad (5.13) \qquad (4.16)$$

$R^2 = 0.719,$
$DW = 2.036.$

Case B

$$\hat{\pi} = 0.20\hat{Y} + 0.43\widehat{W/P}_{ma(-n)} + 0.13I_{(-n)} - 0.10I_r$$
$$(7.30) \quad (2.57) \qquad\qquad (4.85) \qquad (4.01)$$

$R^2 = 0.722,$
$DW = 1.997.$

Case B'

$$\hat{\pi} = 0.17\hat{Y} + 0.25\widehat{W/P}_{ma(-n)} + 0.14I_{(-n)} - 0.12I_r$$
$$(5.60) \quad (3.36) \qquad\qquad (9.52) \qquad (8.36)$$

$R^2 = 0.938,$
$DW = 2.692.$

to a slowdown in productivity growth, the W/P_{ma} ratio has in recent years diminished significantly. It is well to point out that the decline in this ratio—a rather exceptional occurrence in the economic history of the United States—has been brought about because the price of machines has increased considerably due to increases in energy and raw materials prices, while money wages have increased to a smaller extent.[13] The problem then is to understand why so slow an increase in wages, that is, why since the late 1970s have real wages declined. I think that the main reasons are two: the great influx of workers from Latin America and the rapid absorption of women in services (from 1971 to 1981 total employment in the United States increased by 21 million; of this figure 13 million are women). Although the two phenomena have powerfully contributed to slow down the increase in money wages, at the same time the entry of women into the labor force has raised the number of families obtaining at least two incomes and so has lessened the impact of the decrease in real wages.

In Italy the slowdown in productivity growth has been less pronounced than in the United States. What seems to be the key factor here is that, contrary to what has been happening in the United States, since the late 1970s the relative cost of labor has continued to increase, though at a slower speed than in the past. Real wages, again contrary to what has been happening in the United States, did not decline in the 1970s; only in the first two years of the 1980s has a certain decline occurred, but outside the market (i.e., as a consequence of fiscal drag). (It must be observed, however, that in Italy in the 1970s the level of employment rose only slightly, but in the underground economy, where usually subnormal wages are paid, it expanded.)

Considering the great importance of the W/P_{ma} ratio to the slowdown in productivity growth in Italy and the United States, it may prove promising, after critical appraisal of the implications of the whole productivity equation, to make detailed—possibly disaggregated—empirical analyses for the said two countries and for other developed countries along the lines worked out here.[14]

Notes

I have benefited from the critical comments of Mario Amendola, Jan Kregel, Franco Momigliano, Alessandro Roncaglia, and Enrico Zaghini. I express my deep gratitude also to Sidney Weintraub who, though very ill, from his hospital bed took great pains to revise the original text; with his death, I have lost a great friend.

1. To quote Keynes, "The excess of the value of the resulting output over the sum of its factor cost and its user cost is the profit or, as we shall call it, the *income* of the

entrepreneur" (*General Theory* 1936, 23). "When a man buys an investment or a capital asset, he buys the right to a series of future receipts that he expects to obtain from the sale of its output, after deducting the running expenses incurred to obtain such output, during the life of that capital" (p. 135).

2. Smith writes (Ricardo's views are similar): "The value which the workmen add to the materials . . . resolves itself . . . into two parts, of which the one pays their wages, the other the profits of their employer upon the whole stock of materials and wages which he advanced. He could have no interest to employ them, unless he expected from the sale of their work something more than what was sufficient to replace his stock to him; and he could have no interest to employ a great stock rather than a small one, unless his profits were to bear some proportion to the extent of his stock" (Smith [1776] 1951, 54).

3. If we formalize Marshall's statement, we have

$$w = \frac{\partial x}{\partial L} - e,$$

where w is the rate of wage, $\partial x / \partial L$ is the partial derivative of total output x with respect to total labor, L, and e represents incidental expenses per unit of output. Whereas the relation $w = \partial x / \partial L$ (without e) is consistent with the aggregate production function $x = f(L, K)$, the above relation is not. If the production function is homogeneous of the first degree, we have

$$\frac{\partial x}{\partial L} \cdot L + \frac{\partial x}{\partial K} \cdot K = x$$

which is the general form of the marginalist interpretation of the distribution of income.

In this context it is difficult to speak of a partial derivative of output with respect to labor, since Marshall's incidental expenses imply the use of additional quantities of other means of production, such as raw materials and intermediate products.

4. In 1949, when I was at Harvard on a scholarship, I had Schumpeter as my supervisor. After completing the study of *Business Cycles*, I prepared a paper raising a few questions, among them the one just mentioned. After citing the two passages quoted in note 1, I stated: "This point is not clear to me. The possibility for firms to obtain 'money' more cheaply should give them a slant to increase the demand for all the factors of production, labor included. If the firms prefer to buy more machinery and less personal services, the choice would seem to me to be based on the comparison of the prices of the various factors of production and not on the cheapness of money."

My question I think brought home to Schumpeter that he was using a type of analysis that conflicted with his conception of the rate of interest on loans to firms as the price of using the means of payment to buy all sorts of means of production, including the hire of workers. After reading my question (before replying he would read each point aloud), he said: "But then you reject an essential part of traditional theory?" My reaction was a shrug to indicate that I was not much shaken by his comment. Schumpeter replied, "All right, all right"—and went on. Although he had the patience to devote a considerable amount of time to comment on the paper of that rather impudent young man, he never did answer the question. I think that the only answer is the one I point to in the text.

5. Kalecki's conception is very close to the classical one, as may appear from the following quotation (brought to my attention by Jan Kregel):

The idea that the reduction of the rate of interest stimulates the application of more capital per worker is based on the assumption that the planned *output* of the investing entrepreneur is given. On this condition a lower rate of interest makes it profitable to use more capital and less labor. If we assume, however, that the *capital* available to a firm for financing investment is given, the reduction of the rate of interest has no influence on the choice of the method production when planning investment, because it affects the expected net profit equally, whatever the method of production adopted. . . . The main stimulus to use more capital per worker is provided by new inventions. (Kalecki 1944, 51).

Although Kalecki is right in pointing out the artificial and misleading assumption implicit in neoclassical theory, in presenting his view, he introduces a constraint that is certainly reasonable but, in my opinion, not necessary.

6. See L. L. Pasinetti (1981, esp. 192–197). The origin of the misunderstanding lies in the way "capital" is conceived. The rate of interest can properly apply to capital when it is conceived as purchasing power. When it is conceived as capital goods, changes in wages and the rate of interest modify the very prices of such goods; in the final analysis, this is the reason why it is wrong to compare the interest and the wage rates to analyze the substitution between labor and capital goods. (Between the two conceptions of capital just mentioned there is an intermediate one: "capital" as a putty. Of course this is word play, not a concept, but it points up the confusion still prevalent in this line of economic theory.)

7. S. Weintraub has used such an equation in several of his works; see, e.g., Weintraub, 1969, *Classical Keynesianism Monetary Theory and The Price Level* especially chapter 2.

Another, more complete version of the industrial price equation is

$$P = a\frac{W}{\pi} + bRM$$

where, in addition to the symbols in the text, RM is used for the prices of raw materials and intermediate goods.

8. For Lord Kaldor's writings on this subject, see the spring 1983 issue of the *JPKE*— the special issue in honor of Nicholas Kaldor's 75th birthday.

9. Since the rate of change of total employment is equal to the rate of change of total income *less* the rate of change of productivity, or

$$\hat{N} = \hat{Y} - \hat{\pi}$$

substituting $\hat{\pi}$ with equation (1) and writing $1 - b = b^*$, we have

$$\hat{N} = \hat{Y} - b^*W/\hat{P}_{\text{ma}} - dI_{t-n}.$$

10. The explanation became clear after discussing the matter with Piero Quarantelli, an engineer with wide managerial experience.

11. As is well known, the W/P_{ma} variable is lacking in the productivity equations estimated by economists who accept traditional theory and take the aggregate production function as the starting point in their empirical investigations. However, it is clearly absurd not to consider in such investigations the prices of capital goods, at least as an element in the substitution between capital and labor; several economists have introduced a special variable, the "rental of capital goods," intended to combine the traditional variable—the rate of interest—with the prices of capital goods. In fact this "rental" has been conceived as the product of the said two quantities (some use this "rental" net of taxes but gross of depreciation) (see Jorgenson and Griliches 1967). Yet this concept is open to an objection similar to that raised to Marshall's "net product"—that it is inconsistent with the neoclassical theory of distribution. Indeed, if we define the said rental as $P_K \cdot i$, the relation

$$P_K \cdot i = \frac{\partial x}{\partial L}$$

fails to mesh with the aggregate production function and the theory of distribution derived from it.

12. The following observations (*Economic Report of the President* 1982, 114) are still valid: "There have been concerted efforts to explain the measured slowdown. These efforts have met with only limited success. While there are a number of possible explanatory variables, available studies suggest that none separately nor in combination is capable of explaining more than half of the decline."

13. It has been found that the increase in energy prices has contributed to the productivity slowdown (see Hudson and Jorgenson, quoted in Norsworthy, Harper, and Kunze 1979, 388, 412). This finding is fully consistent with the view put forward in the text. Since machinery and energy are to a large extent complementary inputs, the price of energy is an important part of the running expenses of machines, so the prices of machines could be replaced by an index combining the prices of the two inputs. On the other hand, as already noted, the increase in the price of energy has contributed to push up the prices of machines and thus to pull down the W/P_{ma} ratio. If this is so, then it does not seem to be necessary to consider separately the price of energy in the productivity equation; the ratio W/P_{ma} appears to be adequate. (Strictly speaking, this ratio would have to be modified in the following way: $W/(\alpha P_{ma} + \beta P_{en})$, where P_{en} is the price index of an unit of energy and α and β are appropriate weights). Let us add that, though the increase in the price and in the running expenses of machines has reduced the incentive to substitute machines for labor, it has stimulated the absolute saving of machines (i.e., it has increased the incentive to save the use of machines per unit of output).

14. Since completing this chapter, I have seen the March 1983 issue of the *Economic Journal* in which there are three papers, together with a commentary, on the slowdown in productivity growth that has occurred in recent years in all developed countries. The authors are A. Lindebeck, H. Giersch and F. Wolter, E. F. Denison, and D. J. Morris, who is the author of the comment on the paper by Lindbeck. I recommend that the reader compare my conclusions with those reached in these three papers, which follow the traditional approach.

References

Ferguson, C. E. 1969 *The Neoclassical Theory of Production and Distribution*. Cambridge University Press.

Ferguson, C. E. 1971. "Capital theory Up To Date: A Comment on Mrs. Robinson Article." *Canadian Journal of Economics*, May.

Graham, F. D. 1926. "Relation of Wage Rate to the Use of Machinery." *American Economic Review*, September.

Hayek, F. A. 1942. "The Ricardo Effect." *Economica*, May.

Jorgenson, D. W., and Griliches, Z. 1967. "The Explanation of Productivity Changes." *Review of Economic Studies* 34.

Kaldor, N. 1942. "Professor Hayek and the Concertina Effect." *Economica*, November.

Kalecki, M. 1944. "Three Ways to Full Employment." In *The Economics of Full Employment*. Blackwell, Oxford.

Keynes, J. M. 1936. *The General Theory of Employment Interest and Money, The Collected Writings of J. M. Keynes*, Vol. 7. Reprint. Macmillan, London, 1973.

Maddison, A. 1982. *Phases of Capitalist Development*. Oxford University Press.

Marshall, A. 1890. *Principles of Economics*. Reprint. Macmillan, London, 1949.

Nelson, R. R. 1981. "Research on Productivity Growth and Productivity Differences: Dead Ends and New Departures." *Journal of Economic Literature*, September.

Norsworthy, J. R., and Harper, M. J. 1979. "The Role of Capital Formation in the Recent Productivity Growth Slowdown." *Working Paper 87. Bureau of Labor Statistics*, January.

Norsworthy, J. R., Harper, M. J., and Kunze, K. 1979. "The Slowdown in Productivity Growth: Analysis of Some Contributing Factors." *Brookings Papers on Economic Activity* 2.

Pasinetti, L. L. 1981. *Structural Change and Economic Growth*. Cambridge University Press.

Ricardo, D. 1821. *On the Principles of Political Economy and Taxation, The Works and Correspondence of D. Ricardo*, Vol. 1. Ed. by P. Sraffa with the assistance of M. Dobb. Reprint. Cambridge University Press, 1951a.

Ricardo, D., 1951b. *Speeches and Evidence, The Works and Correspondence of David Ricardo*, Vol. 5. Ed. by P. Sraffa with the assistance of M. Dobb. Reprint. Cambridge University Press.

Salter, W. E. G. 1969. *Productivity and Technical Change*. Cambridge University Press.

Schumpeter, J. A. 1912. *Theorie der wirtschaftichen Entwicklung*. Duncker-Humblot, Berlin. (English translation. *Theory of Economic Development*. Harvard University Press, Cambridge Mass., 1934.

Schumpeter, J. A. 1939. *Business Cycles: A Theoretical, Historical, and Statistical Analysis of the Capitalist Process*. McGraw-Hill, New York.

Shaikh, A. 1974. "Laws of Production and Laws of Algebra: The Humbug Production Function." *The Review of Economics and Statistics*, February.

Smith, A. 1776. *The Wealth of Nations*. Reprint. Methuen, London, 1961.

Sraffa, P. 1960. *Production of Commodities by Means of Commodities—Prelude to a Critique of Economic Theory*. Cambridge University Press.

Sylos-Labini, P. 1974. *Trade Unions, Inflation and Productivity*. Lexington Books, Lexington, Mass.

Sylos-Labini, P. 1980. "Progresso tecnico, preços e crescimento: uma introducão." In *Progresso Técnico e Teoria Economica*. Editoria Hucitec. Universidade Estadual de Campinas, Saõ Paulo.

Tarantelli, E. 1970. *Produttività del lavoro, salari e inflazione*. Ente Luigi Einaudi, Rome.

Verdoorn, P. J. 1949. "Fattori che regolano lo sviluppo della produttività del lavoro." *L'industria* 1.

Weintraub, S. 1961. *Classical Keynesianism Monetary Theory And the Price Level*. Greenwood, Westport, Conn.

Wicksell, K. 1926. *Lectures on Political Economy*. Reprint. Routledge, London, 1934.

Sources of the Statistical Data

Italy.
Ministero del bilancio. *Relazione generale sulla situazione economica del paese*, various years.
For investment and fixed capital: Confederazione generale italiana dell'industria, Ufficio studi, Roma, 1982.

United States
Economic Report of the President. Washington, D.C., 1982, tables B-37, B-38, B-42, B-48, B-57.

III

Changes in Market Structure

5. The Theory of Prices in Oligopoly and the Theory of Growth

5.1 Competition and Oligopoly

Under competition, since the entry of new enterprises is free, profit can only temporarily exceed a level that induces enterprises to continue production. Under all other market structures, in particular under oligopoly and monopoly, entry is not free; there are obstacles. Therefore profit can, even in a lasting way, exceed that minimum level which, in practice, is determined by the rate of interest.

For prices in competitive markets I adhere to the classical, or more precisely, the Ricardian view: in the short run prices depend on supply and demand, and in the long run they depend on costs. Naturally, this implies constant returns, but, as Sraffa has demonstrated in his article of 1926, it is the only hypothesis compatible with competition.

In markets not governed by competition, things are different. In the discussion that follows, I show that, in the case of oligopoly, prices depend on costs in the short run and in the long run on demand. However, one must allow for two important qualifications: (1) costs and profits of various enterprises differ; (2) as a rule enterprises that benefit from the highest protective barriers succeed in obtaining the largest profits. In the long run demand tends to influence prices in the opposite sense: the more rapid the expansion of demand, the greater the technical and commercial economies of scale that enterprises, considered in isolation, can obtain and the less—prices of factors of production being equal—the costs and hence prices.

One can yet subscribe to the tripartite scheme of Colin Clark and maintain that, in general, competition is the most frequent market structure in primary sectors (agriculture and mining), and oligopoly the most widespread market structure in industry. Markets of tertiary activities (services) are characterized by remarkable imperfections and some features of oligopoly (one might call these imperfect oligopolies). As long as very small firms prevail—whether managed by their owners or organized into companies consisting of a small number of partners—competition predominates also in industry. In the most advanced capitalist countries the phase of individual enterprise lasted until the 1870s or 80s. Then a process of concentration occurred in several branches of industry and finance, primarily for technological reasons, and a relatively small number of large firms became dominant. Such firms were organized as share companies and corporations controlling several firms—cartels, trusts, holdings and, more recently, conglomerates. In this second phase one can observe that oligopoly prevails in industry in various forms and with different types of barriers to entry.

Given a particular market size in industries with a relatively homogeneous product, the main barrier to entry depends on the minimum quantity that can be produced at costs that stand up to competition. This is the technological barrier. Many basic industries belong to this category. In industries with differentiated products the main barrier to entry is given by the size of expenditure on sales promotion and advertising a firm has to incur to penetrate markets and then to extend or at least to maintain its market share. This is the commercial barrier. Expenditure on sales promotion and advertising is analogous in character to fixed costs. The larger it is, the larger must be production to obtain a sufficiently low average cost, even if technical motives are left aside. The size of the market renders the commercial barrier more or less effective. Many, perhaps most, nondurable consumer goods belong to this category. I call "homogeneous," or "concentrated," oligopoly a market situation where the technological barrier is the most important; "differentiated," or "imperfect," oligopoly a market situation where the commercial barrier predominates; and "mixed" oligopoly a situation where we find a combination of both categories of barriers (most consumer durables and mechanical products belong to this category).

In addition to technological and commercial barriers there are financial barriers which protect in particular the largest firms. These barriers are responsible for the difficulties small firms encounter when they seek access to the financial market or to bank credit; the large firms are definitely favored. Financial barriers are especially important in the case of integrated groups of industry, whether vertically or horizontally, which organize finance companies for the purpose of supplying funds to the enterprises they control or granting credit to the buyers of the products. Such a practice is widespread in the automobile industry.

5.2 The Formation and Variation of Prices under Oligopoly

Again given a particular market size, the various barriers give rise to different profit rates, and since they operate with different intensity in each industry, firms obtain average profit rates of a different size, in both the short and the long run.

Under these conditions supply is administered so as to administer prices. When demand falls, production is reduced proportionately so as to maintain prices; when demand expands, production is generally increased to a corresponding degree. To face demand expansion in the short run, large firms dispose of unutilized capacities; they calculate the "standard costs," which they use as point of departure for the administration of prices, in reference to the standard volume of production, which exceeds the quantity corresponding to the "break-even point" but remains below the maximum possible output. In addition the large firms build their plants in the expectation of the probable expansion of demand in the long run, not only because the gestation period of investments is usually long but also because unutilized capacity can serve to discourage potential competitors. Therefore in the short run price variations depend on those of costs, although the two do not vary systematically in the same proportion. It is only in special circumstances, when in the majority of enterprises demand expansion exceeds expectations and full capacity is reached, that demand can contribute to determine variations (increases) in prices.

In a given situation the technical conditions of production, the size of the market, the elasticity of demand for the products of the industry, and the barriers to entry explain the level of the price, whereas the differential effects of barriers to entry due to technical and commercial economies of scale explain the various cost levels of different firms (costs of production and distribution). To study price formation, one has to use the concepts of "entry-preventing price" and "elimination price." [1]

With prices and the level of costs as already determined, the large firms, which usually play the role of "price leaders," use the proportional margin between cost and price (the markup) to make the price vary when market conditions change, and in particular when costs vary due to changes in the price of the means of production. In other words, the so-called full-cost principle, though meaningless in relation to the analytical problem of price formation, assumes all its significance in the problem of price variations in the short period. Its rational basis becomes evident not in a static but a dynamic context. Contrary to what the expression "full-cost principle" suggests, the base used to apply the markup is not the full—direct plus indirect—cost but only direct cost, which consists of unit wage cost and materials cost. Fundamentally, the reason is that direct cost changes are frequent and affect all firms, though to somewhat different degrees; the differences depend especially on the divisor of unit wage cost, direct labor productivity, which varies among firms. Overhead costs are much more differentiated, and their changes do not affect all firms at the same time. Under oligopoly, changes in direct costs necessitate a price change for reasons of oligopolistic rivalry.

The principle of full cost can then be expressed by the equation:

$$P = v + qv,$$

where v is the direct cost—the sum of labor cost (ratio between wage and labor productivity, W/π) and raw material costs (RM)—q is the proportional margin, and qv serves to cover fixed unit costs relative to the standard volume of production (k/x_n) and to yield a predetermined profit per unit of output (g). One can say that firms that use this formula to vary prices when direct costs vary follow a target markup pricing policy.

If enterprises follow a target return pricing policy, we have

$$r = \frac{Px - vx - k}{K},$$

where r is the target rate of profit and K the invested capital. The said formula implies the following equation:

$$P = v + \frac{k}{x_n} + r\frac{K}{x_n}.$$

The first equation gives the same results as the second on the assumption that v, k, and K vary in the same proportion. Salaries, which account for a non-negligible share of overhead costs, k, tend to vary in the same proportion as wages. Another part of k (which covers depreciation) and K (the value of capital goods) vary in the same direction as labor and raw material costs but not necessarily in the same proportion. All in all, the assumption that v, k and K tend to vary in the same proportion is not strictly accurate though somewhat justifiable. In a first approximation, then the two equations used to analyze the variations of P can be considered equivalent.

The markup on direct costs is not constant. More precisely, though it tends to remain relatively stable over the long run (a cycle of several years), in the short run (from year to year) it is variable, tending to diminish when direct costs increase and to increase when they diminish.[2]

I attempted tried to demonstrate this thesis elsewhere.[3] Here I limit the discussion to the fact that when the direct cost increases, the markup tends to diminish, that is, the price increases proportionately less than direct cost, and this for various reasons: for certain reasons which are independent of firm decisions (foreign competition and internal oligopolistic competition), and for reasons which lie within the power of large firms (enterprises wishing not to check demand expansion and at the same time to reduce the risk of invasion by other firms, a risk that tends to increase when demand rises rapidly). There is further an aggregate effect if one considers one industry or even the whole industrial sector: variations in productivity and hence labor costs differ substantially among firms, and it is often precisely the largest firm that oobtains the most rapid increases in productivity and has consequently less reason to increase prices when wages and raw material prices rise (as a rule the largest firms are "price leaders").

When direct costs diminish, prices decline on average less than proportionally—and the markup increases—because (1) foreign and internal competition may not operate or play only a weak role and (2) because the large firms may reduce prices only to the extent they consider necessary to prevent an invasion by other firms. In addition the innovations these firms are in a position to introduce are often inaccessible to small firms just because of their size, and they can therefore be more or less certain that the increase in profit margins does not involve risks of an invasion of their market, at least in the short run. Further *the large firms that play the role of price leaders aim at achieving a certain profit rate over a certain number of years, not in a single year. Therefore the growing profit margins obtained when direct costs diminish serve to compensate for the smaller earnings when direct costs increase.*

For instance, General Motors administers the prices of its products with a view toward "the highest attainable rate of return on capital." This, however, constitutes a long-term objective: "the company does not necessarily try to maximize its return in any given year, but rather over a period of years which may be characterized by wide fluctuations in output." [4]

Thus in the short run the sum of the coefficients of direct costs is less than unity, but in the long run, and on average, it tends to approach unity, in which case costs and prices tend to vary in the same proportion. Indeed, if in the long run costs increases more than prices, the least efficient firms, those that have the highest costs and do not succeed in obtaining even the minimum profit, are driven out of the market; as a result in a given industry, average costs are pulled down and brought again in line with prices. On the other hand, if on the average the rate of profit remains at a level considerably above the minimum for a long time, new firms are attracted to the market, and the price falls. In brief, this mechanism is similar—though not identical—to that of strict competition.

5.3 Profit Maximization and Sales Maximization

Recently, some economists like Baumol, Marris, and Galbraith have doubted whether the objective of firms is that of maximizing profit; the objective would rather be to maximize sales, or more precisely, their rate of growth. Since those economists have maintained that such an objective is valid for large firms organized in the form of share companies, I shall refer in the discussion to firms of this type.

With the exception of Marris, those who put forward this view neglect the fact that profits serve to finance development. The two objectives of maximizing profits and the rate of growth of sales would coincide if all investments were financed from profits. It is true that finance in part can be external, but one can and must suppose that, according to Kalecki's "principle of increasing risk," the external debt cannot exceed certain limits. This is why, from a dynamic point of view, there is a definite link between these two objectives, so that as a rule they can be considered equivalent.

However, not all profits are available for self-financing: some goes to paying dividends and some to the interests on borrowed funds. Mathematically,

$$A = G - \sigma K' = iK'',$$

where A is self-financing, G total profits, K' capital invested by shareholders, K'' borrowed capital, σ the rate of return to share capital, and i the rate of interest. To simplify, one can assume that the two rates are equal and write

$$A = G - \sigma(K' + K'') = G - \sigma K.$$

The maximum level external finance can attain without danger to the enterprise can be considered as a multiple of self-finance:

$$E = mA.$$

Therefore the maximum potential level of total financing is given by

$$F = G - \sigma K + m(G - \sigma K)$$
$$(G - \sigma K)(1 + m).$$

On the other hand, firms can use their internal funds and the money they borrow not only to enlarge their productive capacity but also in other ways: (1) to launch advertising campaigns to accelerate the expansion of demand for already produced goods or to "create" a demand for new products, (2) to set up subsidiaries, (3) to acquire other firms and absorb them, (4) to make investments abroad, and (5) for purely financial investments and uses.

In view of all this the thesis that, over time, the objective of sales maximization diverges from that of profit maximization does not appear to be sustainable. The calculations given in table 5.1 clarify this issue. Accordingly, we make the following assumptions:

1. The value of capital equals that of sales.

2. The rate of interest of borrowed external funds (equal to the yield of the share capital) is 5 percent.

3. The internal and external financing potentially available during period t is used totally or partially to finance investment in period $t + 1$ (maximum limit of total financing).

4. The external debt can attain a maximum amount equal to the funds available for self-financing so that $E = A$ and $F = 2A$.

5. Total average cost is constant so that when production increases, total cost increases in proportion.

6. If prices and distribution costs remain equal, demand tends to increase by 10 percent each year.

In the table the initial situation is summarized in case 1. The situation in case 2 arises if the firm does not take certain measures concerning prices or distribution costs. Sales increase by 10 percent, total profits also by 10 percent, but the rate of profit is 15 percent. The actual financing is below the maximum: the expansion of productive capacity in period $t + 1$ is financed entirely from internal funds.

In cases 3 and 4 we have two situations where sales expand by 20 percent instead of the 10 percent in case 2. In case 3 the expansion of sales is obtained through a price reduction (from 10 to 9.45), and in the case 4 through an advertising campaign (pushing up average cost from 8.5 to 9). Afterward the rate of expansion of sales may go back to 10 percent, but this rate will apply to an increased volume of sales. Therefore period by period the total value of sales will exceed that which would have been obtained by maintaining the succession of cases 1 and 2, but for the problem of financing. Investment, which during the period $t + 1$ is 200 in cases 3 and 4 (200 being the maximum limit of financing determined by the profits obtained in the initial period), during the following period $(t + 2)$—not considered in the table—declines in both cases to 120, since this represents the new maximum limit of total financing.

Cases 3 and 4 are equivalent in their results; case 4 has been presented here because it is more realistic for modern times and also because it opens the way to my discussion in section 5.4. For simplicity, in the rest of this section I will consider only case 3 and not case 4.

Table 5.1

	(1) Sales $p \cdot x = S$	(2) $\Delta S/S$	(3) Cost $c \cdot x = C$	(4) Profits $S - C = G$	(5) ΔG with respect to 1	(6) Self-financing $G - 0.05K = A$	(7) Maximum financing $F = 2A$	(8) Investment $I = \Delta K$	(9) Capital $S = K$	(10) Rate of profit $G/K = r$
1. Initial period (t)	$10 \times 100 = 1{,}000$	—	$8.5 \times 100 = 850$	150	—	100	200	—	1,000	15%
2. Normal increase in demand, prices and distribution costs remaining equal (period $t+1$)	$10 \times 110 = 1{,}100$	10%	$8.5 \times 110 = 935$	165	15	110	220	100	1,100	15%
3. Increase in demand caused by a decline in prices, variations in prices, variations in relation to t (period $t+1$)	$9.45 \times 127 = 1{,}200$	20%	$8.5 \times 127 = 1{,}080$	120	−30	60	120	200	1,200	10%
4. Increase in demand caused by an advertising campaign, variations in relation to t (period $t+1$)	$10 \times 120 = 1{,}200$	20%	$9 \times 120 = 1{,}080$	120	−30	60	120	200	1,200	10%
2a. As 2 + an additional investment of 100 with a yield of 6% (period $t+1$)	$10 \times 110 = 1{,}100$ + 100 ——— 1,200	20%	$8.5 \times 110 = 935$	165 6 —— 171	15 6 —— 21	110 1 —— 111	220 2 —— 222	100 100 —— 200	1,100 100 ——— 1,200	15% 6% ——— 14.25%

In case 3, then, the rate of expansion of sales increases compared to case 2, passing from 10 to 20 percent; however, total profits fall from 150 to 120 or from 165 to 120, depending on whether one compares it with case 1 or 2. Thus the rate of profit declines from 15 to 10 percent. According to Baumol, the modern firm prefers the alternatives given by cases 3 and 4 to case 2: the decline in profit, both total and proportional, would be compensated by a greater expansion of sales, which is what really matters for the firm's well-being.

This thesis, however, neglects the fact that profits serve as a basis for financing investments. In case 2, during the period $t + 1$ the firm could invest 200 (maximum financing permitted by the profits obtained in period t), but it limits itself to an investment equal to 100. If we compare cases 2 and 3, the choice may appear to be indeterminate, since in case 2 profits are higher though sales are lower, and of course the preference of managers cannot be determined a priori. Yet the argument of Baumol and the other economists mentioned is by no means farfetched. When considering a longer period, however, the terms of the choice change. In fact in period $t + 2$ the firm can invest more when its background is given by case 2 than when it is given by case 3, precisely because total profits are higher. This becomes clearer if we assume (case 2a) that the firm finds a way to carry out an additional investment equal to 100, for example, by producing a new good; it is enough that the firm expects to earn a profit at least a little higher than the rate of interest $(6\% > 5\%)$. Now, there is no difference between cases 2a and 3 as far as sales maximization is concerned—the expansion of sales is 20% in both cases. However, in case 3 profits fall from 150 to 120, whereas they rise from 150 to 171 in case 2a. Since profits indirectly determine the maximum limit of financing, case 2a is to be preferred when referring to the long run. In this case the two objectives coincide.

The conclusion is that the choice is indeterminate when there are no investment opportunities except those created by the "normal" increase in demand. In practice, however, large firms often have a range of investment opportunities so the problem of choosing between the two objectives may be indeterminate only in the case of small firms. For large firms the two objectives—sales or profit maximization—generally do coincide, contrary to the view of the economists mentioned here. If managers intend to maximize sales in the short run (cases 3 or 4), letting down total profits provided these do not fall below a certain minimum—this is Baumol's thesis—they in fact have renounced maximization of sales in the long run.

In the example given, the relationships and alternatives that I have considered can be translated into precise quantities only by assuming that the

Table 5.2

	Two highest rates		Average rates	Two lowest rates	
1947	20.1	17.0	11.9	6.0	6.6
1948	22.9	18.9	13.1	.6.8	7.4
1949	31.3	19.1	11.7	3.7	5.3
1950	34.9	24.6	13.4	1.8	4.7
1951	20.0	18.5	11.2	3.6	6.2
1952	20.5	18.5	10.3	5.9	4.1
1953	20.0	17.3	10.8	6.0	5.2
1954	22.6	20.6	10.6	4.5	5.1
1955	26.6	21.9	12.7	6.0	6.6

managers of the firm have a perfect knowledge of market conditions and are able to make perfect forecasts. Of course this assumption does not correspond to reality, since in the real world uncertainty rules. Incomplete knowledge on the part of the firms and a continual change in market conditions forces the firm to follow a "simple" rule that maximizes profits and sales over time while minimizing different kinds of risks: invasion of their market by other firms, immobilization (which would result from too high a leverage), public intervention if the firm fixes prices that are "too high." The latter risk is particularly great in the case where the firm produces a "basic" commodity such as steel.[5]

The simple strategy for enterprises endowed with market power is to fix prices with a view toward a target markup or a target rate of profit. This is not a *minimum* rate of profit but the rate rendered possible by the protective barriers from which the firm benefits. Since these are different between markets and even within a market, profit rates taken as a target will also be different. The target rate is pursued by a given firm not by year but in the course of successive years, thus from one year to another, profits can be below or above a certain target rate. However, in each year for an industry or the economy as a whole, one will observe a range of profit rates. It must be presumed that the highest profits and those relatively most stable are obtained by firms that play the role of "price leaders."

For instance, let us look at table 5.2 which reports the profit rates of twenty-two enterprises examined by Kaplan, Dirlam, and Lanzillotti for the period 1947 to 1955, in terms of the two highest, the two lowest, and the average rate for each year.[6] One might think that the differences depend mainly on the degrees of risk attached to various productive activities and investments. But it can easily be seen that this is not the case. The highest profits are almost without exception those of very large companies, like General Motors, General Electric, and Dupont de Nemours, which clearly do not make very high profits because of relatively higher risks. In fact we find higher profits in certain companies even over a large number of years. Such a relatively stable difference of profits characterizes precisely the markets not governed by competition or markets sheltered by more or less high barriers. Under competition the highest profits last only for a short time, even if the difference tends frequently to reappear.

The simple strategy just mentioned—that of a rate of profit taken as a target—does not mean exclusion of discretionary elements in the management of firms, particular the large ones. In the main, the choices to be made concern the policy to follow in order to expand sales (by lowering prices and/or launching advertising campaigns), the critical "leverage" ratio, and decisions on dividends to be distributed and hence on the rate of return of share capital. All these factors in turn are not only conditioned by the knowledge of data and risks but also by the initiative and the ability of managers.

The basic target of maximizing total profits and sales over time implies a global strategy which includes several interdependent decisions, among which we find (1) the problem of determining and varying prices and the amount of expenditure on advertising, (2) the problem of the diversifying of production and penetrating new markets, and (3) the problem of financing investments.

Profit maximization over time, or "long-term profit maximization," is therefore considerably removed from the profit maximizing techniques of marginal analysis, which refer to a given point of time or, more realistically, to a very short period: in theory the solution supplied by this analysis is perfectly determined but it is of little value in interpreting reality.

Certain patterns of bahavior, however, clash with long-term profit maximization. One can quote the example of a financial speculator who succeeds in gaining control of a share company with which he does not "identify" himself; he intends to use that control for obtaining gains in the immediate future; in fact as soon as he can he sells his shares to realize capital gains. Persons of this type are regarded contemptuously as adventurers by "serious" industrialists, that is by those who identify themselves with the companies they operate (an expression used by Simon and Galbraith). Another example is given by a situation in which struggles and conflicts among managers and technicians (inevitable in complex organizations such as large share companies) become so acute as to reduce the efficiency and the dynamics of the enterprise and hence its capacity to make profits. Again should a struggle take place between an external group wanting to take over a company and the one having the control, the target of long-term profit maximization is set aside for as long as the struggle lasts.

There is further a very important point. Barriers to entry do not necessarily give rise to more than normal profits. The search for all opportunities of gaining profits presupposes an energetic and incessant effort by managers. Paradoxically, the higher the barriers that shelter enterprises from pressures of rival competition pressures, the greater can be the temptation for the leading group of managers to pursue a policy of ease and to slack off. In other words, the target of long-term profit maximization is pursued with all the stronger effort, the greater the pressure of competition and hence the threat of rivals. If this threat is not restrained it will bring a loss of autonomy, culminating in the financial control and the absorption by other companies.

However, in addition to the differences in the pressure of external competition, there are differences in the taste for, or aversion against, risk as well as in the abilities of managers. In the final analysis, the size of the firm, as Maffeo Pantaleoni wittily observed, depends on the size of the brain of the entrepreneur. The heroic times of the development of a given firm may be those when a certain manager or an extraordinarily capable or dynamic group of managers is in charge; the successors can, in large part, trade on their accomplishments. It may also happen that a certain firm that was once efficient and dynamic falls at a certain moment into the hands of incapable or lazy managers due to inheritance or an erroneous policy of co-optation by the managing group. It is not that such individuals do not intend to maximize profits, but they pursue this policy within the narrow limits set by their capacities, or they have an excessive predilection for "weekends" and holidays.

Not all managers therefore aim at long-term profit maximization; financial speculators do not even consider it. Such a target when intensely pursued by industrialists results in profits and growth that are all the more positive, the stronger the pressure of oligopolistic competition.

Industrialists who "identify" themselves with the firm are induced to maximize profits in the long run, either for a immediate financial interest or, and even more so, for reasons of security, independence, and power. In effect the target in question implies a logic that conditions the behavior of all managers considered as a group: *it is a target of the company, not of individuals.*

The immediate financial interest derives alternatively or simultaneously from two sources: administrators are often at the same time shareholders, though generally only of a relatively small part. They share in the profits even more often through remunerations directly linked to average profits, or through bonus payments or in other ways. As a rule both remunerations and bonus payments are decided on by the managers themselves, who can take the lion's share in the distribution of profits. Constraints introduced by law, as unanimously admitted by lawyers, are not very effective, but this varies from country to country. In fact the remunerations fixed by the managers are usually very high. They incorporate a part of the monopolistic or oligopolistic above-normal profits of many large firms and serve, rather than for economic ends, to determine the *status* (as sociologists say) of the managers; thus within certain limits they become almost a necessity of the system.

On the whole, however, such behavior does not seem to reduce significantly the capacity of large firms to expand. The fact is that the main motive of the policy of long-term profit maximization is not the material interest of the managers but the fact that profit constitutes the principal source of financing development. Development is as a rule desired by the managers because, by expanding the firms they operate and with which they identify themselves, they can obtain or increase their personal prestige, their own influence, and finally their own "power" in the outside community. They can especially improve their chances of making a career inside the firm, and this ensures that they can maintain themselves as an autonomous group. If in fact the firm does not grow or grows at a lower rate than that of its big rivals, the risk of absorption of the firm by other, more dynamic, organizations increases as do also the chances of being taken over by a financial group. If one of the two risks materializes, the managing group loses its autonomy, and without autonomy it loses everything. Profit maximization as a means of maximizing the growth of the firm is thus necessary for the survival of the managing group as such. If this is true, one must suppose that the target of profit maximization is associated with the policy of maximizing undistributed profits and of plowing them back into the firm. This is exactly what seems normally to happen.

5.4 The Limits of Growth: Profits and Demand

The growth of a large firm has then two constraints, the volume of profits and that of demand. We have thus far been concerned with the former; we shall now deal with the latter.

In theory the firm can choose between two sales policies: a passive one limited to ordinary commercial expenditures, or an aggressive one. It is clear that the former only makes sense if demand for the products of the firm, "special" demand, tends to grow by itself at a rate considered satisfactory; generally, such a steadily expanding demand will only take place if global effective demand tends on its part to grow at a high rate. In that event an aggressive sales policy will have all the more chances of success. One can state in formal terms that the rate of expansion of special demand is a function both of commercial expenditure and of global effective demand.

At the time when small individual firms predominated in industry and product differentiation was not pronounced, variations in effective demand had a very modest effect on production, in particular on its expansion: firms made their production decisions on the basis of prices, which they could not influence, and costs, which they could influence through improving methods of production.

However, in modern times the large industrial enterprises operating in oligopolistic markets are no longer compelled to consider prices as given but can influence them by administering supply so as to obtain a predetermined mark up (or a predetermined profit rate) not each year but on average in a certain number of years. The principal stimulus for innovation does not come from the tendency of prices to fall but from the tendency of wages to increase. In fact, the enterprises that succeed in increasing their productivity more rapidly than others do not make a strong resistance to trade union demands for wage increases; they may even take the initiative in increasing wages so as to attract additional workers or to keep the net margin from growing too much in relation to costs and thus deter the invasion of other firms. Trade unions have by now become strong enough to be able to generalize wage increases and to accelerate them. To a large extent the development of trade unions is the result of the same process that has increased the market power of firms in a large sector of the economy.[7]

In our times many firms are in a position to influence supply in relation to variations of demand so as to administer prices, particularly in industry. This fact has very important consequences both in the short and long run.

In the short run a drop in demand, whatever its cause, is accompanied not by a fall in industrial prices (except in the case where costs decline, and even then, to a limited extent) but by a corresponding decline in production; that is, in the short run industrial prices become *flexible in relation to costs and rigid in relation to demand*. However, in the long run it is effective demand that becomes the main determinant of the development of production and employment.

5.5 The Movement of Prices in the Last Century and in Our Century

We cannot develop the conceptions we have just put forward any fuller. I think, however, that it will not be useless to reflect on the movement of prices since the nineteenth century.

As is well known, during most of the last century wholesale industrial prices showed a descending trend; the prices of agricultural products and primary materials also declined but less rapidly, so that the terms of trade between the two groups of commodities shifted in favor of agriculture and raw materials.

In general, national income increased throughout the century; it continued to increase, and often even more rapidly, in periods when prices declined than in the much shorter ones when they rose.

In our century, however, prices, whether industrial or agricultural, have tended to rise; this trend has been accentuated since the second world war. Between the two wars prices declined sharply form 1929 to 1933 and only recovered their 1929 level at the threshold of World War II, in 1939. In this period, in contrast to what happened in the last century, during phases of price declines national income, and above all industrial production, fell as much as or even more than prices. Agricultural prices declined much more sharply than industrial prices, though agricultural production did not fall at all. In our century we have no example of a long-term fall in prices accompanied by an increase in industrial production. And the terms of trade favor industrial products instead of primary commodities despite support policies applied by numerous governments.

During the cyclical crises of the last century a fall in effective demand (or in total expenditure expressed in monetary terms) provoked a decline in prices rather than in production, because in industry as in agriculture production units were small and unable to influence prices. In certain cases a fall in demand could even go hand in hand with an increase in production, because producers, when seeking to reduce the damage inflicted on them by the fall in prices, tended rather to raise production, at least as long as the price left some margin above cost. In our century a decline in demand in industry brings about a fall in production rather than in prices. Moreover an initial drop in demand sets off a depressive spiral of demand itself through the decline in employment and hence in the wage bill. The spiral becomes particularly serious because in our century industry has assumed greater importance in terms of production and employment than during the previous century.

A comparison between the great depression of the last century, lasting from 1873 to 1879, with that of our century can serve to illustrate this point. I consider the United Kingdom and the United States, distinguishing the percentage variations of price and production in industry and agriculture. It must not be forgotten that after the first world war the United Kingdom suffered a much more serious and longer crisis than the United States, but the depression of 1929 to 1932 was relatively less severe there (see table 5.3).

In both countries the depression of 1873 to 1879 was longer but much less

Table 5.3

	Industry			Agriculture	
	Prices	Production	Wages	Prices	Production
United Kingdom					
1873–79	−29%	− 5%	−10%	−18%	Moderate rise
1929–32	−21%	−16%	− 4%	−44%	Stationary
United States					
1873–79	−33%	− 5%	−35%	−31%	Moderate rise
1929–32	−23%	−48%	−18%	−54%	Stationary

severe than that of 1929 to 1932: unemployment was considerably lower, and the recovery was more rapid and much more sustained. In the last depression unemployment remained at a very high level until the World War II. Agriculture was affected rather similarly in the two depressions, production, despite a fall in prices and a very sharp one in 1929 to 1932, did not decline and even increased in the two periods. In industry, by contrast, during the depression of 1873 to 1879 prices and wages fell sharply in both countries, while production declined much more moderately. During the depression of 1929 to 1932 prices and wages fell considerably less, while production declined considerably more—in the United States the drop was near catastrophic.[8]

To clarify in a very simple manner one of the main points put forward, let us consider as an index of monetary expenditure for acquiring industrial production the price index multiplied by that of quantities, and let us consider, for the two depressions and the two countries, the ratio between the percentage decline in production and the sum of the two percentage declines. This ratio indicates to what extent the decline of total monetary expenditure can be attributed to production (table 5.4).

The comparisons of these two depressions refer mainly to long-term consequences. In the view of the author, the Great Depression of our century was not simply caused by speculative madness followed by an unprecedented collapse; neither did it result from the inefficiency (or badly conceived policy) of the monetary authorities nor the simultaneous occurrence of downturns in cycles of different durations, as Schumpeter saw it. I rather see it as a consequence of the fact indicated earlier: in modern times a fall in demand, whatever its origin, provokes a corresponding decline in production and, because of the tendency of productivity to increase, an even sharper fall in employment. More precisely, the last depression was prepared by an enormous shift toward profits in the distribution of incomes (see chapter 9); it

Table 5.4

	A Expenditure for industrial products	B Percent of fall in A imputable to that of production
United Kingdom		
1873–79	-33%	15%
1929–32	-34%	43%
United States		
1873–79	-36%	13%
1929–32	-60%	67%

Sources: For United Kingdom, on prices see Imlah (1950) and Martin (1948); on industrial production see Hoffman (1954), League of Nations (1933, 1939), Economic Commission for Europe (1949), H.M. Stationary Office (1955), United Nations (1961, 1966); on wages see Layton and Crowther (1935) and Phelps, Brown, and Hopkins (1950); on agricultural production see Ojala (1952). For United States see U.S. Department of Commerce (1960); on the depression of 1929–32, see Means (1935).

became so severe, in terms of output and employment, for the reasons just mentioned. In the new conditions, then, the decline in the level of activity is not automatically followed, as in the past, by a full recovery and by a resumption of the development process. A kind of stagnation can take place, unless an impulse external to the system of private enterprises comes into operation. Such an impulse can be determined by an increase in public expenditure. Seen from this angle, not only is the deep-seated cause of the gravity of the 1929 to 1932 crisis brought to light but also the reason for the serious insufficiency in the subsequent recovery. In fact the increase of public expenditure provoked by Roosevelt's New Deal was entirely inadequate, as Keynes was to point out.[9] The recovery and the subsequent expansion did not take place until the outbreak of the World War II which brought in its wake an enormous increase in public (military) expenditure.

5.6 The Expansion of Demand and Economic Growth

I maintain that in the long term the problem for private enterprise generally will be an increasing inability to bring about, in an endogenous manner, an expansion of demand. An expansion of demand is what will lead to a sustained increase in production, sufficient on its part to cancel the negative effect of increases in productivity on the level of employment and to absorb natural additions to the labor force. If I am correct, the expansion of demand must come from stimuli that are external to the system of private enterprise. These can be of two types: public expenditure and foreign demand. In the postwar period in the United States the impetus to expansion came mainly from public expenditure, which was in large part due to the increase in military expenditure. In an economy where exports account for only 4 percent of gross national product, these was, and there is, not much to be expected from foreign demand. In contrast in West Germany and Japan foreign demand has played a dominant role in determining an expansion that has been truly extraordinary.

In the last analysis, the expansion of foreign demand has depended essentially on three factors. First, the creation of the Common Market has brought with it an enlargement of economic space which has stimulated endogenously the expansion of oligopolistic industries. Second, in recent times backward and socialist countries have rapidly increased their purchases on the international market; in both the principal, and often the only, push has come from public decision centers. Third, the American economy has expanded at a sustained rate; there is no doubt that had this expansion not taken place, the international trade of the western world and of Japan would not have increased at the high rate we have observed.

Of greatest importance has been the expansion of the U.S. economy, which in fact has been stimulated mainly by an increase in public expenditures—for military, social, and productive purposes. Yet such expenditure does not and cannot increase continually over time at the exact pace required to keep the economic machinery going at the desired speed—which we might call "the optimum rate of expansion of public expenditure."[10] Since the forces and interests of public expenditures do not follow a rigorous economic logic, and since in the case of military expenditure there exists a larger strategic design, it is probable that in certain periods public expenditure grows too slowly and in others too rapidly. It is precisely the second case that has occurred in recent times, and this has contributed to the inflationary process.

5.7 The Structure of Contemporary Industry

According to the views presented in this chapter, in large part elaborated in previous studies of the author, the oligopolistic structure of contemporary industry is the outcome of a process of concentration that started to take shape in the last twenty years of the past century and whose roots are essentially technical. Technical progress accompanied and conditioned by the evolution of small enterprises has led to large plants, hence to large firms, and hence to large financial concentrations. This evolution naturally has continued to give birth to new forms of organization—"conglomerates," multinational corporations, and oligopolies (notably in oil, steel, glass, certain chemical products, motor cars, tires, and electronic computers) which have succeeded in spreading over the whole western world and part of the Orient. As a result economic integration among the industrialized capitalistic countries has spread, and among these the United States is the leader country.

Again, if my observation is correct, then it follows that although the new industrial structures can do miracles with technical progress and means of production, *left to themselves*, they cannot ensure a general expansion of production; they only bring it about on condition that an external force stimulates a sufficient expansion of effective demand. In the major capitalist countries this impetus has been provided by the second world war and after the war, by the increase in military expenditure (and such paramilitary expenditures as space exploration) and by a rapid increase in welfare expenditure. For many years the expansion of public spending, however determined, has been favorable to economic growth. Beyond some point such expansion, as I have observed, has tends to overshoot the target, giving rise to a systematic increase in public deficits which for political reasons are very difficult to manage and which have contributed to inflation.

However, these reflections go beyond the scope of my study of certain relations between market structures and economic development. I return to it briefly before concluding in order to stress the necessity for economists to tackle a fundamental subject systematically, that is, to take account of market structures other than competition in models of general microeconomic analysis.

5.8 Brief Remarks on Models of General Analysis

In both micro- and macroeconomic analyses some headway has been made on the subject of market structures and issues related to price formation and price changes. But almost everything still remains to be done in the field of general microeconomic analysis: we have not yet succeeded in inserting the noncompetitive market forms into models of this type. However, economists, when leaving purely abstract models, agree almost unanimously on the fact that today in nonagricultural activities competition is the exception rather than the rule. At least so far, the traditional general equilibrium model of Walras-Pareto has turned out to be refractory to the introduction of market forms other than competition. The author suspects that the difficulties are insurmountable because they stem from the structure of these models itself and not from more or less serious analytical obstacles. I maintain that there is no difficulty in treating market structures other than competition in the model of general microeconomic analysis elaborated by Piero Sraffa in *Production of*

Commodities by Means of Commodities and that this is precisely the most promising way to achieve this integration. The fact is that the model contains a degree of freedom, so it is possible to consider either the rate of profits or the rate of wages as given. This characteristic of the Sraffa model does not constitute an element of inferiority compared to the Walras-Pareto general equilibrium model. It is, on the contrary, an element of superiority, since it permits one to look at the distribution of income as it really is, that is, determined, among other factors, by the conflict between the various parties concerned (two, in the highly simplified version; several, in successive approximations).

To introduce into the Sraffa model market forms other than competition would suggest, first of all, to suppose that there is no unique rate of profit but a range of rates that can be taken as given. Such a hypothesis can be justified by an analysis similar to that which has been briefly recalled in this chapter; such an analysis leads to the conclusion that firms operating in these markets aim at maximizing profits not in the short but in the long run and that to this purpose they adopt a strategy that involves a certain target rate of profit, which is the rate made possible by protective barriers and in general by conditions of entry into the market. This position is perfectly compatible with that which considers various rates of profit as given. Alternatively, instead of rates of profit one can consider as given a range of "coefficients of divergence," which would depend on the degree of monopoly inherent in different markets, whereas the reference rate or the "normal" rate of profit would depend on the action of monetary authorities.

In an analysis of this type the first steps do not present any difficulty. Let us consider the simplest case: two commodities, no fixed capital, no land as a constraint, a single technique, and a single product for each industry. Assuming a unique rate of profit (r) and taking the price of commodity A as numeraire $(P_a = 1)$, we have

$$\begin{cases} (A_a + B_a p_b)(1 + r) + L_a w = A \\ (A_b + B_b p_b)(1 + r) + L_b w = B p_b, \end{cases}$$

where the known data are the quantities produced of the two commodities (A, B), the quantities (of the same commodites) utilized as means of production in the two industries, the quantities of labor employed, L_a and L_b and r, the rate of profit. The price of B and the wage rates (w) are the unknowns.

If we assume that there are two rates of profit, the first "normal" $(r_a = r)$ and the second superior to the first $(r_b = rm$, where m is larger than unity), the number of knowns increases (in addition to r there is m), but the number of the unknowns remains the same. With the help of a numerical example of these two cases—a unique rate and two rates of profit—it is easy to see that in the second case (1) the relative price of commodity B is higher, (2) the wage, which is equal in the two industries, is lower, and (3) the sum of profits is larger.

One must not lose sight of the fact that the original schema of Sraffa aims at explaining the essential features of an economic system by considering given quantities of commodities apart from the behavior of returns and market structure. More precisely, Sraffa deliberately limits his analysis to the effects of variations in the distribution of income on relative prices, on the assumption that the quantities are fixed. However, Sraffa's schema is consistent with the hypothesis that returns are constant—as Sraffa himself warns the reader—and a capitalist economy is implied, one in which competition prevails in all markets (this is the meaning of an unique rate of profit). Nevertheless, there seem to be no logical difficulties in introducing noncompetitive market structures by assuming a variety of profit rates: the simple example presented here suggests that the possibility is open.

Although Sraffa does not consider simple reproduction nor reproduction on an enlarged scale (accumulation), his conception of a "self-replacing state" presents several points of contact with the schema of simple reproduction. Yet it does not coincide with it, because by excluding the variations of quantities produced, he also excludes the possible repercussions that the variations in income distribution can have on the "basket" of commodities which constitutes national income. Nevertheless, the possibility is also there for introducing the hypotheses to approach progressively real situations. In successive approximations one can introduce noncompetitive market forms and also allow for the possibilities of change in composition and volume of national income and in coefficients of production. In other words, it is possible to use Sraffa's schema as a point of departure to combine an analysis of noncompetitive market forms with the analysis of growth and technical progress in a general microeconomic framework.

Notes

1. See the author's monograph, *Oligopoly and Technical Progress* (Harvard University Press, 1969 edition; orig. Italian edition 1956) and "Industrial Pricing in the United Kingdom," *Cambridge Journal of Economics* 3 (1979): 153–163.

2. If one considers annual variation rates of industrial wholesale prices and of the two elements of direct cost, that is, of the cost of wage labor $(L = W/\pi)$ and that of raw materials, one has

$$\hat{P}_i = a\hat{L} + b\widehat{RM}.$$

The value of each coefficient can be viewed as the weight of each cost element multiplied by an index of variation measuring the degree to which the change in each cost element is shifted onto price. Then, if the sum of the two coefficients is equal to one, the shift in variations of direct cost onto price is complete; otherwise, it is partial. The thesis adopted in the text is that $a + b < 1$ in the short run and $a + b = 1$ in the long run.

3. See the author's *Trade Unions, Inflation and Productivity* (Lexington Books, Lexington Mass., 1974), ch. 1.

4. U.S. Congress, Senate, Committee on the Judiciary, Report of the Subcommittee on Antitrust and Monopoly, *Administered Prices: Automobiles*, 85th Cong., 2d sess., 1958, S. Res. 231, p. 106. Other large enterprises tend to follow the target markup pricing policy, which, as we have seen, generally can be considered as practically equivalent to the target return pricing policy. It seems that these criteria are used in mature industries which year after year produce the bulk of industrial products. Firms operating in new industries use different criteria, as was shown by Dirlam, Kaplan, and Lanzillotti, *Pricing in Big Business, A Case Approach* (The Brookings Institution, Washington, D.C., 1958), ch. 2. However, these other criteria do not differ much from the one noted here, or they simply consist of "following the leader."

5. This risk in fact preoccupies the administrators of enterprises that are public in character because they produce basic commodities. This comes out clearly in the responses made by the managers to inquires; see Dirlam, Kaplan, and Lanzillotti, *Pricing in Big Business, A Case Approach*, pp. 166–175. It is significant that these authors, in explaining the price policy of the U.S. Steel Corporation, speak of "inhibitions of a public utility." The managers avoid a policy of high prices because they fear government intervention which could impose from outside precisely that regulation of prices usually applied to public utilities or nationalized firms. The "self-restraint" in price policy does not therefore depend on the fact that the administrators are particularly enlightened or concerned with the public good but on the instinct of a private and autonomous group which intends to remain so. It is correct to state that they seek to maximize total long-term profits "subject to the inhibitions of a public utility." (It is not improbable that a case study of the type mentioned here has led some economists to abandon the hypothesis of profit maximization.)

6. Ibid., pp. 313–319.

7. It is a mistake to think that the increasing margins, due to the increasing bargaining power of the firms operating in certain branches of economic activity, necessarily become above-normal profits; they can as well become above-normal wages, and owing to the barganing power acquired by the trade unions in the labor markets, this possibility is more and more frequent. In a sense the trade unions tend to expropriate a part of the market power of the firms. (It is worth noticing that the possibility that high margins due to monopoly power can become high profits or high wages was explicitily considered by Adam Smith; as quoted in section 1.5 of this book.)

8. It is interesting to point out that in the United States the fall in industrial prices during the depression of 1929 to 1932 (about 20 percent) can be explained by the fall in direct costs, which in its turn can be attributed almost completely to the fall in agricultural and mineral raw material prices (about 50 percent). The behavior of the two categories of prices is fully consistent with the model briefly recalled in the text.

9. J. H. Williams, "Deficit Spending," in *Readings in Business Cycles Theory* (Blakiston, Philadelphia, 1944), p. 284.

10. P. Sylos-Labini, *Oligopoly and Technical Progress*, pp. 202–203 and 211. This issue concerns not only the rate of expansion of *total* public expenditure but also the *composition* of the said expenditure (productive and unproductive), which we do not consider here but which is no less important.

References to Table 5.3

Economic Commission for Europe. *Economic Bulletin for Europe*. Geneva, 1949.

H. M. Stationary Office, *Annual Abstract of Statistics of the United Kingdom*. 1955.

Hoffman, W. "Ein Index der industriellen Produktion für Gross-Britannien seit dem 18. Jahrhundert." *Weltwirtschaftliches Archiv* (September 1954).

Imlah, A. *"The Terms of Trade of the United Kingdom 1793–1913."* *Journal of Economic History* 2 (1950).

Layton, W. T., and Crowther, G. *An Introduction to the Study of Prices*. London: Macmillan, 1935.

League of Nations. *Statistical Yearbook*. Geneva, 1933, 1939.

Martin, K., and Thackeray, F. G. "The Terms of Trade of Selected Countries 1870–1938." *Bulletin of the Oxford Institute of Statistics* (November 1948).

Means, G. "Price Inflexibility and the Requirements of a Stabilizing Monetary Policy." *Journal of the American Statistical Association* (June 1935).

Ojala, E. M. *Agriculture and Economic Progress*. Oxford University Press, 1952.

Phelps Brown E. H., and Hopkins, S. V. "Wage-Rates in Five Countries 1860–1939." *Oxford Economic Papers* No. 2 (1950).

United Nations. *Statistical Yearbook*. New York, 1961, 1966.

U.S. Department of Commerce. *Historical Statistics of the United States: Colonial Times to 1957*. Washington, D.C., 1960, pp. 115, 139.

6

Rigid Prices, Flexible Prices, and Inflation

6.1 Analytical Problems

Introduction

The notion of a general price level may be of some use, though to a limited extent, in purely statistical and descriptive studies, but it is dangerous and deceptive in theoretical analyses that aim at explaining price variations. To be meaningful, these analyses must, as a first approximation, distinguish between two kinds of markets—those for raw materials and those for manufactured goods—and as a second approximation between at least five—three whole-sale markets for agricultural, mineral, and industrial products and two retail markets primarily for agricultural and industrial products and, second, for services; the labor market calls for separate consideration. The analysis must be differentiated in this way, because in the short and long run the mechanisms of price formation and variation are different for reasons connected with the market structures and the types of goods. Here I will devote special, though not exclusive, attention to the dichotomy in raw materials and manu-factures as regards goods. I shall introduce another dichotomy with reference to the labor market. The logical basis for the double dichotomy is given by the degree of flexibility of prices and earnings in relation to demand.

Prices of Agricultural Products in Domestic Markets and Prices of Raw Materials in International Markets

We shall therefore begin with the prices formed in wholesale agricultural markets. As a rule these markets operate in conditions close to competition, in the sense that entrance is free and the producers, even when they are relatively large (various multinationals are now operating in agriculture), are not in a position to exercise a substantial influence on prices. Under these circumstances the propositions of the classical economists are valid: prices in the short run depend on demand and supply and in the long run on costs of production. Similar propositions hold good, in principle, for the prices of mineral products. However, important qualifications must be made for both categories of prices.

In the first place it is essential to distinguish between the prices formed in international markets from those in domestic markets. For the same products prices will tend to vary together, but the link will be very close in the case of domestic markets which are not protected by customs duties (i.e., protected solely by the cost of transport and by other obstacles defined as "natural"). However, the link will be looser in the case of protected markets.

Thus it may be assumed that in individual domestic markets the prices of agricultural products depend on demand and supply and on the international prices of these products, subject in any case to the constraints of custom duties, and in the case of Europe, to the regulations of the Common Market.

Demand for purposes of production (and consumption) is to be distinguished from demand of a speculative nature. For empirical tests, the index of industrial production can be used as a variable representing the demand for agricultural products, since two important industries, food and textiles, employ agricultural raw materials (alternatively, aggregate internal demand or overall demand for consumers' goods could be used). As for speculative demand, it is not really important in internal markets of agricultural products; it is more relevant in internal markets of mineral products (which are easy to preserve). In general, however, speculative demand is more important in international markets of all raw materials and especially minerals. Thus, when we refer to internal markets of agricultural products, speculative demand can be neglected. Supply depends on the volume of harvests and on stocks, but stocks can change due to harvests or to changes in demand. Owing to this ambiguity, it is probably advisable not to consider stocks in empirical tests.

To conclude, in order to analyze the variations in the prices of agricultural products in the short run, within domestic markets in the short run, we have an equation of the type

$$P_a = a_1 + b_1 PD - c_1 O_a + d_1 P_{Ai},\tag{1}$$

where P_a is the index of agricultural products, PD is an index of demand for purposes of production, O_A is an index of supply and P_{Ai} is an index of the international prices of the said products. Considering that in our time all the variables of equation (1) tend to grow, we should use either the deviations from the trend of these variables, or even better, the rates of variation.

Let us consider now the agricultural products sold and bought in the international markets. Here demand for productive purposes can be expressed by the advanced countries' index of industrial production. As for speculative demand, I have already suggested that it has always been more important in international markets than in domestic markets, for several reasons: the size of transactions, the large variety of subjects involved, the greater uncertainty. In fact the greater the uncertainty, the higher the chances of gain for those businessmen who succeed in making the right forecasts. Uncertainty both in commodity markets and in foreign exchange markets, and therefore the incentives to speculate, have become decidedly more important after the weakening of the dollar as a reserve currency (Biasco 1979, 85). Speculative demand can be seen as a function of (1) the difference between the expected rate of change of prices and the short-term rate of interest, which represents the main financial cost of holding stocks, and (2) the expected quotations of the dollar, which is the means of payment more generally used in international raw materials transactions. In the interpretation of short-term variations in the prices of mineral products, supply can be assumed constant and therefore neglected.

To conclude, for variations in the international prices of agricultural raw materials, RM_A, in the short term the following equation holds good:

$$\widehat{RM}_A = a_2 + b_2 \widehat{WIP} - c_2 \hat{O}_{Ai} + d_2 (\widehat{RM}_A{}^* - i) + e_2 DO^*. \tag{2}$$

For the international prices of mineral products, RM_M, this equations applies:

$$\widehat{RM}_M = a_3 + b_3 \widehat{WIP} + c_3 (\widehat{RM}_M^* - i) + d_3 DO^*, \tag{3}$$

where the cap over a variable indicates a rate of change, the star indicates an expected value, WIP is the index of world industrial production, O_{Ai} is the index of world production of agricultural raw materials, and i is the rate of interest, and DO is the weighted average of the quotations of the dollar in the main financial markets. The uncertainties for the dollar as reserve currency began when the dollar was unhooked from gold (August 15, 1971). The institutional support for that role was then suppressed—a support consisting of a provision in the Bretton Woods agreements (see Siglienti 1981); the crisis in the international monetary system was confirmed by the general abandonment of fixed exchange parities. For these reasons the variable DO must be brought into econometric analyses for periods later than 1971. The weakening of the dollar as a reserve currency and an accumulator of value and the adoption of flexible exchange rates accentuated the speculative component in international markets. This is shown by the fact that the fluctuations in the

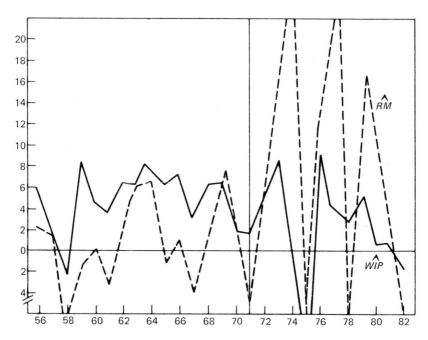

Figure 6.1
Industrial production and prices of raw materials (variation rates)

prices of raw materials traded in international markets became much more marked after 1971; see figures 6.1 and 6.2. Of the independent variables only the index of world industrial production (OECD index) is considered in these figures, and it shows that up till 1971 the rates of variation in world industrial production (OECD index) are almost always higher than those for prices of raw materials (IMF index). After 1971 the price fluctuations are from four to five times greater; moreover, unlike what happened previously, these fluctuations are for the most part positive. Figure 6.2 illustrates these relations from another point of view; it compares the two orders of rates of variations—for industrial production and prices of raw materials. All raw materials are considered regardless of whether they are agricultural or mineral. The only independent variable used is the demand index. Hence the relations derived from the comparison are very approximate. However, there is a clear difference between the regression lines for the two periods—one from 1958 to 1971 and the other from 1971 on. Both the constants and the coefficients are different:

For 1958 to 1971
$$\widehat{RM}_{AM} = -5.1 + 0.9\widehat{WIP}.$$

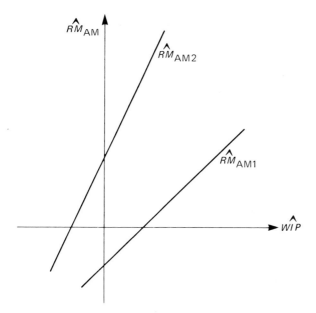

Figure 6.2

For 1972 to 1980
$$\widehat{RM}_{AM} = +9.1 + 2.4\widehat{WIP}.$$

The term RM_{AM} is the price index of *all* raw materials—agricultural and mineral, excluding oil which is to be considered separately.

The contrast between the two relations provides a basis for the analysis of the nexus between the short- and the long-term variations of prices in the international raw materials markets, taking into account that these markets are as a rule competitive.

Since great importance is attached to speculative demand in this explanation of the sharply contrasting behavior of raw materials prices before and after 1971, it is worthwhile to reflect more closely on this question.

The holding of stocks for productive and speculative purposes implies not only financial costs but also real costs—transportation and storage. However, it is well to concentrate our attention on the financial cost, which in the course of time is the most important and fluctuates the most, and in particular on the short-term rate of interest. Now, before 1971 the rate of change in raw materials prices, excluding oil, oscillated between -9 and $+8$ percent and the short-term rate of interest between $+2.5$ and $+5.5$ percent; since 1971 the rate of change in prices has been oscillating between -18 and $+28$ percent, with a peak of 54 percent in 1973, and the rate of interest between + 5.5 and + 16 percent. This means that in the years of rising prices it is very easy for speculators to gain, provided they are able to forecast well in advance that the price rise in going to exceed decidedly the short-term rate of interest. Upward price movements are more pronounced than downward movements since speculation works more vigorously in the upward direction. There are at least two reasons for this pattern of behavior: (1) this type of speculation is much easier than the opposite one and (2) the rate of interest cannot fall below zero, whereas the rate of price change can well become negative and thus render very burdensome the financial cost of holding stocks.

Price Variations under Competitive Conditions in the Long Period

It may seem from the preceding considerations that the shift in the function linking the rates of variation in demand to the prices of raw materials depends solely on the speculative factor, which has been stimulated by the weakening of the dollar as reserve currency. This, however, is only one of the factors explaining the shift. There is at least a second factor that makes its influence fully felt in the long term but can have a certain effect in the short term as well. This is the trend in the cost of production. In reality the classical proposition that in the long run, under competitive conditions price depends on the cost of production still holds good. This is because if the increase in demand causes the price to rise, above-normal profits appear which induce existing firms to expand production and new firms to enter the market. (For the classical economists the essential characteristic of competition is not the large number of producers, but free entry.) A certain time is needed in order to expand production—at least a year in the case of agriculture and, as a rule, more than a year for mining and industry where the period cannot be defined (it is a question of enlarging equipment and plant and installing new facilities.) As production increases, the price tends to fall. All other things being equal, excluding demand, the price tends to fall to its initial level, which covers the cost of production and permits profits not higher than the normal ones. An inverse process takes place where demand shrinks. As the price falls, a certain number of firms suffer losses, and some withdraw from the market. Production declines, so the price tends to revert to its level at the start. The process is not exactly symmetrical, since there is even more uncertainty about the time needed for the drop in production to take place.

It is not easy to identify the empirical correlate of the "short" and the "long" period. In agriculture the difficulties do not seem serious, since in most cases the productive cycle is an annual one. Hence the year is the short term.

For the long term a triennium can reasonably be assumed. Taking account of the fact that in extra-agricultural activities decisions on equipment and plant are usually taken once a year at budget time, a similar criterion may be adopted for these activities as well. Hence in the short-term case we can take annual data (equations 1, 2, and 3); for the long term we should use moving three-year averages, both of prices and the main cost factors. These belong to two classes: labor and the means of production.

For the long-term variations of agricultural prices the following equation may hold:

$$P_{A(l)} = a_6 + b_6 W_{A(l)}/\pi_{A(l)} + c_6 MP_{A(l)} + d_6 P_{Ai(l)},\tag{4}$$

where W_A is the wage in agriculture, π_A the output per worker, MP_A the price index of the means of production, and P_{Ai}, as has been seen, the index of international prices of agricultural products.

For the long-term variations of the prices of agricultural and mineral raw materials traded in international markets, the following equations apply:

$$RM_{A(l)} = a_7 + b_7 W_{A(l)}/\pi_{A(l)} + c_7 MP_{A(l)},\tag{5}$$

$$RM_{M(l)} = a_8 + b_8 W_{M(l)}/\pi_{M(l)} + c_8 MP_{M(l)},\tag{6}$$

where W, π, and MP express weighted averages of wages, output per worker, and means of production in the main producing countries. Prices and wages are expressed in dollars. (It should be pointed out that these relations, which use averages relating to different products and countries, can furnish only very general interpretations. If more precise interpretations are desired, disaggregated analyses are needed.)

It is important to note that the means of production employed by the producers of agricultural and mineral raw materials are largely industrial goods. Hence in the long term the trend in raw material prices depends both on that of the cost of labor and on that of industrial prices.

Variations in Industrial Prices in the Short and Long Period: Theoretical Aspects

In modern industry, competition is the exception. The rule is oligopoly in its three forms—concentrated, differentiated, and mixed. In the first of these cases the firms involved are few and large, and the product is homogeneous. In the second case the products are similar but differentiated, and the market is subdivided into a large number of small markets, each of them protected by barriers of various kinds, usually determined by publicity. The third case constitutes a combination of the two preceding cases.

For reasons that I have tried to analyze in different studies (Sylos-Labini 1956, 1974, and chapter 7), prices are determined on the basis of direct costs, to which a markup is applied. This, however, does not remain constant over time, especially in markets open to foreign competition. Hence for manufacturing as a whole, short-term price variations depend not only on those in direct cost items but also on those in international industrial prices (the asterisk on the two last variables indicates that international prices must be translated into lire at the prevailing exchange rate):

$$P_i = a_9 + b_9 W_i / \pi_i + c_9 R M^*_{AM} + d_9 P^*_{ii} \tag{7}$$

The relation now indicated, which does not include demand in the explanatory variables, assumes that at the present time firms operating in the manufacturing sector normally have unused capacity. Thus, if demand increases, production can be expanded without a rise in prices. Demand can influence prices only intermittently, when unused capacity falls to a low level in most industries, and there are obstacles in the way of imports.

These observations apply to the manufacturing industry. It is different with the building industry. In that industry one cannot speak of unused capacity in the same sense as in the manufacturing industry. In addition land, which constitutes a substantial proportion of the cost of housing, is not a reproducible good. As a result the prices of housing are affected in the short term by demand and supply, like goods produced in a competitive market, even if in the long term the scarcity factor tends to cause a systematic increase in the absolute and relative prices of housing. This is as true today as it was in the past.

In the long term the variations in the prices of goods produced by the manufacturing industry also depend on variations in costs. In the long term, however, total costs are considered:

$$P_{i(l)} = a_{10} + b_{10} W_{i(l)} / \pi_{i(l)} + c_{10} M P^*_{i(l)} + d_{10} P^*_{ii(l)}. \tag{8}$$

If it is recognized that both direct and indirect costs evolve in a fairly similar way, there may not seem to be any great differences between short- and long-term variations in the prices of manufacturing products. But that is not so. In fact the evolution of costs, and hence prices, in the manufacturing industry in the long term would be different if the short-term prices did not depend on costs but, as is the case in a competitive market, on demand and supply.

Let us consider a market in isolation where conditions of oligopoly prevail. In the short term, if demand increases, production will rise without an increase in price, assuming that in general there is unused capacity and that it is too risky for each of the oligopolists to try to exploit the situation by raising prices. However, if there is a fall in demand, there will be a proportionate drop in production, but prices will not decline. Prices will fall only if costs decline, and costs, generally speaking, decline when the prices of raw materials fall or when money wages increase less than productivity. Yet for reasons into which I cannot enter here, the prices will fall much less than proportionately to costs (Sylos-Labini 1979b). Most important, wages normally increase at a rate equal to or higher than the rate of increase in productivity, owing to the bargaining power acquired by the labor unions which, partly at least, reflects the power acquired by the oligopolistic firms in the markets for the products. The result is that the unit cost of wage labor either remains constant or increases, and falls only in exceptional cases. The short-term variations in costs and prices condition the long-term trend. All things considered, costs and hence prices remain constant or increase contrary to what happens in competitive conditions. The case, in generalized competition—competition in the product and labor markets—is that money wages tend to remain stationary or to increase less than productivity. At the same time the prices of the means of production—raw materials, intermediate products, and capital goods—tend to fall. As a result the long-term price trend will be downward, as Adam Smith had maintained with reference to the conditions of his time (Sylos-Labini 1976). According to Smith, however, in generalized competition the fall in prices tends to be faster for manufactures than for raw materials (both agricultural and mineral products), since the increase in productivity is faster in manufacturing. Indeed the prices of minerals can even show a rising trend if the exhaustion of known mines is not offset by the discovery of new ones. As for agricultural raw materials, at least vegetables, prices tend to fall but more slowly than those of manufactures, since the possibilities of subdividing and specializing labor in agriculture are less than in the manufacturing industry.

Empirical Aspects

According to Smith, then, the conditions of generalized competition differ for the two sectors: raw materials and manufacturing. Although in both sectors prices tend to fall, they fall more slowly in the former than in the latter. And this is precisely the picture offered by the evolution of prices during most of last century, a period when competition was the most frequent market structure in both sectors. The evolution of the two categories of prices is the one indicated in figure 6.3; the period being considered goes from the beginning of the nineteenth century to 1897, a year when the long-term fall in prices came to an end. Over the whole period, though amid wide fluctuations,

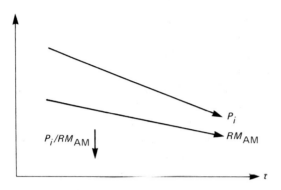

Figure 6.3

the ratio between the two categories of prices varied with respect to industrial prices $(P_i/RM_{AM} \downarrow)$.

In the present century the situation has changed. It would seem that the critical period was the last ten or twenty years of the nineteenth century, when the process of concentration was speeded up, and in the more advanced countries large limited liability companies, trusts, and cartels came to the fore, especially in finance and industry. In the industrial sector what is called the competitive market gave way to the one termed oligopolistic. As a result a dichotomy between the two sectors emerged. In the industrial one the prevailing market structure became oligopoly (in the first stage, concentrated oligopoly and, in the second, with the commercial revolution and with the spread of the so-called mass media, differentiated and mixed oligopoly). In the agricultural and mineral raw materials sector, however, the prevailing market structure has remained competitive, even though in certain cases companies of a monopolistic type operate.[1] Because it must coexist with a sector that is no longer competitive, the raw materials sector finds itself in a rather peculiar situation, and the evolution of prices reflects this over time. In the short run prices have still fluctuated according to the variations in demand and supply, but in the long term, as can be seen from equations (4), (5), and (6), the price trend has been stationary and, more often than not, upward, since the prices of part of the means of production, which are industrial products, tended definitely to rise. As a result the evolution of the two categories of prices in the present century has usually been as shown in figures 6.4 and 6.5. It must be borne in mind that the years from 1929 to 1938 were overshadowed by the Great Depression and formed a kind of intermezzo. In that decade the variations are those shown in figure 6.6 (the minima are the levels reached in 1933). (We shall not discuss this when we examine the fundamental trends of the two categories of prices.)[2]

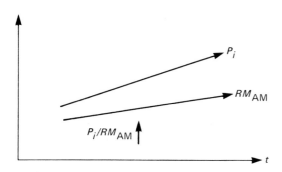

Figure 6.4

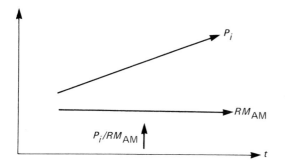

Figure 6.5

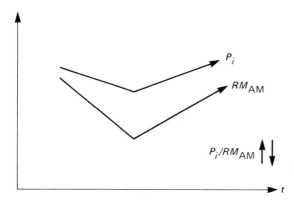

Figure 6.6

Thus with reference to the present century, and more precisely the period beginning in 1897 and ending in 1971, it may be said that for the prices of raw materials the evolution of curve RM_{AM} in figure 6.4 has been the one noted in those countries such as the United States which produce both industrial goods and raw materials, whereas the evolution shown in curve RM_{AM} in figure 6.5 has been the one relating to the prices of the raw materials produced in backward countries. In both cases the ratio of industrial prices to raw material prices increases or varies with respect to raw materials. But in the former case the increase is less, and in the second it is greater. As regards the reasons for the increases in industrial prices, we have already discussed the point. In industrial countries the prices of raw materials increase because the prices of the means of production supplied by industry increase, whereas in the past century these prices tended to fall. At the same time wages rise at a rate similar to, and even higher than, that of productivity, since in the sectors producing raw materials as well, labor is relatively scarce, and trade unions have achieved considerable bargaining power. Thus in the United States from 1897 to 1971, prices of raw materials have increased, even if to a lesser extent than industrial prices; as a consequence, the ratio P_i/RM_{AM} has increased by about one-third (during the Great Depression, as we have seen, that ratio increased sharply at first and then decreased). In contrast, during that same period, 1897 to 1971, the prices of raw materials produced in backward countries (especially those in the tropics) remained practically stationary, presumably because the increase in the prices of the means of production supplied by industry has been offset by the fall in the cost of labor: $\uparrow\widehat{MP} + \downarrow \widehat{W/\pi} = 0$. Such an evolution of the cost of labor is to be imputed to an increase in productivity, with stationary money wages. The stationary level of wages in turn is to be ascribed to a situation that A. W. Lewis (1954) sums up in a hypothesis on the economically unlimited supply of labor. Indeed, it seems that in backward countries the worsening of the terms of trade for these countries began as early as the seventies of the past century. Prices continued to decline, as in the preceding decades, but those of industrial products declined more slowly than those of raw materials, since in backward countries producing raw materials, wages continued to remain stationary, while in developed countries they started to increase at a brisk rate as a result of the transformations in the structure of production and in the labor market.

I have dwelt at such length on this matter because in my opinion this is essential for an understanding of the trends underlying all prices. If we term inflation a process characterized by a systematic increase in prices, we must call deflation the opposite process, and we must say that the past century has been dominated by a long process of a deflationary type. In the present

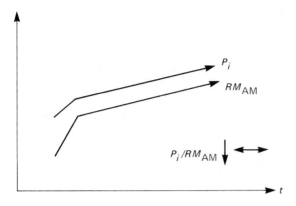

Figure 6.7

century the picture has been reversed, even if up to 1971 the inflationary process in industrialized countries had not reached the extremely high rates that it did after that year. It is important to understand why.

The Evolution of Prices after 1971: The Crisis of the International Monetary System and the Action of the Oil Cartel

The evolution of industrial and raw material prices underwent a profound change after 1971 and, in particular, after 1973. In 1971 there was the disengagement of the dollar from gold and the end of the system instituted by the Bretton Woods agreements. One of the consequences was the intensification of the burst of speculation in raw material markets to which we have already referred. This stimulation, which operates far more upward than downward, accentuated the worldwide inflationary process which had previously been under way. But inflation was greatly accelerated by the explosion of prices of raw materials and, in particular, of oil. The evolution of raw material prices, including those of oil, from 1971 to 1980 is illustrated in figure 6.7. As readers will see, the most violent spurt in the prices of raw materials took place in 1973.

In order to understand the reasons for this burst of inflation, we must take account of three events: (1) the 1972 to 1973 biennium was a period of rapid growth in all the industrialized countries and hence rapid expansion in the demand for raw materials (see figure 6.1); (2) 1973 saw the outbreak of the Arab–Israeli war which disrupted the flows of oil between Arab and industrialized countries; and (3) in the same year the United States liberalized imports of oil, and thus exacerbated the expansion of total demand for this fundamental source of energy. These events must be seen within the framework of the crisis of the dollar as reserve currency, which intensified speculative pressures precisely when the world demand for raw materials, including oil, was expanding. In particular, as regards oil, the price before that tremendous surge had remained practically stationary for a number of years. To be more precise, from 1950 to 1971 it had increased but moderately, and independent of the fluctuations in demand. This evolution is characteristic of a commodity produced in conditions of oligopoly. None of the large oil multinationals considered individually was inclined to raise the price for fear lest the rivals should not follow suit. The fact is that in oligopoly as a rule the price is varied only if the cost varies. But the costs of oil production, which are largely imputable to the expenses of prospection and to plant designed to last for a considerable time, varied very little; already on an average they were substantially lower than the price. In addition there were political reasons that prevented the large companies from reaching agreement to form a genuine cartel. Among other things there had already been in the United States a lawsuit against the agreement reached between a certain number of large companies, mainly American ones, after the first world war. (As to the oil-producing countries, even before 1973 there was a cartel between these countries, but it proved of very slight effectiveness in practice.) All these obstacles were overcome in 1973 owing to the circumstances recalled earlier and, in particular, to the Arab-Israeli war which had led the Arab countries, already stronger in the international sphere, to coalesce in order to use oil as a weapon of political pressure. For their part the large companies had no reason to oppose the Arab countries' action. Indeed, they had every interest to support it by placing at the Arabs' disposal their international commercial network; thus the profits of these companies increased enormously after the increase in the price of oil. It must, however, be recalled that, though it is true that the great surge took place in 1973 and continued in 1974, back in 1971 and 1972, in connection with the crisis in the international monetary system, the price of oil had been raised by 30 and 15 percent, respectively.

Hence in the period after the second world war and up to 1971, the evolution of the price of oil is that characteristic of a commodity produced at stable costs and sold in conditions of oligopoly. After 1971 and until recently, it is that of a commodity sold in conditions characterized by a monopoly-type cartel, even if the market power of this cartel has varied considerably in the course of time and the features of the oligopolistic competition tend to reappear (see Roncaglia 1983). In effect in monopoly, as Ricardo had already noted, price depends, as in a competitive market, on demand and supply. In conditions of competition, however, that is true solely for the short term. In addition in a monopoly, unlike what happens under competition, the supply does not vary freely because of the action of a large number of producers but is more or less effectively controlled by a single decision-making center, and it is controlled precisely with a view toward making the highest possible total profit. However, two qualifications must at once be made: (1) the control may be effective if the demand is rigid for a relatively large part of the curve, and (2) the degree of elasticity of demand does not remain stable over time. If in a given period it is low or very low, as was precisely the case and to a fair extent still is for oil, as time goes by, it may increase, thanks to savings in oil consumption and to the process of dynamic substitution—both stimulated by the high price. The increase in the elasticity of demand and the difficulty of controlling supply may gradually reduce the bargaining power of the cartel. Still with reference to the particular case of oil, we must bear in mind two factors: the objective pursued by the producer countries of keeping the "real" price of oil (the ratio of nominal oil prices to prices of manufactured goods) at least stable over time, and the comparison anticipated yield (delayed extraction).

In general, we may then speak of both "oligopolistic" and "monopolistic" phases in the international oil market. In fact for many decades oil was produced under conditions of oligopoly, where the large companies sought to reach agreement for common action in different sectors of activity: production, transport, wholesale trade, processing, and of course prices. In other words, there has always been a monopoly-type component. We may say that after 1973 this component was strongly accentuated because of the international situation.

Prices and Wages: The Double Dichotomy

The arguments developed in the previous sections lead us to believe that, at the present time, cases where demand affects prices have become more and more rare. The major cases are three in number. First, if domestic demand increases, there may be a rise in the prices of agricultural products and raw materials produced at home, provided the other variables, supply and international prices, do not work against them with equal or greater force. Second, if there is an expansion in most of the industrialized countries and an increase in the world demand for raw materials, costs will rise and hence, as an indirect result, so will the prices of industrial products provided there are no offsetting pressures arising from other variables. Third, if the form of the market is changed, for example, from oligopoly to monopoly, the increase in world demand will reinforce an increase in prices which, but for this change, would not have taken place or would have been much more modest and of a relatively short duration.

In contrast, in the markets for manufactures as a rule demand will not directly affect prices. It may drive prices up only in individual industries or even in the manufacturing industry as a whole in periods of rapid expansion when unutilized productive capacity shrinks. However, this holds good for countries with a high tariff wall; for the others an increase in demand leads to a rise in imports. Otherwise demand may drive up prices in an international boom. Such situations are by no means frequent. The usual pattern is the one outlined earlier. In any case the increase in domestic demand tends to swell imports. Such an increase can give rise to a foreign deficit of such magnitude that the currency falls in value vis-à-vis other currencies. In this way the prices of imported finished products rise, as do those of raw materials, with as a consequence an increase in costs and in the prices of industrial products.

We must therefore distinguish between two major categories of prices, on the one hand, agricultural and mineral products and, on the other, manufactures. The alternative to an analysis of the "general price level" is not necessarily therefore the analysis of individual prices. If there are valid theoretical reasons, the alternative may be the analysis of wide categories of prices; in the case which we are considering, only two of them. As already suggested by me many years back (Sylos-Labini 1956, 16–17 and 167), the dichotomy must be related not only to the market structure but also to the technical conditions of production and to the type of goods. Arthur Okun (1981) has recently again put forward this dichotomy, relating it rather to characteristics of the goods (whether homogenous or differentiated) than to the market structure, with producers who are "price takers" or else "price makers," a dichotomy which in fact presupposes different types of market.[3]

As we have seen, for manufacturing as a whole, foreign competition acts as a brake on attempts to pass on to prices increases in costs (see equation 7). Referring to the well-known distinction between protected markets and those exposed to foreign competition, we must assume that in protected markets the markup on direct costs remains relatively stable, even when it declines in nonprotected markets, except where there is a devaluation in terms of foreign currencies. In addition it is more probable that demand has some influence on prices, even if only intermittently, in protected markets rather than in exposed ones. We can assimilate the sector of consumable services to the protected industrial subsector.

For goods and services, then, the dichotomy in question holds good. The labor market in general has characteristics close to those of the goods and services sector whose prices are hardly affected by variations in demand. However, it is essential to distinguish between manual and intellectual labor. In the former variations in demand, expressed inversely by those in unemployment, have some, if only a limited, effect on wages, whereas in the latter the effects are negligible or nil.

Let us go deeper into the matter. In the last century wages were markedly flexible, in the sense that they responded to variations in the demand for labor. At that time, at least as a first approximation, the Phillips relation normally applied to short-term fluctuations. In the present century, and especially after the first world war, that relation became insufficient. As a result of the power acquired by the trade unions (at least in democracies), it became necessary to include variations in the cost of living in the wage equation.[4] In the last ten or fifteen years it became at least useful to include in addition a variable expressing the intensity of trade union action; the unemployment variable gradually becomes less important and in any case has to be corrected in order to make account of multiyear contracts, wage increases arranged beforehand, and those mechanisms such as subsidies and unemployment relief which attenuate the consequences of variations in unemployment on wages. In other words, the Phillips relation, like all economic relations, is historically conditioned.[5] In the past unemployment constituted an important factor in "disciplining" workers. Nowadays, with the creation of the mechanisms under reference and with the increase in family incomes—all of which are the result of economic growth—to a not inconsiderable extent unemployment has lost that distressing effectiveness. In any case the remaining effectiveness of unemployment takes the form of its influence only on short-term wage variations. On this point I agree with the monetarists.[6]

Summing up, the effects of variations in the demand for labor on short-term wage variations have now become very uncertain. I advance the hypothesis, which needs to be verified, that in present conditions variations in unemployment up to a critical threshold have either very slight effects on wages or even none at all. The effects may be substantial only after unemployment has passed a certain critical threshold.

Whatever the cause, a wage increase can influence prices in the first place through costs (if the increase is greater than that of productivity). This applies to industrial products. As regards agricultural products and raw materials produced domestically, the increase in wages may lead to an increase in demand (if employment does not fall in the same proportion or even more than proportionately). And the increase the demand may have the effects indicated earlier.

Since no one doubts that the variations in the costs of living influence those in wages—with a greater or lesser intensity depending on the strength of the trade unions and the different institutional or organizational patterns—all variations in prices included in the cost of living cause variations in wages. Among these factors the prices of public services and administered prices call for special consideration. It may happen, and on several occasions it actually has happened, that to reduce the public deficit (which is regarded by certain schools of thought as the main cause of inflation), prices of public services and indirect taxes have to be raised, with the result that inflation is aggravated either directly or indirectly through increases in wages.

On short-term wage variations, then, the influence of demand is usually slight, and it is even slighter on the variations in private employees' salaries, and practically nil in the case of civil servants. It should be clear that the flexibility in question is only that relating to variations in demand. Earnings are not at all rigid in relation to the cost of living, and the prices of manufactured goods are not at all rigid in relation to the costs of production and, in particular, to direct costs, even if this flexibility is high where these costs increase and low where they decline.

All this applies in the short term. Undoubtedly, trade union action and the support of various kinds afforded to the trade unions by the public authorities have helped to create a systematic increase in money wages. In the long term there are two other factors to be considered—the increase in productivity, on the one hand, and, on the other, in countries with a relatively high and rising per capita (and hence family) income, the slow but growing reluctance to accept manual jobs and repetitive or unpleasant types of work. This appears to have been only partly remedied by the immigration of foreign workers from poor and backward countries. As a consequence the relation of workers' earnings (wages) to those of employees (salaries) has been varying in favor of the former. Since the whole system of long-term prices is crucially dependent on the prices of agricultural and industrial commodities, this systematic upward pressure, both absolutely and relatively, as regards wages has injected into the system a further element of inflation.

Inflation and Demand: Five Propositions of Monetary Theory

The double dichotomy which has played a fundamental role in the analysis appears neither in the neoclassical models, including those of the monetarists, nor in the Keynesian models. The neoclassical models, which presuppose generalized conditions of competition and introduce special hypotheses regarding the evolution of costs, assume flexibility of prices and wages. The Keynesian models, on the contrary, assume rigid wages and prices in relation to demand up to the level of full employment. There are therefore three groups of economists: (1) those who assume flexible prices in relation to demand, among them being the monetarists; (2) those who assume rigid prices, among whom are the Keynesians; and (3) the economists who feel that it is essential to distinguish between different categories of prices and wages, and among these is the writer of the present study. The classification is schematic, but I trust not misleading. Thus Friedman (1968, 103) warns us that the fixing of a legal minimum wage and the action of the trade unions drives up the "natural" level of unemployment which tends to assert itself in the long term. But in the short term he does not consider any important limit to flexiblity vis-à-vis demand, either for wages or for the prices of commodities.[7]

For the old-style monetarists the link between the amount of money and demand was given by the velocity of circulation, which was taken to be relatively constant. For Friedman and the new monetarists, however, the value of this velocity is not stable, but the function of the demand for money *is*. This, he considers, ensures a fairly stable link between money and income.

A monetary expansion is therefore translated, after a certain interval, into an increase in money income, owing both to an increase in real income and to a rise in prices. However, according to Friedman, that is true only in the relatively short run. In the long run the growth of income and the level of employment depend on real factors. Monetary policy is powerless. Thus, if it is desired to accelerate growth and reduce unemployment by reducing interest below the normal or natural level, such a reduction will not last long (less than a year), mainly because the expansion in the amount of money following the reduction of the interest rate will lead to a rise in prices. This will be bound to cause an increase in interest, which will revert to its initial level and will even tend to exceed it. The reduction in the level of unemployment, too, which is initially assumed to be at the normal or "natural" rate, will not last for long, owing to a sort of comedy of errors based on expectations of wages and prices. To start with, real wages fall, making it possible to reduce unemployment. But they will soon go back to their original level, as will unemployment. That could be kept below the initial level, which by assumption is also the "natural" level, only at the cost of a gradual acceleration of the inflationary process.

Now it is possible to accept all the three propositions put forward here (a relatively stable link between money and income, weak direct long-term effects of monetary policy on interest and unemployment) without necessarily accepting the specific arguments that Friedman adduces to justify them or two other fundamental monetarist propositions, namely (1) variations in total demand bring with them variations in the same direction as prices in a proportion that is all the greater, the longer the period considered, and (2) the link between the amount of money and income points mainly in the direction $M \rightarrow Y$.

In principle, the first proposition is admissible in an economy where prices, at least in most cases, are flexible vis-à-vis demand. It does not apply in industrialized countries where at the present time the double dichotomy referred to earlier has appeared to have taken root. In such an economy since prices and earnings, which do not react (or react only slightly) to variations in demand, constitute the main share in terms of income and employment, a restrictive monetary policy will have as its main consequence the reduction of investments and employment; the downward thrust on the rate of increase in earnings and in prices cannot but be very limited. This, in my opinion, is the main reason why in modern industrialized economies the social cost of a restrictive monetary policy proves so high and the results so slight.

For the sake of clarity, and indeed honesty, we must strongly emphasize that usually the social cost cannot but be very high. In fact it is precisely because of the mechanisms and shock absorbers referred to in the preceding section that unemployment can have much more serious effects on wages than on salaries, that is, once it has crossed the critical threshold or after a *massive and prolonged* increase. Such an increase can comply with this definition if it occurs not only because of dismissals carried out by firms reducing their output but also because of firms going bankrupt. The resulting drop in earnings and prices or, more probably, the also substantial drop *in the rate of increase* in earnings and prices will take place only after the trade unions have received a crushing blow (see Kaldor 1980). Ultimately this becomes the meaning, which is not at all technical, of the delays and "lags" to which Friedman refers. The paradoxical aspect of the matter is that, if the monetary squeeze is kept in force for a sufficiently long time and there is a massive rise in unemployment, the resultant fall in the rate of price increases is *not* determined by variations in the demand for products, as some monetarists contend, but by the fall in the rate of cost increase. A decline in the rate of cost increase is in turn caused by the drop in the demand for labor. In the labor market, however, there is no competition. If anything, there are the conditions formalized in models of bilateral monopoly.

Only in two cases can the social cost of a restrictive monetary policy, at least as regards its duration, be somewhat less serious. The first is the case of a country producing a large proportion of the agricultural products and raw materials used in its industry. If a restrictive monetary policy is adopted, the economy sags (on this all economists are agreed). This decline will lead to a fall in the prices of agricultural products and raw materials. Through the cost of production, the prices of industrial products too will tend to fall, though to a limited degree (for raw materials form only part of the cost) and in a smaller proportion (Sylos-Labini 1979b). All this is assuming that wages grow in step with productivity and that hence unit cost of labor does not vary nor the prices of public services.

The second case is one where the restrictive policy is followed by all industrialized countries. The fall in world demand for raw materials will drive the prices down, and this fall will gradually tend to depress the prices of industrial products, assuming there is no change in the unit cost of labor. It should be stressed that more recently this has hardly been the case; there has not been a reduction, even a limited one, in prices but rather a slower increase. It should also be emphasized that the slackening of growth caused by the restrictive policy may have negative effects on productivity, which constitutes the denominator of the cost of labor.

In general monetarism cannot admit that cost inflation can take place. In a country that imports a large part of its oil and raw materials, the upward thrust of the prices of finished products caused by increases in the prices of these goods must obviously be regarded as a particular case of cost inflation. A similar consideration applies to pressures on prices caused by wages, when wage increases depend on rises in the cost of living not due to demand. The monetarists admit the existence of cost inflation only to the extent that money makes it possible; money allows costs and prices to increase, so that it would still be the monetary pressure that is decisive. Such is not the case, however. If, with pressure flowing from costs, the quantity of money is reduced, cost inflation takes place, but the level of activity is reduced. What in fact happens is a variant of the well-known present-day phenomenon (one unknown in the past) called stagflation which in certain cases, such as the one under consideration, should be called "recession with inflation." An inflation, it is worth repeating, can within limits be restrained by a ferocious monetary squeeze and a prolonged depression, marked by contractions of production and bankrupticies.

This analysis brings out an important lesson. According to the monetarists, when the real level of unemployment approximates its "natural" level, labor costs per unit of product and prices tend to remain stable. In present-day conditions, however, the "natural" level of unemployment cannot but be so high as to reduce the power of the trade unions to a minimum, a power that to a considerable extent is based on social transfer expenditures and on public measures of protection. Such a level, which can be tolerated for a long time under a dictatorship, may prove socially and politically incompatible, except for limited periods, with democratic patterns, which include in their essential institutions genuinely representative trade unions. However, this means that, if the trade unions and political parties that support them wish to avoid more directly dangerous reactionary pressures, they must learn how to control the dynamics of wages and social expenditures, including those for rescue operations, so as to reduce the temptation to have recourse to policies capable of raising actual unemployment to the level of "natural" unemployment, which cannot be defined but is certainly dramatically high.

The Interpretation of the Money-Income Nexus

The most controversial proposition sustained by Friedman is the one referred to earlier which says that the link between amount of money and income is mainly in the direction $M \rightarrow Y$, where Y is money income (i.e., real income Y_R multiplied by the price level, P) and M is the quantity of money, often indicated by M_1, and is the sum of what is called monetary base in the hands of the public (MB) and credit money in the strict sense of the word (demand deposits, DD). Since, according to Friedman, there is normally a very close relation between MB and DD, it can be said that the main casual nexus is $MB \rightarrow Y$. Granting, for the sake of argument, that this is so, the question arises: Are the variations in the quantity of money affecting mainly real income or prices? As Sidney Weintraub has rightly pointed out, monetarism leaves this absolutely crucial question undetermined. Friedman (1970a) has tried to answer only on the empirical plane by arguing that, in the first instance, the variations in money income are due almost exclusively to a variation in real income ($M \rightarrow Y_R$) since, initially, prices vary "imperceptibly." "The effect on prices becomes manifest, on an average, after other 6 to 9 months," so that, between the variations of M and the variations of P as a whole, some 12 to 18 months pass. This is why, says Friedman (1970), it is so difficult to stop an inflationary process.[8] Every time an economist has raised his voice in criticism of this interpretation, Friedman, citing some writing of his own, has shown that he has always recognized that, if there is a link $M \rightarrow Y$, there is also a link $Y \rightarrow M$. However, in the end he invariably concluded that the main link was the first one and that M, or in particular MB, is an exogenous variable, that is, one determined, at least as a rule, by autonomous decisions of the central bank.

This thesis, as formulated by Friedman, is unacceptable, even if it must be recognized that critics such as Kaldor (1970) have gone too far in defense of the opposite view. To put the problem in its proper focus, we must consider not only the relations of cause and effect but also the reactions, whether they be purely mechanical or discretionary. Hence the cases are three, expressed in symbols as $M \rightarrow Y$, $Y \rightarrow M$, and $Y \rightleftarrows M$. In the third case the reactions of M on Y may be of varying intensities. An idea of this type may be found in Friedman's writings and in those of his critics, but it is not clearly or distinctly expressed, and in any case it does not receive the emphasis it deserves. The emphasis is placed either on the first relation or the second; the third case is practically ignored. The fact is that a systematic analysis is needed of the reasons why the monetary base or deposits are created. Such a creation depends on the stimuli coming from business, which needs money for its activity, including the reimbursement of loans and the settlement of foreign transactions and from the Treasury. There is in addition another particular case where the autonomous or discretionary element seems actually to be only one: the purchase and sale of public bonds by the central bank. But even such an operation is not unrelated to the other two reasons, since the sale of bonds, other things being equal, drives interest up and hence tends to act as a brake on the creation of money for business. In any case the purchase and sale of bonds constitutes an operation in which the autonomous decision-making element clearly prevails. When money is created to meet the demands of business and of the Treasury, the stimulus is external to the banking system. The question is: How do the banks respond to these demands? If they are accommodating and respond, as it were, passively, sequence $Y \to M$ prevails; if, on the contrary, the response is active, in a restrictive or expansionary sense, sequence $M \to Y$ prevails. In addition there are all the intermediate possibilities. Given the contiguity of the Treasury and the central bank, the creation of money on behalf of the state may be equated to a discretionary decision, so that in this case sequence $M \to Y$ tends to prevail (the extreme case is that of a war economy). When, on the contrary, the most vigorous thrust comes from business, sequence $Y \to M$ prevails. This is the sequence theorized by Schumpeter, and it is surprising that, in his works, apart from some marginal quotations, Friedman ignores the great theorist and historian of cyclical development. Anyone who knows Schumpter realizes full well that the variations in M, when they are stimulated by *business*, may take place *before* a variation in income. The fact is that the sequence $Y \to M$ is particularly important in the case of bank money, that is, demand deposits (DD) which are affected to a limited extent and indirectly by the discretionary component discussed earlier and are, on the contrary, affected much more strongly by a stimulus coming from business. Moreover in periods of monetary restrictions even the bills of firms can to some extent be used in place of money. All this would not create serious difficulties for the monetarist theories if bank money (in the strict sense, demand deposits and the bill used as money) would vary in the same direction of the monetary basis. Now, although little is known of the bills used as money, it is known that *in general* the monetary basis and bank money vary together; the problem is that this does not happen precisely in crucial periods, as, for example, in the decade from 1929 to 1938. On various occasions Friedman has maintained that the Great Depression should be attributed "in great part" to the errors of monetary policy and, in particular, to the fact that the Federal Reserve System "forced or permitted a sharp reduction in monetary base" (Friedman 1968, 97). It is on this ground that Friedman (1970a, 17 and 8) goes so far as to state: "If Keynes had known the facts about the Great Depression, as we now know them, he could not have interpreted that episode as he did," with the consequence that "if Keynes were alive today, he would no doubt be at the forefront of the counter-revolution [in monetary theory]."

Now, as Kaldor has pointed out (1980), the affirmation regarding the reduction of monetary base does not square with the facts. This can be seen even from the statistical data presented by Friedman and Schwartz (1963, 803–804). Monetary base remains constant from 1926 to 1929 (in the very period of the most rapid expansion) and increases by 15 percent from 1929 to 1932. Conversely, bank money falls, in the second period, by 30 percent. (The ratio of M to MB then crumbles from 4.0 to 2.4 in 1933. The contraction of M depending on that of DD expresses essentially that phenomenon Schumpeter defines as the "autodeflation" of the business system, a phenomenon that implies precisely the sequence $Y \rightarrow M$.) In his reply Friedman (1970b) ignores Kaldor's criticism, which is well founded and very serious.

A final critical observation is called for. Friedman makes a sharp distinction between the long and the short term. Monetary policy is effective in the short term but impotent in the long term (even if it can cause damage in the form of a persistent inflationary process). In the long run the real phenomena—growth of income and level of employment—do not depend on money but on other factors which Friedman refers to in extremely vague terms. Right off the distinction itself is analytically deceptive. As we have seen in the preceding subsections, the prices of the various categories do not vary with the same speed in the short or the long run. In particular, the variations in the ratio of industrial prices to prices of raw materials influence income distribution, and the variations in this distribution influence the speed and the type of accumulation and growth (see chapter 7). Moreover, if wages grow more rapidly than productivity, it is not only prices that vary but also income distribution, again with effects on accumulation and growth and hence also on the level of employment. In fact the increases in the prices of raw materials, including oil, have indirectly aggravated clashes of interest between industrialists and workers, and more generally between producers of raw materials and the other two categories of subjects. This is a trilateral conflict which when the raw materials are produced in the third world, takes on international dimensions (Sylos-Labini 1979b, 18). This conflict helps to fuel the inflationary process, as should be clear from all the preceding analysis (see also Rowthorn

1980); at the same time this conflict has contributed to slow down the rate of growth in developed countries.

The decisive errors of monetarism, however, are the ones discussed earlier. Two of them concern us in particular. The first consists of minimizing the sequence $Y \rightarrow M$; the second is the assumption that as a rule prices and earnings are flexible vis-à-vis variations in demand. Anyone wishing to realize the real meaning of flexibility in prices need only take a look at figure 6.1, from which it is obvious that in the international raw material markets fluctuations in demand are accompanied, without dubious delays, by fluctuations in prices. Anyone wishing to be convinced that industrial prices and wages are *not* flexible, in the sense that they do not respond or respond only very irregularly to variations in demand, is invited to make a graph of the rates of variation in production and those in prices and wages in the industries of the major developed countries. As to variations in salaries, the relation to variations in demand is negligible and in most cases non existent.

We should be quite clear about this. The idea, which is as old as economic theory, that a fall in demand can lead to a fall in prices is not wrong. Only it is valid in the short run and under conditions of competition which, among other things, presuppose homogeneous products. In the past these conditions were the rule, whereas nowadays, in industry, they are the exception. At the present time these conditions can be found in many agricultural productions and in certain types of mineral productions. Even where monopoly-type conditions prevail, demand brings on variations in prices but in a different way.

Only in certain countries and under certain conditions, as has already been noted, can variations in demand have relatively widespread effects on prices, and hence a restrictive monetary policy may have a certain degree of effectiveness. It is no accident that in the United States, where monetarist theory was born and developed, demand proves to have some influence, though a modest one, on the prices of industrial products (see Gordon 1975; Sylos-Labini 1979, 159). The fact is that the United States produces a considerable part of the agricultural commodities and raw materials it needs. Moreover the American economic situation influences the international one and hence the world demand for raw materials. However, monetarism has not spread in the United States alone. A factor operating in favor of this school of thought has also been the rapid expansion in all industrialized countries of the public deficit. This expansion in its turn has been determined by social pressures which, thanks to the spread of a certain crude type of Keynesianism, have enrolled the active backing of the most differing political parties. Now there is no need to be a supporter of monetarism to recognize the damage that a large and growing public deficit may cause the economy. Given certain conditions, such a deficit can make an inflationary process worse, not only because it can contribute to the expansion of the quantity of money and to price increases (especially in the case of agricultural commodities and raw materials), but also because by increasing the demand for all products including imported ones, it causes a balance of payments deficit and pushes foreign exchange rates up, and hence also the prices of all imported goods. In addition a growing public deficit involves as a rule a growing issue of securities to pay for the public debt. Sooner or later, but not always and not necessarily as the monetarists seem to believe, this leads to a crowding out of part of private investments. For where the public deficit is not financed by taxes or loans, the variations in monetary base depend on the *political* authority (government or parliament). *Monetary* authority is forced to reduce the creation of money for business, if it wishes to influence monetary base; to do this, it has to fix the rate of interest at a high level. However, crowding out depends not only on the volume of the deficit financed by loans but also on the type of financing—whether bank loans or public bonds, which are short and long term, respectively.

Although a restriction in demand has modest effects on prices, and under certain circumstances, none, it has a powerful impact on imports and hence on foreign accounts, and through them, on tha rate of exchange. Such a restriction can be obtained either by monetary policy, which normally has direct effects on investments and indirect ones on consumption, or by fiscal policy, which acts in the opposite way, or more frequently by a combination of both policies. Such a combination in this case would settle the differences between monetarists and Keynesians. As for monetary policy, a restriction is carried out essentially by fixing a high rate of interest; this is precisely the crucial decision variable, not the quantity of money (which is an extremely ambiguous notion, not only because, as I recalled earlier, even the bills of firms can be used in place of money but also because in the course of time the number of substitutes for money is steadily increasing).

In general the origins of the worldwide inflation in recent times are to be found in the explosion of oil prices and in the crisis in the international monetary system. The monetary crisis was characterized by the severing of the link (a limited but important one) between the dollar and gold and the end of the system of fixed parities.[9] It should be observed that this view has nothing to do with the monetarist theories. Surely it is true that originally the dollar crisis went from bad to worse because of huge American foreign deficits and an abundance of dollars (though the measures to cope with it could have been different, leading rather to a sharp increase in the dollar price of gold); it is also true, however, that lately an abundance of dollars can no longer be considered a problem. To be more specific, the problem is not the weakness of the dollar but its instability. The dollar, which still retains its role of a currency used for international transactions especially in the markets for oil and raw materials, does damage when it loses its value in terms of the other currencies and gold, and it also does damage in the opposite direction, that is, when its value goes up in terms of other currencies and of gold.

Friedman has dwelt not only on the question of the quantity of money but also on the advantages of flexible parities. Thereby he bears the heavy responsibility of diverting attention from the central problem, which is cutting generalized inflation at its root and, among other things, bringing back the speculative factor to its pre-1971 intensity through a reform of the international monetary system. In my opinion, we must go back to a system linked in one way or another to gold, even if within narrow limits, and to a system of fixed partities; we must recognize that the disadvantages of flexible parities are overwhelmingly greater than their advantages.

6.2 The Reform of the International Monetary System

The Behavior of Raw Materials Prices

Let us go back to the behavior of raw materials prices in the last twenty-five years. A view quite widespread among economists is that the extraordinary rise in the prices of oil and raw materials in 1973 and 1974 is to be attributed to certain erratic events such as the 1973 world boom, the Yom Kippur War, crop failures in certain parts of the world (especially the U.S.S.R.), and, finally, the abundance of dollars due to the large deficits in the U.S. balance of payments in 1971 and 1972.

A glance at figure 6.1 persuades one to reject this view. There is no doubt that those incidents have intensified the rise in raw materials prices in 1973 to 1974; but that rise was followed by others in 1977 and 1979, which were less impressive but no less extraordinary when compared with the pre-1971 fluctuations. How can this sharp contrast be explained?

The reason that comes naturally to mind is that such a contrast must have something to do with the 1971 crisis of the international monetary system which brought an end to dollar convertibily and fixed exchange rates. More precisely, my view is that the speculative factor in the international markets of raw materials has become much stronger as a consequence of these changes in the international monetary system. The dollar as a reserve currency and accumulator of value has weakened, so to some extent certain raw materials have assumed these roles. Speculation has also become much stronger in foreign exchanges. It should be noted that the flexibility of exchange rates works asymmetrically; it works more easily in an upward than in a downward direction. This applies even more to speculation in the markets of raw materials. Speculation in foreign exchanges and speculation in raw material markets, however, often combine. Even when the raw materials prices are expected to be stable, it is possible to observe speculation in these markets if the dollar is rising in terms of the other currencies, since most of the transactions in raw materials markets are carried out in dollars. All this has contributed to determine a worldwide process of inflation.

The Role of Gold

Under the new conditions, then, all prices have shown a systematic tendency to rise. In particular, the rise in raw materials prices has, by way of costs, pushed up the prices of manufactured goods and thus the cost of living. The rise in the cost of living has pushed up wages, in turn reinforcing, by way of costs, the increase in industrial prices. Such a process has taken place in all industrial countries, but the speed of increase in prices and wages has been different in each country, as it depends on the structure of production, public spending, the strength of trade unions, and the institutions involved. In certain countries with deficits Triffin's vicious circle has occurred (rising exchange rates, prices, etc.). In short, directly or indirectly, the worldwide inflation of the last ten years is largely to be attributed to the crisis in the international monetary system, but the degree of inflation has depended on the particular conditions of each country.

The way out of the strong inflationary pressures of our time appears to lie in a reform of the international monetary system, one capable of bringing the intensity of speculation back to what it was prior to 1971 when , despite all sorts of problems, wholesale prices of all commodities in the industrial countries were increasing very slowly or, in certain years, even slowly falling. The dollar, as a reserve currency and an accumulator of value, was working relatively well; at present it has ceased to be a reliable unit. We have to find a substitute. It seems difficult to imagine a relatively stable and reliable international monetary unit completely dependent on the discretionary policies of internal and international monetary authorities. If we want to have such a unit, those policies should be in some way conditioned by an objective standard, and it is difficult to imagine an objective standard different from gold.

However, the conditions for the working of the gold standard are gone forever. Strictly speaking, that monetary system implied the convertibility of bank notes into gold coins of a given weight for everyone, banks, companies, and individuals. As for the gold exchange standard, historically we have known at least two varieties of such a system. The first, which was adopted in several countries after World War I, called for a gold standard in at least one country; in the other countries the bank notes were convertible into bank notes and credit instruments of the country with the proper gold standard. In the countries adopting the gold exchange standard, the convertibility into gold coins was not only indirect but also restricted to companies and banks; in practice, individuals were excluded. Under these conditions gold did not circulate, and therefore, strictly speaking, was not money but a medium performing certain monetary functions. It has been said that the Bretton Woods agreements reintroduced the gold exchange standard after World War II. This is true only if it is specified that we have here a second variety of the gold exchange standard, since the leading monetary unit, the dollar, was convertible into gold bullions, not gold coins, and was not open to all but only to central banks and at particular conditions.

It is probably now worth discussing the possibility of establishing a third variety of the gold exchange standard, one where the convertibility of the monetary unit—be it the ECU, the dollar, or another unit—would be (1) restricted to central banks, (2) admitted only at given intervals, and (3) introduced gradually after creating a forward line of defense based on the strong currencies. Of course the new arrangement would reintroduce the system of fixed exchange rates.

At various times Keynes proposed buffer stocks schemes to stabilize the prices of raw materials, and every time these met with very cool receptions (Keynes 1980, 25 esp. 72 ff.; 26, 111ff; Higonnet 1981). Recently Kaldor has correctly pointed out that such schemes were strictly related to Keynes's projects for reforming the international monetary system, including the project presented at Bretton Woods. Kaldor reproposes Keynes's scheme to stabilize the prices of raw materials, emphasizing that this is in the vital interest of both developing and developed countries, "since it is a precondition for securing long-term investment necessary for sustained industrial growth" (he refers to the investment necessary to expand raw materials and the sources of energy). In addition he proposes creating a new international currency convertible into primary commodities (Kaldor 1983). I fully agree with Kaldor. I only note that, despite all the limitations and cautions hinted in my earlier discussion, the chances of success for the reform would be greater if the new currency is made convertible first and foremost into that singular mineral commodity—gold.

The World Inflation and the Slowing Down in the Process of Growth

If in fact the origins of worldwide inflation are as I have described them, money management in individual countries cannot be the solution. In particular, monetary policies, even if very restrictive, are bound to have effects that are limited in terms of inflation and at the same time costly in terms of production and employment.

As regards the link between variations in the quantity of money and those of total demand, we can accept the proposition that variations of total demand bring with them variations, in the same direction, of prices *if* demand fluctuations influence prices and earnings in general, as they did in the past century. However, that proposition is not acceptable in an industrialized twentieth-century economy, where a double dichotomy has arisen and taken root. Since prices and earnings, which do not react or react only slightly to variations in demand, constitute the main share in terms of income and employment, a restrictive monetary policy at the present time will have as its main consequence the reduction of investment and employment; the downward thrust in the rate of increase in earnings and in prices cannot but be very limited. This, in my opinion, is the main reason why the social costs of a restrictive monetary policy prove so high in modern industrialized economies, and the results so slight as far as the inflationary process is concerned. Yet the results are remarkable when that kind of policy is aimed at the reduction of a foreign deficit, precisely because a restrictive monetary policy strongly affects the level of activity.

In the past century the picture was different. A restrictive monetary policy, which was usually adopted by raising the rate of discount, was followed by considerable and quick results in reducing a foreign deficit (which in the gold standard implied an outflow of gold coins). Moreover these results were obtained not only, as is now the case, by reducing total demand and therefore the volume of imports but also prices. Such policy could then foster the international competitiveness of the economy because prices were flexible in relation to demand. In other words, a reduction of prices, and not simply their rate of increase, was obtained as a byproduct of that policy. In fact a policy specifically intended to combat inflation was exceptional, since inflation itself was a rare occurrence due to events external to the economic system, like a war. Today, particularly in the last ten years, inflation has become the norm. This does not mean that inflation is now to be regarded as a physiological phenomenon. It is as pathological as in the past, and its most damaging consequences become evident as time goes on. The main damage lies in the serious slowing down of the rate of growth in industrialized countries considered as a whole, due to a process of stop and go at the world level.

In fact today every worldwide economic expansion tends to bring with it a remarkable rise in the raw materials prices. In turn this rise tends to determine or to aggravate a deficit in the balance of payments of the industrialized countries. To reduce this deficit the governments of those countries will adopt restrictive credit or fiscal policies. As a consequence a worldwide recession becomes inevitable. Let us not forget that after the slump of 1975 the recovery of the industrialized economies was strong but short-lived (see figure 6.1) and that a new recession took place only three years later, in 1978. In 1979 there was a new recovery, followed very soon by a new recession. Each recovery was accompanied by a remarkable rise in the price of raw materials much higher than before 1971, and by increasing deficits in the balance of payments in the majority of industrialized countries. Each recession, like the one in which we are living, was accompanied by a fall in raw materials prices. It appears, however, that the rise is greater than the fall; it appears too that this fall can determine a reduction in the rate of increase in industrial prices and in the cost of living but is unable to determine an absolute fall in these prices because, among other things, money wages continue to increase more than productivity. The overall results of these variations are continual inflation, though at a varying speed, and a slowing down in the process of growth, since the periods of expansion tend to become shorter and contractions more pronounced.

Policies to Combat Inflation

The slowing down in the process of growth depends not only on the recurring deficits of the balance of payments but also on policies intended primarily to combat inflation, which are based, at least in part, on monetarist theories. In the last few years policies of this kind have been adopted by the United States and the United Kingdom.

If the monetarist prescriptions are to be rejected, what is then the line to be followed? The answer to this question depends on the diagnosis. We have to separate the two problems. On the one hand, there is world inflation to be considered and, on the other, the inflation differentials. I have discussed the origins of world inflation in section 6.1; the causes of the inflation differentials I have analyzed elsewere (Sylos-Labini 1974). In brief, my conclusions are that the world inflation that started in 1971 has been fueled primarily by the new behavior of raw materials prices, whereas the inflation differentials depend on the behavior in each country of public deficits and wages.

The public deficit can contribute to the inflation differential of a country fundamentally in three ways: (1) by pushing up imports, with the consequent appearance of a deficit in the balance of payments and a rise in foreign exhange rates, (2) by pushing down (via high interest rates) private investment and, in this way, the increase in productivity and (3) by stimulating (via the expansion of the monetary base) the demand for products with flexible prices. In fact the prices of the two categories of goods, though interrelated, play different roles in the inflationary process.

The prices of raw materials in a given country can rise either because they rise in the international markets or because the internal money unit falls in terms of foreign exchanges.

As for the prices of manufactures, their tendency to rise depends, first of all, on the rise of raw materials prices and prices of imported manufactures and, then, on the behavior of wages. Wages are conditioned by a variety of factors, among which are the actual and the expected variations in the cost of living index, particularly if a system of wage indexation is in operation; trade union aggressiveness; unemployment; duration of labor contracts; and intervals between labor bargainings sessions.

Under present circumstances inflation can slow down at the world level—as has happened in the last two years—but only if there is an economic recession and a fall in raw materials prices. However, such a slow down in the process of growth would clearly lower the demand for raw materials, including oil, and, together with high rates of interest adopted by the principal capitalist countries to combat inflation, would create an untenable external debt situation in several third world countries.

If it is true that during worldwide economic recovery and prosperity the tendency of raw materials prices to rise considerably, even to explode, depends fundamentally on the malfunctioning of the international monetary system, then to combat *this* source of inflation, a new Bretton Woods type of agreement is necessary, and both industrialized and developing countries ought to participate to discuss not only the reform of the international monetary system but also a new arrangement of external debt. With a view toward such a conference, a more limited agreement is further desirable between European countries and Japan, on the one side, and the United States, on the other, to fix the margin of oscillations of the dollar in terms of other currencies. Otherwise, just as a recovery comes into sight, the prices of raw materials rapidly increase and/or in the United States the rate of interest rises, ostensibly caused by anti-inflationary monetary restraint, and these events are likely to render the recovery weak and short lived. Clearly an increase in the rate of interest in the United States, by attracting foreign capital, pushes up the dollar in the international financial markets, and this gives a new push to inflation in countries using the dollar to buy a significant share of their imports.

At the national level inflation can be treated either by a reduction in public deficit or a reduction in the rate of increase of money wages, or both. To be effective, the reduction in the public deficits should be carried out not so much by reducing expenditure as by reducing the rate of increase, by shifting expenditure from unproductive to productive purposes, so as to contribute to the expansion of income and receipts. If, on the contrary, expenditure is severely cut, a vicious circle can be set into motion. It will induce a recession, but eventually not a reduction, rather an expansion of the deficit.

To reduce the rate of increase in money wages some economists, namely Weintraub and Wallich, have proposed an income policy based on taxes (see Weintraub 1981). I would surmise a proposal logically similar to this one but, I believe, much simpler. As long as the inflationary process goes on, the problem of the fiscal drag due to progressive income taxes is a serious social problem, so much so that the governments, though irregularly, are bound to intervene in any case. My proposal is to "administer" the tax adjustments on condition that the trade unions and the firms accept certain guidelines in their wage negotiations.

To a good extent national and international measures are interdependent. In order to have a vigorous recovery of the world economy, an international discussion of the reforms mentioned earlier ought also to aim at coordinating the economic policies of the different countries. In any case the individual countries will only be able to participate in a world recovery, be it vigorous or weak, if they are able to reduce or to keep constant their public deficits and to reduce the rate of increase of money wages.

Notes

I am grateful to Professors Mario Arcelli, Paolo Baffi, Salvatore Biasco, Alessandro Roncaglia and Luigi Spaventa for their criticisms and suggestions. Naturally, they bear no responsibility for what I have written.

1. These cases are to be found only in mining. In agriculture one can note large companies with transnational interests and various forms of vertical integration, which obtain considerable advantages in terms of efficiency and, when operating in backward countries,succeed in obtaining monopsony earnings in the purchase of raw products. However, except in special cases, these companies are not in position to control sales prices in the international markets.

2. As I have already noted (chapter 5, n.8), the drop in industrial prices (of about 20 percent) should be attributed not to the drop in demand but to the drop in direct costs, which in turn is caused mainly by the fall in prices of raw materials (50 percent), and it is here that demand has been operative; this applies not only to the period as a whole— 1929 to 1932—but also to the year to year variations.

3. The dichotomy indicated here not only coincides with the one in Okun but

corresponds as well to those put forward in 1935 by Gardner Means and in 1943 by Michal Kalecki (prices determined by demand and prices determined by costs), and more recently by Sir John Hicks (1965, 1974), who distinguishes between "flexprices" and "fixprices," by Lord Kaldor (1976), and by J. Robinson (1977); I myself used this dichotomy in my monography on oligopoly. It should be borne in mind that price rigidity vis-à-vis demand may depend not only on the structural conditions connected with economic and social evolution (concentration of production and differentiation originated by advertising) but also on public regulation, which may be modified without too much difficulty but is often introduced when structural conditions do not allow market forces to function automatically.

4. "The importance of $\dot{P}$ as an explanatory variable has greately increased compared with the pre-war period. This indicates a substantial movement in the direction of a one-to-one relation between changes in prices and changes in wages. This is an extremely interesting change. [$\dot{P}$ is the rate of variation in the cost of living]." LIPSEY (1960, p. 26). See Sylos-Labini (1980) and Fratianni-Spinelli (1980).

5. Briefly, the three wage equations corresponding to the three historical stages alluded to in the text are as follows:

$$\hat{W} = a - bU^{-1},$$
$$\hat{W} = a - bU^{-1} + c\hat{V},$$
$$\hat{W} = a - bU^{-1} + c\hat{V} + dTUP,$$

where the first equation is the Phillips relation and the second the relation set forth by Lipsey and where the symbols W, U, V, and TUP indicate, respectively, the wage rate, unemployment, the cost of living, and the pressure of the trade unions (e.g., expressed by the number of days lost for strikes); the cap over a variable indicates a rate of change. See Sylos-Labini (1980).

6. In backward countries where the supply of labor is unlimited in the sense used by A. Lewis (1954), in the long run the increase in wages is held down by the pressure of unemployment, which in practice merges into employment in the traditional sector.

7. See the critical observations of Franco Modigliani and the replies (which are quite unsatisfactory) by Friedman in the debate reproduced in Modigliani-Friedman (1977, 13); the criticism had been put forward by Modigliani (1977).

8. The empirical indications of these lags are, on Friedman's own admission, extremely uncertain and ambiguous, to the point that various economists of whom I am one, are convinced that these delays are a myth. Nevertheless, the lags hypothesis has played an important part in the practical applications of this doctrine. Considering the effects of restrictive monetary policies in certain countries such as England (disastrous on income and employment and slight on prices), it can be said that this doctrine would long have been discredited, but for this hypothesis. The fact of having postulated these lags, which are not short and are of varying length, has enabled the monetarists to proclaim: clench your teeth, wait and see. See in particular Friedman (1969).

9. The crisis in the international monetary system in its turn was provoked by a number of events, among which, as noted by Biasco (1979, 101), we also have to include the wage explosion of the triennium 1968 to 1970.

References

Biasco, S. 1979. *L'inflazione nei paesi capitalistici industrializzati. Il ruolo della loro interdipendenza 1968–1978*. Milan: Feltrinelli.

Fratianni, M., and Savona, P. 1972. *La liquidità internazionale*. Bologna; Il Mulino.

Fratianni, M., and Spinelli, F. 1980. "Sylos-Labini on Fratianni and Spinelli on Inflation: A Reply," *Banca nazionale del lavoro Quarterly Review* (December).

Friedman, M. 1969. *The Optimum Quantity of Money and Other Essays*. Chicago: Aldine. (This volume includes, among others, the following two essays: "The Lag Effect of Monetary Policy," dated 1961, and "The Role of Monetary Policy," dated 1968.)

Friedman, M. 1970a. "The Counter-Revolution in Monetary Theory". Institute of Economic Affairs–Occasional Papers, No. 33.

Friedman, M. 1970b. "Reply to Kaldor." *Lloyds Bank Review* (October).

Friedman, M., and Schwartz, A. J. 1963. *A Monetary History of the United States 1867–1960*. Princeton: Princeton University Press.

Gordon, R. A. 1975. "The Impact of Aggregate Demand on Prices." Brookings Papers on Economic Activity. No. 3.

Grilli, E. 1982. *Materie prime ed economia mondiale*. Bologne: Il Mulino.

Grilli, E., and Maw-Cheng Yang. 1981. "Real and Monetary Determinants of Non-Oil Primary Commodity Prices Movements." The World Bank. Working Paper. No. 6.

Higonnet, R. 1981. *Keynes and the Gold Exchange Standard*. Discussion Paper No. 1. International Banking Center and Department of Economics. Florida International University, Miami, November.

Hicks, J. 1965. *Capital and Growth*. Oxford University Press.

Hicks, J. 1974. *The Crisis in Keynesian Economics*. Oxford: Basil Blackwell.

Kaldor, N. 1970. "The New Monetarism" and "Reply to Friedman." *Lloyds Bank Review* (July–October).

Kaldor, N. 1976. "Inflation and Recession in the World Economy." *Economic Journal* (December).

Kaldor, N. 1980. *Memorandum of Evidence on Monetary Policy to the Select Committee on the Treasury and Civil Service* (HMSO).

Kaldor N. 1983. "The Role of Commodity Prices in Economic Recovery." *Lloyds Bank Review* (July 1983).

Kalecki, M. 1971. *Selected Essays on the Dynamics of the Capitalist Economy 1933–1970*. Cambridge: Cambridge University Press. (This volume includes the essay "Costs and Prices," dated 1943.)

Keynes, J. M. 1980. *Activities 1941–1946. Shaping the Post-War World. Bretton Woods and Reparations. The Collected Papers of J. M. Keynes*, Vol. 26. London: Macmillan.

Lewis, A. 1954. "Economic Development with Unlimited Supplies of Labour." *The Manchester School* (May).

Lipsey, R. G. 1960. "The Relation between Unemployment and the Rate of Change of Money Wage Rates in the United Kingdom, 1862–1957: A Further Analysis." *Economica* (February).

Means, G. C. 1935. *Industrial Prices and Their Relative Inflexibility*. Senate Document No. 13. 74th Cong., 1st Sess., Washington, D.C.

Modigliani, F. 1977. "The Monetarist Controversy, Or Should We Forsake Stabilization Policies?" *American Economic Review* (March).

Modigliani, F., and Friedman, M. 1977. "The Monetarist Controversy. A Seminar Discussion." *Economic Review*, Supplement, Federal Reserve Bank of San Francisco (Spring).

Okun, A. M. 1981. *Prices and Quantities—A Macroeconomic Analysis*. Oxford: Basil Blackwell.

Quadrio Curzio, A. 1981. "Un diagramma per l'oro tra demonetizzazione e rimonetiz-zazione." *Rivista internazionale di scienze economiche e commerciali* (October–November).

Robinson, J. 1979. "What are the Questions." 1977. Reprinted in *Collected Economic Papers*, Vol. 5. Oxford: Basil Blackwell.

Roncaglia, A. 1983. *L'economia del petrolio*, Bari: Laterza (Engl. tras. forthcoming, London: Macmillan).

Rowthorn. B. 1980. *Capitalism, Conflict and Inflation—Essays in Political Economy*. London: Lawrence and Wishart. (This volume includes the essay "Conflict, Inflation and Money," dated 1977.)

Siglienti, S. 1981. "The Future of the Dollar as a Reserve Asset." In *Europe and the Dollar in the World-Wide Disequilibrium*. Edited by J. R. Sargent. Alphen aan den Rijn, The Netherlands: Sijthoff and Noordhoff.

Sylos-Labini, P. 1969. *Oligopoly and Technical Progress*. Cambridge, Mass.: Harvard University Press (1st ed., 1956).

Sylos-Labini, P. 1974. *Trade Unions, Inflation and Productivity*. Lexington, Mass.: Lexington Books.

Sylos-Labini, P. 1976. "Competition: The Product Markets." In *The Market and the State—Essays in Honour of Adan Smith*. Edited by T. Wilson and A.S. Skinner. Oxford: Clarendon Press.

Sylos-Labini, P. 1979. "Industrial Pricing in the United Kingdom." *Cambridge Journal of Economics* (June).

Sylos--Labini, P. 1980. "Spinelli and Fratianni on Inflation: A Comment." *Banca nazionale del lavoro Quarterly Review* (December).

Weintraub, S. 1981. *Our Stagflation Malaise*. Westport Conn.: Greenwood Press.

IV

Changes in Income Distribution

7

Prices and Income Distribution in the Manufacturing Industry

7.1 Wages and Prices: Theoretical Hypotheses

Adam Smith maintained that, given the "productive powers" of labor, an increase in wages would be completely passed on in higher prices. David Ricardo maintained that an increase in wages would *not* increase the prices of commodities but would cause profits to be reduced. Karl Marx advanced a proposition similar to Ricardo's. Keynes took up Smith's position that, in a closed economy, a change in wages would produce a proportional change in prices. Keynes's position had a practical motivation, however: Keynes wished to show that the remedy of wage reduction could not provide a cure for the depression, since it would bring a proportional reduction in prices with no appreciable variation in output and employment (1936, ch. 19).

Two years later Kalecki (1938a), examining the price consequences of the strong increase in hourly wages (around 60 percent) decided by the Blum government, concluded that Keynes's position was substantiated.

Is the Keynesian position still valid? What, then, is the behavior of the cost-price relationship?

The answer cannot be general and unequivocal. Empirically, the solution might appear to be easy today, since the number of price equations worked out by econometricians in the last decade or so is very large indeed. Yet the matter is not so simple, for as a rule such equations include among their arguments not only cost elements but also demand variables, so that the interpretation of the cost-price relationship becomes obscure.

Fortunately, in the case of modern industry it seems justifiable to limit the analysis, at least in a first approximation, to the relation between prices and direct costs, that is, labor costs and the costs of raw materials. In fact a theoretical model can, I think, provide the necessary framework (Sylos-Labini 1969, 1974).

The preliminary assumption is that competition (in the classical rather than the neoclassical sense) prevails in agriculture and in many raw materials markets, whereas the prevailing market form in the manufacturing industry is oligopoly, of which there are three varieties: concentrated oligopoly (in industries producing major producer goods), differentiated oliogopoly (in nondurable consumer goods), and mixed oligopoly (concentration *cum* differentiation, especially in durable consumer goods). Quasi-competitive conditions can be observed for some nondurable consumer goods and in satellite activities.

The main assumptions of the oligopoly pricing model are the following:

1. Given the price of the means of production, and wages, the short-run marginal cost is constant and therefore equal to direct cost.

2. The long-run marginal cost curve is *L*-shaped.

3. Only large firms can influence prices directly, while small firms can exert indirect influence by means of variations in combined output.

4. A new firm does not enter the market unless it expects to sell at a price that can give at least a minimum rate of profit; any price below this level can be considered an "entry-preventing" price. In the long run the entry-preventing price becomes an "elimination price," for an existing firm of a given class will abandon the market if it is persistently unable to earn the minimum profit.

5. An existing firm is forced to suspend its activities if the price falls below direct cost per unit; a price lower than this level, even in the short run, is an elimination price.

6. If new firms enter the market, existing firms continue to produce as much as before, not only to discourage the entry of new firms but also to avoid raising unit costs.

The following four propositions are worth considering here:

Proposition 1
The equilibrium price is determined primarily by the conditions of the market, including technology and the price of the means of production and wages, on the one hand, and the position and shape of the demand curve, on the other. The largest firms, however, can affect price and market conditions to some extent.

Proposition 2
The discretionary power of firms becomes more important in considering price variations carried out on the basis of the markup resulting from the equilibrium price. (This implies that the so-called full-cost principle is meaningful only in a dynamic context.) The equilibrium price must be

changed when at least one of these conditions changes. The oligopolistic interdependence becomes fully relevant even in the short run when the change affects all firms. As a rule changes in direct costs—labor and raw materials costs—belong to this category. The markup then is applied to direct cost, which is taken as the reference cost by firms endowed with market power.

Proposition 3
The market power of the oligopolistic firms does not necessarily yield above-normal profits; it can mean above-normal wages, given the historic conditions of the labor market.

Proposition 4
Since in industrial production full capacity is reached only in boom periods and in a limited number of industries, as a rule an expansion of demand does not affect industrial prices. In an open economy the expansion of demand does not necessarily affect prices even in industries where full capacity is reached; such an expansion tends rather to speed up imports. All things considered, at least to a first approximation, the determinants of industrial wholesale prices are the cost elements, with demand left on one side. This proposition is similar to the Keynesian proposition that changes in demand normally affect the level of activity, but not prices. It refers to the short period (the year) and applies to manufacturing industry, but not to agriculture and mining where competition often prevails, and in the short period price variations depend on supply and demand.

In this chapter, attention is concentrated on the manufacturing industry, which is the most dynamic sector of the economy.

7.2 Wages and Prices: Empirical Analyses

Empirical analyses show that industrial prices respond to changes in costs, but not completely in the short period; in the long period the situation may be different.

For empirical tests, annual data represent a reasonably good solution of the "normalization problem."[1]

The following relation incorporates the full-cost principle in its simplest form:

$$P = av, \tag{1}$$

where P is price, a is the markup over cost, and v is the direct or variable cost, equal to the sum of labor costs and raw materials costs per unit of output:

$$v = (W/\pi) + RM,$$

where (W/π) is the ratio of hourly money wages and hourly productivity in real terms and RM is the unit cost of raw materials, which can be expressed by the appropriate price indexes if, as seems reasonable, the inputs of raw materials are assumed constant in the short period.

To analyze the behavior of the cost-price relationships in manufacturing industry, the following simple equation can be used:

$$\hat{P}_i = a(\widehat{W/\pi}) + b\widehat{RM}, \tag{2}$$

where the cap over a variable indicates the rate of change.

The equations were estimated as follows (the value of Student's t is given in parentheses beneath each coefficient):[2]

1. *Italy, 1951–1975*
$$\hat{P}_i = 0.383 + 0.367(\widehat{W/\pi}) + 0.433(\widehat{RM}),$$
$$(0.97) + (8.98) \qquad\qquad (22.53)$$
$$R^2 = 0.977,$$
$$DW = 1.700.$$

2. *United States, 1948–1976*
$$\hat{P}_i = 0.688 + 0.492(\widehat{W/\pi}) = 0.439(\widehat{RM}),$$
$$(2.09) + (5.60) \qquad\qquad (10.35)$$
$$R^2 = 0.876,$$
$$DW = 1.520.$$

3. *United Kingdom, 1954–1973*
$$\hat{P}_i = 0.671 + 0.521(\widehat{W/\pi}) + 0.215(\widehat{RM}),$$
$$(1.42) \qquad (14.00) \qquad\qquad (16.06)$$
$$R^2 = 0.822,$$
$$DW = 2.442.$$

4. *West Germany, 1953–1973*
$$\hat{P}_i = 1.062 + 0.313(\widehat{W/\pi}) + 0.491(\widehat{RM}),$$
$$(2.21) \qquad (2.95) \qquad\qquad (9.89)$$
$$R^2 = 0.883,$$
$$DW = 1.643.$$

5. *Argentina, 1955–1972*
$$\hat{P}_i = 0.610 + 0.505(\widehat{W/\pi}) + 0.492(\widehat{RM}),$$
$$(0.631) \qquad (4.95) \qquad\qquad (6.94)$$
$$R^2 = 0.957,$$
$$DW = 2.341.$$

Attempts were made to include the degree of capacity utilization as a proxy for the relative pressure of demand. The results for Italy and the United Kingdom were negative, however, confirming the result reported by Coutts, Godley, and Nordhaus (1978) for the United Kingdom. In the U.S. industrial sector the relative pressure of demand does have statistical significance (see the works cited in the References, especially Solow 1969). This conforms to the hypothesis allowing for a (limited) influence of demand on industrial prices in relatively closed economic systems. Nevertheless, none of the equations examined for the United States showed any crucial importance for demand: the percentage of explained variance seems to remain high even when demand variables are omitted.

In all cases except Argentina, changes in costs seem to be only partially shifted onto prices. The proportion ranges from 74 percent in the United Kingdom to 93 percent in the United States.

Three important questions must be answered. First, why is the shift only partial? Second, is the partial adjustment symmetrical? Third, are all types of costs shifted onto prices in the same proportion?

In trying to answer these questions, we must consider the pressure of foreign competition and the dispersion of productivity increases.

Apart from customs duties, national producers are favored by various kinds of "hidden protection," due to factors such as lower transportation costs, better knowledge of the markets, some kind of control over the channels of retail trade, and so on. All these circumstances—plus, of course, product differentiation—can allow a (limited) divergence between prices of home products and foreign goods. Still imports act as a brake on the shift of cost variations onto prices.

Let us now consider the dispersion of productivity increases.

Changes in wages and in the prices of raw materials affect all firms in an industry and therefore modify the equilibrium price (proposition 2). But unit labor cost also depends on productivity, which seldom changes at the same rate in all firms since certain innovations are not equally accessible. If the unit labor cost increases in all firms in a given industry, and the firm acting as the price leader obtains the highest or near highest rate of productivity increase, then the product price will rise less than the average of the industry cost increase even if the price leader completely shifts *its own* cost increase. On the other hand, if the unit labor cost decreases in all firms and, again, the firm acting as the price leader achieves the highest rate of productivity increase, this firm can reduce the price only in relation to the (smaller) productivity increase accessible to all other firms. This tends to make the shift not only partial but also asymmetrical.

In a wider world perspective, changes in raw materials costs tend to be fully shifted onto prices because they also affect producers in competing countries;

in this case the shift can be incomplete only as a result of differences in the industrial structures of the different countries. Also productivity and wages vary worldwide at very different rates. Therefore when domestic labor costs jump faster than those in competing countries, they cannot be shifted fully onto prices. On the other hand, given the power of trade unions in the industrialized countries, a decrease in labor cost can scarcely take place simultaneously in all countries; thus there is no international pressure to shift onto prices a decrease in labor cost occurring in a single country.

We conclude that, whereas the shift of raw materials costs onto prices tends to be approximately complete and symmetrical, the shift of changes in labor costs tends to be partial and asymmetrical.

7.3 Shifting: Partial and Asymmetrical

Emprical tests support the view that foreign competition acts as a brake upon prices. In these equations an index of prices of industrial products in international markets takes into account the price limits posed by international competition:

6. *Italy, 1952–1977*

$$\hat{P}_i = 0.062 + 0.299(W/\pi) + 0.387(\widehat{RM}) + 0.276\hat{P}_{ii}$$
$$(0.11) \quad (6.12) \quad\quad (14.03) \quad\quad (2.23)$$
$$R^2 = 0.981,$$
$$DW = 1.552.$$

7. *United Kingdom, 1954–1973*

$$\hat{P}_i = 0.939 + 0.262(W/\pi) + 0.293(\widehat{RM}) + 0.254\hat{P}_{ii'}$$
$$(2.84) \quad (3.33) \quad\quad (4.19) \quad\quad (2.34)$$
$$R^2 = 0.855,$$
$$DW = 2.428.$$

The fact that the third variable is clearly significant, and that the sum of the three coefficients is closer to unity than the sum of the two elements of direct costs, indicates that the transfer is partial mainly because of foreign competition. Moreover if we compare empirical equations 6 and 7 with equations 1 and 3, we must notice that the coefficient of labor costs varies much more than that of raw materials costs, showing that foreign competition affects mainly the shifts of changes in labor costs.

The sum of the coefficients is also nearer unity in the United States and Argentina, where foreign competition exerts a relatively small influence. Other evidence concerning Italy shows that changes in prices in periods of cost increases in 14 industries and the pressure of foreign competition were inversely correlated (Sylos-Labini 1974).

Finally, cited earlier is the evidence presented by Kalecki with respect to France in the period from April 1936 to April 1937: the shift was practically complete, but in that period France could be considered a closed economy.

The price adjustment, however, is not only partial but asymmetrical. Can we find empirical evidence in support of this assertion?

For Italy and the United States, the first equation that follows uses only the rates of increase in costs; the second uses only the rates of decrease. The division between periods of cost increases and periods of cost decreases was made on the basis of total direct costs, composed of a weighted average of labor and raw materials costs. For cost decreases the number of observations is lower than that required for statistical validity (18 observations in the case of cost increases and 9 observations in the case of cost decreases for Italy, and 18 and 12 observations for the United States).[3]

Italy

8. Cost increases
$$\hat{P}_i = 0.346 + 0.377(\widehat{W/\pi}) + 0.430(\widehat{RM}),$$
$$(0.62) \quad (18.03) \quad \quad (21.64)$$
$$R^2 = 0.981,$$
$$DW = 1.862.$$

9. Cost decreases
$$\hat{P}_i = 0.068 + 0.191(\widehat{W/\pi}) + 0.432(\widehat{RM}),$$
$$(0.04) \quad (0.55) \quad \quad (4.25)$$
$$R^2 = 0.277,$$
$$DW = 2.212.$$

United States

10. *Cost increases*
$$\hat{P}_i = 0.674 + 0.548(\widehat{W/\pi}) + 0.419(\widehat{RM}),$$
$$(1.06) \quad (4.31) \quad \quad (6.53)$$
$$R^2 = 0.810,$$
$$DW = 1.641.$$

11. Cost decreases
$$\hat{P}_i = 0.385 + 0.139(\widehat{W/\pi}) + 0.333(\widehat{RM}),$$
$$(2.47) \quad (2.09) \quad \quad (7.21)$$
$$R^2 = 0.695,$$
$$DW = 2.963.$$

In both countries the correlation is much higher for cost increases than for cost decreases, and the drop in the correlation is connected primarily with labor costs. The shift is asymmetrical: for Italy the sum of the coefficients is equal to 0.807 for cost increases and 0.623 for decreases. For the United States the two values are 0.967 and 0.472, respectively. Further the values of the two coefficients vary, with that of labor costs fluctuating much more than that of raw materials costs. To interpret these results properly, we must keep in mind that the value of each coefficient can be viewed as the weight of each cost element multiplied by an index of variation measuring the degree to which the change in each cost element is shifted onto price.[4] If we give total direct cost a value of unity and if, on the basis of the input-output tables, we attribute to direct labor a weight only limitedly greater than that of raw materials—say, 0.55 and 0.45, respectively—then we see that the coefficient of raw materials does not diverge much from the presumed value of its weight and varies relatively little, regardless of whether costs increase or decrease; the coefficient of labor cost, on the other hand, appears to be always lower than the weight and varies considerably, depending on the direction of the change in costs (in Italy, $0.38 \rightarrow 0.19$; in the United States, $0.55 \rightarrow 0.14$). These results are consistent with our expectations: almost complete shift in the case of raw materials; partial and asymmetrical shift in the case of labor cost. (It is well to point out that the resistence of firms to trade union claims would be incomprehensible were the shift of labor cost increases on prices complete and rapid.)

7.4 Consequences of Partial and Asymmetrical Shifting

The fact that in the short run the shifting of changes in direct costs onto prices is partial leads to variations in the markup over costs that are opposite in direction to the changes in direct costs, since margins diminish when costs increase and increase when costs diminish. The asymmetry does not modify this conclusion, but indeed reinforces it. The asymmetry is relatively weak in the case of Italy, while it is quite strong for the United States. This signifies that in Italy margins fall more in periods of rising costs and rise by less in periods of decreasing costs. This phenomenon takes on major importance when one considers that the markup over direct costs serves to cover overhead costs and to provide profits. As a group, Italian manufacturing industries are damaged more than those in the United States (a more nearly closed economy) in periods of rising costs and benefit less in periods of falling costs. Indeed, it seems that when costs rise, American firms taken together succeed in shifting nearly all of their higher costs onto prices, while the Italian firms cannot achieve such complete cost shifts.

The partial nature of cost shifting could produce fluctuations around an overall tendency toward a stable share of industrial profits, with the share decreasing when costs increase and rising when costs fall. The actual trend, however, depends on the intensity and relative duration of the periods of cost increases and decreases. When, as in recent years, direct costs increase without interruptions over a significant number of years, the markup tends to fall, and since usually the shift is incomplete, the profit margin and the profits share too tend to fall. But this is but one of the causes of a fall in the profit share. Actually, though providing profits, the markup serves primarily to cover overhead costs made up of the salaries of managerial, administrative, and technical personnel and capital consumption allowances. At this point then we have to enlarge our analysis and devote some attention to overhead costs, a topic much neglected by economists.[5]

7.5 Overhead Costs and Prices

Changes in direct costs are shifted onto prices in the short run, though not completely, because they affect all firms and therefore the equilibrium conditions of the market (proposition 2). Changes in overhead costs are very different among firms, at least in the short run, and thus do not affect the market equilibrium, and they cannot be shifted onto prices in the short run. What, however, happens when in the long run unit overhead costs increase in all firms, though to different degrees and in different ways?

The increase in unit overhead costs can be covered by an increase in the markup, that is, the price/direct cost ratio. Under such circumstances a fixed markup implies a fall in the profit margin, while a prolonged increase in direct costs a fall in the profit margin through a fall in the markup. But the profit margin cannot go on falling for a long time, otherwise a serious profit squeeze takes place. Since we are talking of the average profit margin, a prolonged fall of this margin implies that an increasing number of firms is undergoing losses, a situation that cannot last for long. Thus the problem is how the profit margin is to be restored. There are two possible ways to do it: one, raise the markup if the cause of the fall is an increase in unit overhead costs and, two, reinstate the markup if it has decreased because of a prolonged increase in direct costs. For simplicity, I consider only the second case; nonetheless, the two cases are similar in every respect as far as our problem is concerned.

When the profit margin tends to fall, the least efficient firms are driven out of the market. At the same time, those firms that see their price/direct cost ratio falling to a dangerously low level try to speed up the increase in productivity. Both, as a result of the disappearance of the least efficient firms and of the acceleration in the productivity increases in other firms, the average price/ direct cost ratio is pushed up. Thus the recovery of the markup is due, not to an increase in price—and the shifting process consists precisely of this—but to a decrease in costs.

A full shift of cost increases onto prices can take place only when especially favorable circumstances occur (since here I consider a long period, I refer to total average costs). Particularly favorable circumstance arise when the government decides a devaluation or when demand expands very rapidly in all or in most advanced countries. Under such circumstances prices can rise worldwide, since competition among countries is thwarted—in fact, as I have already pointed out, under such circumstances, which are to be considered exceptional, demand can affect prices.

In the period we are considering, that is, the three decades after the second world war, the markup has not declined for a long number of years either in Italy or in the United States. Yet it seems that unit overhead costs have increased in both countries. The result would have been a fall in the profit margin and in the profit share; but in the United States the markup has increased, whereas this does not seem to be the case in Italy (see table 7.1 in the appendix). In fact the profit share has fallen in the manufacturing industries of both countries, but more in Italy than in the United States.[6] However, the estimates of total direct costs and of the profit share are liable to a considerable margin of error over relatively long periods; year-to-year variations are more reliable.

In any case there is no doubt that after the second world war unit overhead costs have tended to increase both in Italy and the United States, and likewise, it seems, in all industrialized countries. This trend is due to the fact that the growth in the number of engineers and in the clerical and technical staff has been more rapid than the growth in the number of manual workers. There has also been a spurt in the salaries of top management, who fix the salary levels for themselves and other high-level managers, so that profits of corporations are in part institutionalized and transformed into salaries for top management. This is an important phenomenon, for the high earnings of a few tend to have a demonstration effect on other salaries and also to erode the capacity of the firm to finance investment internally.

The trend of unit overhead costs has been on the increase because total overhead costs have risen more rapidly than total output. In the last ten years the increase in unit overhead costs has been speeded up by the slowdown in the growth of total output. But to clarify this type of problem a particular analysis will be worked out.

7.6 Markup and the Distribution of Income

To assess the relation between prices and the distribution of income in the short run in manufacturing industry, the Kalecki model (1838b) is developed and modified. We start from equation (1), which we rewrite in the following way:

$$P_i = a\left(\frac{W}{\pi}\right) + aRM. \tag{1a}$$

When we move from rates of change to absolute levels of the variables, we must refer to the census of industrial production for the values of the indexes in the base year. In round numbers the values of the variables for the manufacturing industry are $P_i = 180$ for Italy and 175 for the United States; $a = 1.80$ and 1.75, respectively; $W/\pi = 55$; and $RM = 45$. The base year is 1953 for Italy, and 1950 for the United States (see table 7.1 in the appendix).

Multiplying all the terms of equation (1a) by the volume of output, X, and subtracting the quantity RMX from both sides, we get

$$P_iX - RMX = a\left(\frac{W}{\pi}\right)X + aRMX - RMX.$$

Calling Y_i the difference between P_iX and RMX, which is the value added for the industrial sector, and setting the wage bill $W_T = (W/\pi)X$, we have:

$$Y_i = aW_T + aRMX - RMX, \text{ or}$$

$$\frac{W_T}{Y_i} = \frac{1}{a} - \left(\frac{RM}{P - RM}\right)\cdot\frac{(a-1)}{a},$$

or, calling a^* the ratio $(a - 1)/a$ and D_F the difference between P and RM, which is simply the deflator for value added, we get

$$\frac{W_T}{Y_i} = \frac{1}{a} - \frac{RM}{D_F}a^*, \tag{3}$$

from which it can be seen that the share of wages in value added varies inversely with respect to a and RM. (Since $a > 1$, a^* and a necessarily vary in the same direction.) The markup, a, expresses the degree of market power of the industrial producers. If one considers the industrial sector in isolation, it is evident that this market power can be expressed equally as an ability either to increase prices or to depress wages. The inverse correlation that exists between W_T/Y_i and RM indicates a conflict of interest between industrial workers and the producers of raw materials. In the case of imported raw materials this conflict appears as an aspect of the conflict of interest between industrially advanced countries and the lesser developed producers of primary products.

Total profits, G, are equal to the difference

$$G = Y_i - W_T - C_O, \tag{4}$$

where C_O is the aggregate value of overhead costs. From relations (3) and (4) we then have

$$\frac{G}{Y_i} = 1 - \frac{1}{a} + a^* \cdot \frac{RM}{(P_i - RM)} - \frac{C_O}{Y_i},$$

$$\frac{G}{Y_i} = a^* \cdot \frac{P_i}{D_F} - \frac{C_O}{Y_i}, \tag{5}$$

which indicates the determinants of the share of profits.[7]

Empirically, relations (3) and (4) for the manufacturing industry in the United States and Italy show the following:

Italy, 1952–1977

12. $W_T/Y_i = \quad 0.858(1/a) - \quad 0.491(RM/D_F)a^*,$
$\qquad\qquad\quad (21.06) \qquad\quad (3.41)$
$\qquad\quad R^2 = 0.817,$
$\qquad\quad DW = 0.743.$

13. $\quad G/Y_i = \quad 1.005a^*(P_i/D_F) - \quad 1.010\,C_O/Y_i,$
$\qquad\qquad\quad (48.10) \qquad\qquad\quad (30.62)$
$\qquad\quad R^2 = 0.977,$
$\qquad\quad DW = 1.126.$

United States, 1947–1977

14. $W_T/Y_i = \quad 0.820(1/a) - \quad 0.563(RM/D_F)a^*,$
$\qquad\qquad\quad (17.83) \qquad\quad (3.10)$
$\qquad\quad R^2 = 0.744,$
$\qquad\quad DW = 0.195.$

15. $\quad G/Y_i = \quad 0.928a^*(P_i/D_F) - \quad 0.823\,C_O/Y_i,$
$\qquad\qquad\quad (28.14) \qquad\qquad\quad (19.53)$
$\qquad\quad R^2 = 0.916,$
$\qquad\quad DW = 0.270.$

A conflict exists not only between the markup, a, and the share of wages but also between this share and the price of raw materials. If these prices rise, this share falls, unless a diminishes by an amount sufficient to offset the rise; if a falls, however, the share of profits is reduced. In the case of imported raw materials an increase in relative prices makes the conflict of interest between the workers and the industrial employers more acute.

The grave social and economic difficulties that have befallen the economies of the capitalist countries in recent years are attributable in large measure to the conspicuous advance in the prices of raw materials and the enormous increase in the price of that special raw material, petroleum. The theoretical model proposed here helps to clarify the mechanism through which these difficulties arise. More precisely the problems originated by the rapid increases in raw materials prices depend not so much on a fall in the markup but rather on the slowdown in the expansion of demand caused by price increases, as well as on restrictive policies prompted by trade deficits; both phenomena tend to cause an increase in overhead costs per unit and therefore a fall in the share of profits.

The conflict that has been singled out between countries producing manufactured goods, and those producing raw materials can be examined by means of variations in the ratio RM/D_F in equation (3), which presents a particular way of considering the terms of trade between agricultural and mineral products and industrial goods.

7.7 The Fall in Profits

Manufacturing was chosen for study because this sector is the center of propulsion for technological innovations and capital accumulation. A profit reduction here differs inherently from comparable profit declines in the banking or commercial sectors and is more damaging especially to the process of accumulation, since the basic source of finance tends to dry up and the incentive to invest is reduced. Profits then can be "too low" from the viewpoint of capital accumulation. But profits can also be "too high"; in fact if prices are high relative to costs, they tend to curb the expansion of total demand.

Briefly this is the problem of the "optimum" rate of profit in the theory of accumulation. More precisely we should speak of the optimum *range* of profits, since at any moment in time a variety of profit rates exist; then a low *average* rate of profit implies widespread losses, and a larger dispersion around the mean suggests larger losses.

The behavior of the rate of profit corresponds to that of the share of profits if the capital-output ratio is constant or wavers about a trend. Since in recent years this ratio has revealed a (slow downward) trend, the behavior of the profit share becomes representative of the fluctuation in the profit rate.

In Italy and Great Britain the profit share has shown a tendency to decline, although with fluctuations, for at least ten years. A similar, though less rapid, tendency is also visible in the manufacturing industry in the United States and other advanced capitalist countries. The following explanation can be advanced.

According to the preceding analysis Marx's hypothesis of the increasing organic composition of capital is of little help in resolving this question. Rather the origins of this decline are international competition, on the one hand, and the increased bargaining power of unionized labor as well as the increased market power of certain underdeveloped countries producing raw materials and energy sources, on the other. Finally, the decline of the profit share can also be explained by the fact that, over the long period, overhead costs have tended to increase more rapidly than output (see equation 5); the latter rise seems attributable much more to the relative increase of salaries than to the relative increase of capital consumption allowances. Owing to increased overhead costs, the profit share can remain constant only under a higher gross markup on direct costs; this margin can escalate in the long run only if periods of cost hikes are matched by periods of cost plunges of sufficient intensity and duration.

The share of overhead costs, however, does not ascend without interruption. Advancing in the short period at a relatively stable rate, largely independent of the output growth rate, this share falls when income spurts ahead, as in rapid economic recovery or prosperity. In these periods the profit share grows even with a stable or falling gross markup.[8]

All things considered, the recent decline of the share of profits in several capitalist countries can be attributed to the persistent increase of direct costs in labor, raw materials, and energy and to the increase in unit overhead costs.

In general if the decline in profits is limited and of brief duration, the accumulation process is interrupted, and a "normal" crisis of the capitalist system occurs, during which the conditions for recovery and continued accumulation are recreated. When the decline is strong or of long duration, the crisis takes on abnormal characteristics, as in Italy and the United Kingdom today; nor have other capitalist countries completely escaped the atypical crisis.

7.8 Inflation and the Distribution of Income

In industry the partial shift of direct costs onto prices leads, in periods of inflation, to a progressive erosion of the markup and net profit margin, further accentuated by rising overhead costs per unit of output.

A reduction of the net margin normally leads to a lower profit rate, one of the determinants of industrial investments. Total profits can also fall, damping a second determinant of industrial investment, for total profits constitute the fund of internal finance.

The rise in prices then carries with it a tendency toward worsening of the balance sheets of industrial firms. Yet the price rise also implies a lightening in the real debt burden and thus some improvement in owners' equity. In a period of sustained inflation, however, the negatives will outweigh the positive tendency, obstructing investment. The reduction of profits, which provide internal financing, leads to an increase in indebtedness, and as the demands for bank loans increase, the market power of the banks is enhanced. Banks thus raise their earnings by increasing the difference between their lending and borrowing rates.[9] Total interest charges paid by the firms increase.

In industry investment depends not only on profits but also on the degree of capacity utilization, and thus on demand. Variations in prices, however, are largely independent of demand. When wage costs increase, prices tend to rise even in the face of falling demand; under contemporary conditions wage rises occur even in the presence of high rates of unemployment. It is thus possible to have increasing costs and prices, falling profits, and stationary or falling activity levels. In other words, there is a prospect of stagnation accompanied by inflation (stagflation) or even of recession accompanied by inflation, which many economists view as disconcerting and paradoxical but which present no difficulty of interpretation for the analysis conducted in this study.[10] In the past when trade unions were much weaker, periods of inflation were normally periods of rising profits, because wage costs normally increased more slowly than prices, and firms benefited not only in owners' equity but also on the profit and loss account. Today this generally is no longer true.

Activity can thus decline due to a drop in investment resulting from a cut in profits. It is unlikely, however, that a profit fall alone could provoke a recession. A recession is more probably brought on by restrictive policies meant to reduce the trade deficit caused by an increase in the prices of imported raw materials or by a rise in labor costs, which tends to slow down the expansion of exports and speed up the increase of imports of consumption goods, provided employment does not fall. The system may also be led in this way to a recession accompanied by inflation.

The decline in profit margins can be remedied by a devaluation of the monetary unit, which raises the "ceiling" set by the price of competing imports. In a country that imports substantial raw materials and has strong unions, however, the profit improvement is short-lived, for any additional increase in prices is soon followed by wage claims. This is especially the case if there is a mechanism of wage indexation such as the moving escalator in Italy, which is triggered at short intervals. Profitability can always be restored if the devaluation is repeated, but this may cause an acceleration of the inflationary process and generate a redistribution of income even within the same class of incomes (e.g., between official and black market labor), exacerbating social tensions.

In recent years the lira has been devalued intermittently, twice during 1976. Profits increased temporarily, and industrial profits were higher in 1976 than in the previous year (see table 7.3 in the appendix). Industrial income also grew more rapidly than overhead costs in that year.

A devaluation induces a (temporary) recovery in the profit margin; it may also improve the trade balance by stimulating exports and retarding imports. Nevertheless, it can be quite costly in social and political terms.

7.9 Conclusions

The following conclusions can be drawn from the foregoing analysis:

1. The cost-price mechanism developed here can help to explain why union bargaining power has been growing.

2. Contemporary industrial capitalism has an organic need that periods of increases in direct costs be followed by periods of falling costs, just as whales and dolphins can survive long periods of submersion provided they can surface periodically for air. Since unit overhead costs are rising systematically, unless the markup rises sufficiently, profits fall and the accumulation process is interrupted.

3. Variations in the distribution of industrial incomes can be explained by analyzing variations in prices.

4. In general, given the cost-price transfer mechanism, three forces have operated unfavorably on the share of profits in both the United States and Italy: (a) the increased bargaining power of labor unions, (b) the increased bargaining power of petroleum and other raw materials producers, and (c) the tendency of overhead costs per unit of output to increase systematically. All three of these factors have been fully operative in Italy, whereas the last two have been predominant in the United States.

5. A trilateral conflict of interest exists between workers, industrialists, and raw materials producers. This conflict assumes international proportions when raw materials are imported from foreign countries.

6. In industry the cost-price transfer mechanism helps to explain stagnation accompanied by inflation or recession accompanied by inflation. Such phenomena have ceased to be exceptional in many industrial countries over the past two decades.

7. Under modern conditions inflation is not normally advantageous to the firm. Any favorable effect on owners' equity is overtaken by a negative effect on the balance sheet as a whole. More precisely it is neither necessary nor

inevitable (even in Italy which has a mechanism of transfer particularly unfavorable to the firms) for the margin of profit to fall continuously under inflation. The profit margin can rise if output increases more rapidly than do overhead costs, or if the currency is devalued. All things considered, however, contrary to the dominant thesis, under modern conditions inflation often depress profit margins.

8. More generally, many economists, among them the monetarists, treat real and nominal quantities as if they were fundamentally independent from one another. This procedure is seriously misleading, however, since prices of different categories do not and cannot vary at the same rate, and thus such variations necessarily imply changes in income distribution which in turn necessarily affect current and expected profits, that is, real income and its growth.

Postscript

I have re-estimated the price equations for Italy and the United States up to the period 1982. The results are as follows (to facilitate the comparison, I reproduce the original estimates; for simplicity, constants are omitted):

Italy

1951–1975

$$\hat{P}_i = 0.37(W\widehat{/\pi}) + 0.43(\widehat{RM})$$
$$\quad\quad (8.98) \quad\quad (22.53)$$
$$R^2 = 0.977,$$
$$DW = 1.700.$$

1951–1982

$$\hat{P}_i = 0.42(W\widehat{/\pi}) + 0.44(\widehat{RM})$$
$$\quad\quad (12.33) \quad\quad (22.75)$$
$$R^2 = 0.974,$$
$$DW = 1.689.$$

1951–1975

$$\hat{P}_i = 0.30(W\widehat{/\pi}) + 0.39(\widehat{RM}) + 0.28\hat{P}_{ii}$$
$$\quad\quad (6.12) \quad\quad (14.03) \quad\quad (2.23)$$
$$R^2 = 0.981,$$
$$DW = 1.552.$$

1951–1982

$$\hat{P}_i = 0.28(W\widehat{/\pi}) + 0.34(\widehat{RM}) + 0.53\hat{P}_{ii}$$
$$\quad\quad (22.9) \quad\quad (13.63) \quad\quad (4.74)$$
$$R^2 = 0.985,$$
$$DW = 1.757.$$

United States

1948–1976

$$P_i = 0.49(W\widehat{/\pi}) + 0.44(\widehat{RM})$$
$$\quad\quad (5.60) \quad\quad (10.35)$$
$$R^2 = 0.876,$$
$$DW = 1.520.$$

1948–1982

$$P_i = 0.61(W\widehat{/\pi}) + 0.39(\widehat{RM})$$
$$\quad\quad (7.61) \quad\quad (6.03)$$
$$R^2 = 0.800,$$
$$DW = 2.005.$$

Appendix

Table 7.1
Prices, direct costs, and markup in the manufacturing industry in Italy and the United States

Year	Italy Prices, P	Cost of labor, L	Raw materials prices, RM	Markup, a	United States Prices, P	Cost of labor, L	Raw materials prices, RM	Markup, a
1947					163.92	56.32	42.68	165.57
1948					176.99	56.32	46.48	171.89
1949					171.90	56.42	42.00	174.34
1950					175.00	55.00	45.00	175.00
1951	194.95	54.85	49.65	186.55	191.61	58.37	51.38	174.60
1952	186.89	56.49	45.18	183.24	190.51	61.42	48.05	173.65
1953	180.00	55.00	45.00	180.00	188.51	62.89	46.33	172.35
1954	177.95	52.63	49.96	178.31	188.96	63.14	46.13	172.71
1955	178.84	51.86	45.34	183.93	189.40	62.49	45.69	174.85
1956	179.75	51.81	46.71	182.49	194.72	66.17	46.85	172.23
1957	183.52	51.15	48.05	185.23	201.80	68.25	47.76	173.96
1958	178.31	50.68	45.45	185.41	206.46	69.88	48.57	174.34
1959	175.06	47.13	45.80	188.64	206.01	69.22	48.25	175.40
1960	175.45	47.01	45.77	189.39	207.56	70.09	47.66	176.47
1961	175.98	48.47	44.65	188.80	207.56	70.21	47.24	177.01
1962	178.66	51.35	44.64	185.64	208.23	68.35	47.34	180.03
1963	187.30	56.96	45.78	181.62	207.56	67.72	46.87	181.19
1964	195.41	59.31	46.46	184.07	208.45	66.42	46.90	183.85
1965	197.18	56.23	46.46	191.18	211.99	65.94	48.45	184.96
1966	200.07	56.08	47.30	192.71	218.86	67.90	50.49	184.44
1967	200.08	57.08	45.87	193.45	221.52	70.57	49.26	184.70
1968	200.07	56.49	46.48	193.38	227.94	72.74	50.20	185.34
1969	206.88	58.25	50.20	189.89	236.14	76.12	52.76	183.12
1970	224.85	67.51	51.70	187.47	244.34	77.53	54.75	184.46
1971	234.06	75.87	52.22	181.93	251.87	77.83	56.13	187.63
1972	243.19	78.76	54.31	182.73	259.62	79.91	60.25	184.60
1973	299.61	88.21	76.91	181.35	283.32	82.05	74.31	179.90
1974	436.82	109.29	127.03	184.81	326.74	87.70	88.25	184.87
1975	472.64	142.09	118.41	181.52	361.96	97.85	92.51	188.68
1976	583.24	154.02	159.80	185.82	377.25	97.75	96.23	193.26
1977	677.72	190.83	181.52	182.03	400.06	103.80	100.95	194.05
1978	736.00	225.15	184.02	180.00	431.20	111.58	110.45	192.35

Sources: For *Italy* wholesale prices of industrial commodities and raw materials are taken from Istituto centrale di statistica, *Annuario Italiano di statistica*, various years; Ministero del bilancio, *Relazione generale sulla situazione economica del paese*, various years; hourly earnings and hourly productivity in the manufacturing industry (ratio between value added and the number of hours worked): data of the Ministry of Labor reported in Istituto centrale di statistica, *Annuario di statistice del lavoro*, and in the *Relazione generale sulla situazione economica del paese*.

Table 7.1 (*cont.*)

For *United States* all data, except those for hourly productivity, are taken from *Economic Report of the President*, Washington, D.C., various years; hourly productivity from U.S. Department of Labor, *Handbook of Labor Statistics*, 1977; *Economic Report of the President*, 1978, especially pp. 298, 321, 322. In calculating the cost of labor, the "average gross hourly earnings" and the "output per man-hour," employees, manufacturing, were used. Raw materials prices represent the average of the prices of "crude materials for further processing" and the prices of "materials and components for manufacturing."

Note: The base year is 1953 for Italy; 1950 for the United States.

Table 7.2

Determinants of the distribution of income in the manufacturing industry in Italy and the United States

Year	Italy				United States			
	$1/a$	RM/D_F	$a^\star$	P/D_F	$1/a$	RM/D_F	$a^\star$	P/D_F
1947					0.603	0.352	0.396	1.352
1948					0.581	0.356	0.418	1.356
1949					0.573	0.323	0.426	1.323
1950					0.571	0.346	0.428	1.346
1951	0.536	0.341	0.463	1.341	0.572	0.366	0.427	1.366
1952	0.545	0.318	0.454	1.318	0.575	0.337	0.424	1.337
1953	0.555	0.333	0.444	1.333	0.580	0.325	0.419	1.325
1954	0.560	0.358	0.439	1.358	0.579	0.323	0.420	1.323
1955	0.543	0.339	0.456	1.339	0.571	0.317	0.428	1.317
1956	0.547	0.351	0.452	1.351	0.580	0.316	0.419	1.316
1957	0.539	0.354	0.460	1.354	0.574	0.310	0.425	1.310
1958	0.539	0.342	0.460	1.342	0.573	0.307	0.426	1.307
1959	0.530	0.354	0.469	1.354	0.570	0.305	0.429	1.305
1960	0.528	0.352	0.472	1.352	0.566	0.298	0.433	1.298
1961	0.529	0.340	0.470	1.340	0.564	0.294	0.435	1.294
1962	0.538	0.333	0.461	1.333	0.555	0.294	0.444	1.294
1963	0.550	0.323	0.449	1.323	0.551	0.291	0.448	1.291
1964	0.543	0.311	0.456	1.311	0.543	0.290	0.456	1.290
1965	0.523	0.308	0.476	1.308	0.540	0.296	0.459	1.296
1966	0.518	0.309	0.481	1.309	0.542	0.299	0.457	1.299
1967	0.516	0.297	0.483	1.297	0.541	0.285	0.458	1.285
1968	0.517	0.302	0.482	1.302	0.539	0.282	0.460	1.282
1969	0.526	0.320	0.473	1.320	0.546	0.287	0.453	1.287
1970	0.533	0.298	0.466	1.298	0.542	0.288	0.457	1.288
1971	0.549	0.287	0.450	1.287	0.532	0.286	0.467	1.286
1972	0.549	0.287	0.450	1.267	0.541	0.302	0.458	1.302
1973	0.559	0.345	0.440	1.345	0.555	0.355	0.444	1.355
1974	0.588	0.501	0.411	1.501	0.540	0.370	0.459	1.370
1975	0.617	0.403	0.382	1.403	0.530	0.343	0.470	1.343
1976	0.602	0.459	0.397	1.459	0.517	0.342	0.482	1.342
1977	0.617	0.444	0.382	1.444	0.515	0.337	0.484	1.337
1978	0.625	0.365	0.378	1.273	0.520	0.344	0.480	1.344

Sources: Same as for table 7.1.

Table 7.3
Distribution of value added in the manufacturing industry in Italy and the United States (percentage shares)

	Italy				United States				
Year	Wages and salaries[a]	Wages	Overhead costs, taxes[b]	"Profits"	Wages and salaries[a]	Wages[a]	Overhead costs, taxes[b]	"Profits"[c] (1)	(2)
1947					61.0	41.7	33.2	25.0	
1948					60.5	41.4	33.4	25.2	22.3
1949					60.8	41.4	35.0	23.6	20.9
1950					60.1	40.4	34.6	25.0	22.7
1951	44.5	38.0	31.5	30.5	60.3	40.7	34.1	25.2	22.3
1952	44.6	38.2	32.3	29.5	60.6	41.5	35.8	22.7	19.8
1953	44.6	38.2	33.6	28.2	62.5	42.5	36.7	20.8	18.1
1954	44.7	39.0	32.5	28.5	62.2	41.9	38.5	19.6	17.4
1955	44.5	38.6	30.4	31.0	60.2	40.5	38.8	20.7	19.3
1956	45.3	39.2	30.0	30.8	61.9	40.0	41.5	18.5	17.4
1957	45.7	38.2	31.6	30.2	63.0	40.2	42.2	17.6	16.7
1958	45.8	38.6	32.6	28.8	63.1	38.7	46.3	15.0	15.3
1959	45.7	37.0	32.0	31.0	61.9	38.4	44.1	17.5	17.2
1960	45.6	37.4	31.0	31.6	62.7	38.5	45.6	15.9	15.9
1961	46.3	37.9	31.5	30.6	62.5	38.3	46.4	15.3	15.8
1962	46.9	38.2	35.0	26.8	61.5	37.7	46.4	15.9	16.3
1963	52.2	41.4	36.8	21.8	60.7	37.0	46.9	16.1	16.6
1964	52.8	41.6	40.0	18.4	60.0	36.3	46.8	16.9	17.5
1965	52.6	40.0	41.0	19.0	59.3	36.3	45.7	18.0	18.6
1966	49.6	36.9	42.1	21.0	59.7	35.6	46.7	17.7	18.6
1967	50.4	37.4	41.4	21.2	60.5	35.6	48.7	15.7	17.3
1968	50.2	36.6	42.0	21.4	60.7	35.3	49.1	15.6	16.9
1969	50.9	37.0	44.5	18.5	62.2	35.8	51.1	13.1	14.5
1970	54.3	39.0	45.0	16.0	63.4	36.0	52.9	11.1	12.7
1971	56.2	41.0	46.5	12.5	62.4	35.0	53.5	11.5	13.1
1972	57.2	41.0	45.5	13.5	62.7	35.8	51.4	12.8	13.5
1973	58.5	41.5	43.5	15.0	62.8	34.7	52.0	13.3	13.2
1974	58.3	41.0	46.2	12.8	63.7	33.8	55.3	10.9	10.9
1975	64.8	45.9	45.8	8.3	63.6	33.9	54.2	11.9	11.9
1976	61.1	43.0	44.8	12.2	63.0	33.4	53.1	13.5	13.5
1977	62.0	43.6	45.4	11.0	63.5	33.5	53.1	13.4	13.3
1978	61.8	43.7	45.2	11.1	64.0	33.7	52.6	13.7	13.5

Sources: For Italy, Istituto centrale di statistica, *Annuario di contabilità nazionale*, 1971, pp. 39, 43, 103; 1975, p. 38; *Relazione generale sulla situazione economica del paese*, 1975, 1976. Data for 1970–76 have been adjusted to take into account certain minor changes in the classification of industries. Wages and salaries have been estimated separately using three kinds of data: (1) overall employee compensation; (2) the number of wage and salary earners (from *Censimenti industriali* and *Rilevazione campionaria delle forze di lavoro*, various years); (3) the average wage and average salary in industry (from Istituto centrale di statistica. *Annuario italiano di statistica*, various years).

For United States, 1948–72: *Census of Manufactures and Statistical Abstract of the United States*, various years; Office of Business Economics, *The National Income and Product Account of the USA, 1929–1965: Statistical Tables*, 1966; and Office of Business Economics, *Survey of Current Business*, July, various years. Wages and salaries include supplements, which in official statistics correspond to the difference between total compensation of employees and the sum of wages and salaries; total wages have been estimated by adding 85 percent of these differences to wages proper. Data for profits are from: column (1), Joint Committee of the Council of Economic Advisors, *Economic Indicators*, October 1965; column (2), *Economic Report of the President*, 1973, pp. 37–38; 1976, p. 200.
a. Including supplements (mainly employers' contributions for social insurance and for private pension and welfare funds).
b. Salaries, capital consumption allowances, and net indirect taxes.
c. (1) manufacturing industry; (2) nonfinancial corporations.

Notes

1. The "normalization problem" is the necessary consequence of the adoption of the full-cost principle. In any case the annual data represent a relatively good approximation for aggregate manufacturing industry. See the recent book by Coutts, Godley, and Nordhaus (1978) and the review article by the present writer (1979).

2. Sources of the data for Italy and the United States are given in the footnote to table 7.1 in the appendix. Figures used in estimations for the United Kingdom and West Germany are taken from National Institute of Economic Research (London), *The National Institute Economic Review*, various issues, and United Nations, *Monthly Statistical Bulletin*, various issues. Data for Argentina were supplied by Dr. Carlos Yakubovich, who also estimated the equation.

3. To reduce this uncertainty, an additional test was suggested to me by Dr. Renato Filosa: divide each of the cost elements into two series, the first including the positive elements, with the negative elements made equal to zero, and the second including the negative elements, with the positive elements made equal to zero. In the estimated equation the sum of the coefficients of the positive elements is decidedly greater than the sum of the coefficients of the negative elements, which confirms the asymmetry of the shift. For Italy, the former sum is equal to 0.807, the latter to 0.623; for the United States, the two values, are 0.945 and 0.809, respectively.

4. From equation (1), $P = av$, which we can write as $P = a(L + RM)$, we can get equation (2), $\hat{P} = a\hat{L} + b\widehat{RM}$, in the following way.

Let us take the first derivative with respect to time and divide all terms by P or, what is the same thing, by $a(L + RM)$. If we multiply the first two terms of the second member by L/L and by RM/RM, respectively, we have

$$\frac{dP/dt}{P} = \frac{aL}{a(L + RM)}\left(\frac{dRM/dt}{L}\right) + \frac{aRM}{a(L + RM)}\left(\frac{dRM/dt}{RM}\right) + \frac{L}{L + RM}\left(\frac{da/dt}{a}\right)$$
$$+ \frac{RM}{L + RM}\left(\frac{da/dt}{a}\right).$$

Indicating with a cap the rate of change of each variable (i.e., the ratio between the first derivative with respect to time of each variable and the same variable), we have

$$\hat{P} = \left(\frac{L}{L + RM} \right) (\hat{L} + \hat{a}) + \left(\frac{RM}{L + RM} \right) (\widehat{RM} + \hat{a}).$$

By multiplying the first term of the second number by $\hat{L}/\hat{L}$ and the second term by $\widehat{RM}/\widehat{RM}$, we get

$$\hat{P} = \left(\frac{L}{L + RM} \right) \left[\left(1 + \frac{\hat{a}}{\hat{L}} \right) \hat{L} \right] + \left(\frac{RM}{L + RM} \right) \left[\left(1 + \frac{\hat{a}}{\widehat{RM}} \right) \widehat{RM} \right],$$

where $L/(L + RM) = a'$ is the weight of the cost of labor and $RM/(L + RM) = b'$ is the weight of the raw materials cost over direct cost, and where

$$1 + \frac{\hat{a}}{\hat{L}} = a'' \quad \text{and} \quad 1 + \frac{\hat{a}}{\widehat{RM}} = b''$$

can be viewed as the indexes of variation measuring the degree of shifting onto price of labor cost and raw materials cost, respectively. Setting $a' a'' = a$ and $b' b'' = b$, we get

$$\hat{P} = a\hat{L} + b\widehat{RM},$$

which is precisely equation (2). It is worth noticing that the two indexes of variation, a'' and b'', are equal to one if the markup a does not vary when direct cost varies, and to less than one if, as appears to be the rule, the markup falls when direct cost rises, and vice versa.

(The author thanks F. Padoa Schioppa and E. Zaghini for their help in working out this procedure.)

5. As far as I know, only two economists, Maffeo Pantaleoni and John Maurice Clark, but at different times and a long while back in the past devoted systematic attention to this question (Pantaleoni 1910, Clark 1923). More recently Michal Kalecki has made important but short and isolated observations on overhead costs (Kalecki 1938b). And yet the share of overhead costs in value added is substantial.

6. The following tables shows the distribution of value added in Italy and the United States in the postwar period (sources are the same as those for table 7.3 in the appendix):

		(1)	(2)	(3)	(4) Indirect taxes, other overheads	(5)	(6) "Profits" and c.c. allowances
		Wages	Salaries	Capital consumption allowances		"Profits"	
Italy	1951–52	38.1	6.5	5.6	19.8	30.0	35.6
	1976–77	43.3	18.2	10.5	16.4	11.6	22.1
USA	1951–52	41.1	19.4	6.3	9.2	24.0	30.3
	1976–77	33.5	29.8	11.3	12.0	13.4	24.7

"Profits" also include interest and incomes from individual proprietorships. The latter are, strictly speaking, mixed incomes and are relatively much more important in

Italy than in the United States. The share of profits in Italy is systematically higher than the share in the United States. Considering that the proportion of self-employed laborers in Italian manufacturing industry has fallen from 25 to 14 percent for the observation period, we can conclude that the reduction in the share of profits (excluding the incomes of self-employed laborers) is less than could be inferred from the table. One should also note that in the United States, although the share of profits fell by some 10.6 percentage points from 1951–52 to 1976–77, the share of profits plus depreciation (i.e., "cash flow") fell only 5.6 percentage points from 30.3 to 24.7 percent. In the last ten years, however, the relative importance of interest payments, which were negligible at first, has grown substantially. In the United States interest currently accounts for more than 3 points of value added, so that in 1976–77 profits and depreciation, excluding interest, represented only 21 percent of value added, 9 points less than in 1951–52. In summary, the share of profits has fallen in both the United States and Italy in the last 25 years; the drop was much more pronounced in Italy, even if less extreme than the impression given in the table. Finally, the fall in the share of profits in Italy can be imputed to *both* the relative increase in overhead costs and, at least for the last eight or nine years, to a reduction in the markup. In the United States, on the other hand, the fall is due solely to the rise in overhead costs. Although the markup rose, it was not enough to offset the rise in overhead costs completely.

7. Unlike the price equation, the relations for distributive shares can be interpreted as accounting identities, provided that we use the actual values of a. Such identities can be of great help analytically, since they can bring out the mechanisms through which changes in prices and in their components cause the changes in income distribution. In this case the empirical tests show whether the statistical data are reliable and consistent with the theoretical expectations. Overall, the results seem to be positive.

8. This can explain why Okun and Perry (1970) find a relatively good correlation between the share of profits and the gap between actual and potential output (they refer to all corporations, not to the manufacturing industry; but for this particular question, the general conclusion would not change).

9. This is the dominant tendency under sustained inflation. It is also possible, however, for the gap to increase in periods of recession and decrease in periods of recovery (both under inflationary conditions). If the recovery of profit margins is not sufficient to provide for the increased need for finance, both the demand for loans and the lending rate will increase. On the other hand, the gap is reduced if the government competes with banks for private savings, thus causing them to push up borrowing rates. On the whole the relation between the share of profits in the Italian manufacturing industry and the ratio of net profits of banks to private savings shows an almost perfect negative correlation for the period 1969 to 1977. (See the *Relazione del Governatore della Banca d'Italia*, for 1975, p. 299, and for 1977, p. 279, as well as table 7.3 in the appendix.)

10. Compare the variety of cases in Weintraub (1978, ch. 4) in a policy-oriented analysis.

References

Clark, J. M. 1923. *Studies in the Economics of Overhead Costs*. Chicago: University of Chicago Press.

Coutts, K., Godley, W., and Nordhaus, W. 1978. *Industrial Pricing in the British Manufacturing Industry*. Cambridge: Cambridge University Press.

Dunlop, J. 1938. "The Movement of Real and Money Wages." *Economic Journal 47* (September).

Eckstein, O. (ed.). 1972. *The Econometrics of Price Determination*. Washington, D.C.: Department of Commerce.

Eckstein, O. and From, G. 1968. "The Price Equation." *American Economic Review 56* (December).

Eichner, A. 1973. "A Theory of the Determination of the Mark-up under Oligopoly." *Economic Journal 83* (June).

Eichner, A. 1976. *The Megacorp and Oligopoly—Micro Foundations of Macro Dynamics*. Cambridge: Cambridge University Press.

Fuà, G. 1976. *Occupazione e capacità produttive: la realtà italiana*. Bologna: Il Mulino.

Godley, W. A. H., and Nordhaus, W. D. 1972. "Pricing in the Trade Cycle." *Economic Journal 82* (September).

Glynn, A., and Sutcliffe, R. 1972. *British Capitalism, Workers and the Profit Squeeze*. Baltimore: Penguin.

Kalecki, M. 1938a. "The Lesson of the Blum Experiment." *Economic Journal 48* (March).

Kalecki, M. 1938b. "The Determinants of the Distribution of National Income." *Econometrica 6* (April).

Kalecki, M. 1971. *Selected Essays on the Dynamics of the Capitalist Economy*. Cambridge: Cambridge University Press (Chapter 6: "Distribution of National Income.")

Keynes, J. M. 1936. *The General Theory of Employment, Interest and Money*. London: Macmillan.

Keynes, J. M. 1939. "Relative Movements of Real Wages and Output." *Economic Journal 49* (March).

Marx, K. 1898. *Wages, Price and Profit*. Reprint. 1970. Moscow: Progress Publishers.

Nordhaus, W. 1972. "Recent Developments in Price Dynamics." In *The Econometrics of Price Determination*. Ed. by O. Eckstein. Washington, D.C.

Okun, A. M., and Perry, G. L. 1970. "Notes and Numbers on the Profit Squeeze." *Brookings Papers on Economic Activity*, No. 3.

Pantaleoni, M. 1910. "Di alcuni fenomeni di dinamica economica." In *Scritti vari di economia*. Bari: Laterza.

Ricardo, D. 1821. *On the Principles of Political Economy and Taxation.* Reprint, 1951. Ed. by P. Sraffa. Cambridge University Press, 1951, ch. 1, sec. III, para. 11–14, and ch. 22, para. 14–19.

Smith, A. 1776. *An Inquiry into the Nature and Causes of the Wealth of Nations.* Reprint. 1976. Ed. by E. Cannan. Chicago: University of Chicago Press, ch. 5, para. 11–13.

Solow, R. 1969. *Price Expectations and the Behavior of the Price Level.* Manchester: Manchester University Press.

Sylos-Labini, P. 1969. *Oligopoly and Technical Progress.* 2nd ed. Cambridge, Mass.: Harvard University Press.

Sylos-Labini, P. 1974. *Trade Unions, Inflations and Productivity.* Lexington, Mass.: Lexington Books.

Sylos-Labini, P. 1979. "Industrial Pricing in the British Manufacturing Industry." *Cambridge Journal of Economics* (June).

Weintraub, S. 1978. *Capitalism's Inflation and Unemployment Crisis.* Reading, Mass.: Addison-Wesley.

Williamson, O. E. 1964. *The Economics of Discretionary Behaviour: Managerial Objectives in a Theory of the Firm.* Englewood Cliffs, N.J.: Prentice-Hall.

8

On the Concept of the Optimum Rate of Profit

8.1 Keynes and Kalecki on Effective Demand

John Maynard Keynes formulated his theory of effective demand on the basis of two strong assumptions, constant technology and stable distribution of income. These assumptions reduce drastically the interpretative value of the Keynesian analysis, since technological changes and changes in the distributive shares, due to social conflict, are precisely the main features of a capitalist economy. The assumption of constant technology is usually supposed to be justified in a short-term analysis, because in such an analysis the capital equipment is considered as given; and technological changes depend mainly on new machines. The second assumption is justified on the basis of empirical evidence. Both justifications are very doubtful indeed. The first assumption can be justified on a purely logical plane, but it is unrealistic, because technologies change even in a very short period as a result of new machines introduced in previous periods; the new technologies made possible by such machines are gradually developed in a process of "learning by doing." The stability of the distributive shares has been for a long time a source of misunderstanding. First, the distribution is said to have been "relatively" stable only in the long term, not in the short, and the Keynesian analysis is concerned with the latter type of analysis. However, even in the long term the distribution appears to be "relatively" stable only in certain countries (the United Kingdom and, the United States) and only by choosing certain years, not others. Moreover "relative" stability is an arbitrary concept. Is a change of 3 or 4 points in the share of profits to be considered negligible or relevant? And yet, increases or decreases of that size are frequent. (As we will see, given the key role that must be attributed to the share of profits in a dynamic process, a change of that size is to be considered relevant or very relevant.) Finally, in the postwar period even the "relative" stability mentioned previously seems to be a phenomenon of the past: the share going to wages and salaries has increased systematically in all advanced capitalist countries.

Michal Kalecki worked out a theory of effective demand before Keynes, in which, unlike Keynes, he introduced technical progress and changes in the distributive shares. From this point of view Kalecki's theory is superior to Keynes's. Yet he did not push the analysis of the consequences of both changes very far.

In this chapter I will examine certain relations between the two types of change and the investment decisions, following a course that I deem to be consistent with the one traced by Kalecki, who rightly considered the theory of investment as the pillar of the theory of effective demand. I will refer to the manufacturing industry, because this sector constitutes the center of propulsion of technological innovations and, more generally, of capital accumulation. Moreover I assume that the most frequent market form in modern manufacturing is oligopoly, in its three varieties: concentrated (with homogeneous products), differentiated, and mixed oligopoly.

8.2 The Basic Determinants of Investment

The investment process implies three stages: in the first, the decision is taken; in the second, the spending following the decision takes place; in the third, the final effect of the process occurs, productive capacity increases; as a rule, productivity of labor increases too, since fixed investment, which is the essential part of total investment, consists of machines that almost always are more efficient than the previous ones. For the sake of simplicity I consider as negligible the time lag between the investment decision and investment spending, hereafter called "investment."

The basic determinants of investment and, in particular, of industrial investment are threefold: the expected rate of profit, representing the incentive to invest; total profits, a sizable part of which normally becomes self-financing; and total supply of bank loans, which represents the basis for external financing. In symbols these are

$$I = I\left(\frac{G^*}{K^*}, G, B\right), \tag{1}$$

where I is investment, G^*/K^* is the expected rate of profit, G is the total profits and B the supply of bank loans, or loanable funds. The expected rate of profit, G^*/K^*, is estimated on the basis of the current rate of profit (but under normal conditions the two rate coincide or do not differ very much):

$$\frac{G^*}{K^*} = f\left(\frac{G}{K}\right). \tag{2}$$

Total profits, G, are a function of the degree of utilization of capacity, since as a rule total cost per unit reaches the minimum at the limit of capacity, and of the markup on direct cost, $\alpha = P/D$, which, for a given degree of utilization and therefore for a given value of overheads per unit of output, determines the profit margin:

$$G = F(UT, \alpha). \tag{3}$$

The degree of utilization (UT) can be expressed as the ratio between actual and potential output; potential output (X_p) is the ratio between fixed capital, K_F, and the so-called accelerator, v, that is, the capital-output ratio, where output is potential output:

$$UT \equiv \frac{X_a}{X_p}$$

where

$$X_p \equiv \frac{K_F}{v}$$

and where fixed capital is supposed to bear a constant relation to total capital, or

$$K_F \equiv aK.$$

The degree of utilization, UT, depends on the basic elements of effective demand, (i.e., consumption expenditure, total investment, and exports):

$$UT = UT(C, I_r, E). \tag{4}$$

In turn consumption expenditure depends, first and foremost, on income from employment (wage and salary bill); it also depends on nonlabor incomes:

$$C = C(LI, NLI). \tag{5}$$

Direct cost, D, is given by the cost of direct labor per unit, that is, the ratio between wage per hour and hourly productivity, W/π, and by the cost of raw materials per unit, RM. Therefore

$$\alpha = \frac{P}{W/\pi + RM}.$$

I will assume that the average wage and the average salary change at the same rate. Given the level of employment and the raw material prices, a change in the average wage (and in average salary) implies a proportional change in total labor income. Since the cost of wage labor per unit is equal to the ratio between total wages and output, $W/\pi = W_\tau/X_a$, if W increases less than π, the ratio of labor income to total output decreases. These assumptions and observations will be used in the subsequent analysis. Here I will adopt, without trying to demonstrate it, the proposition according to which α, the markup (equivalent to Kalecki's degree of monopoly), is not constant but varies inversely with respect to D, the direct cost; it decreases when D increases, and vice versa (see chapter 7).

8.3 The Relationship between Wages and Investment[1]

An increase in the wage bill will, *ceteris paribus*, stimulate investment, because such an increase implies a proportional increase in labor income and therefore in consumption expenditure, in the degree of utilization, in total profits and, under normal conditions, in the expected rate of profit. (I assume that the rate of increase of productivity is determined exogenously and is constant; I further assume that wages are the only sources of demand for consumption goods.)

If wages increase more than productivity, the average cost of labor per unit of output increases and (on the basis of the proposition mentioned previously concerning the behavior of α) the markup tends to fall. *Ceteris paribus*, the fall in the markup determines a fall in the profit margin and in the rate of profit. From this standpoint an increase in wages depresses investment. Thus, on the one hand, the increase of wages stimulates investment and, on the other, depresses it. What is the final outcome?

The outcome depends fundamentally on the relative speeds of the wage and productivity increases. As long as the former is lower than the latter, the fall in labor cost will have on investment both a positive effect, by pushing up the profit margin and the rate of profit, and a negative effect, since consumption expenditure will tend to increase more slowly than output. In the course of time the slow increase in consumption expenditure will tend to influence the rate of profits adversely and thus will tend to offset the initial positive effect. When the increase in wages becomes greater than the increase in productivity, the increase in the cost of labor will have the negative effect of reducing the rate of profit and the positive effect of making the expansion of consumption expenditure even more rapid than that of production. However, sooner or later the diminution in the rate of profit will determine a diminution in investment and, eventually, in consumption expenditure, thus canceling out the initial positive effect.

Let us consider, first, the virtual movements of investment depending on

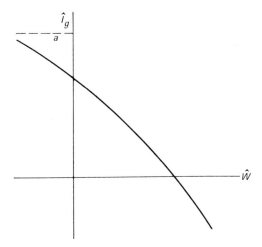

Figure 8.1

the rate of profit and abstracting from demand for consumption goods; we could imagine, for example, that the increasing production would be bought on credit by other countries. Second, let us consider the virtual movements of investment depending on demand for consumption goods and abstracting from the incentive to invest (i.e., from the rate of profit); we could imagine that for a period industrialists go on investing and expanding production, which they can readily sell, despite the decreasing profit rate and after a point, despite losses. In any case investment must be assumed to increase at a decreasing rate because such an increase is bound to meet with increasing frictions, to give only one reason, due to the increasing scarcity of labor.

Let us assume that the investment function can be written as the product of two independent functions:

$$I = I_g \, I_d, \tag{7}$$

where I_g is the function expressing the profit effect and I_d the function expressing the demand effect on investment of changes of W. Under this assumption the rate of change of investment per unit of time can be written as the sum of the rates of each of the two components:[2]

$$\hat{I} = \hat{I}_g + \hat{I}_d. \tag{8}$$

The conditions previously mentioned are satisfied by the exponential curves drawn in figures 8.1 and 8.2. In both figures the rate of change of wages per unit of time

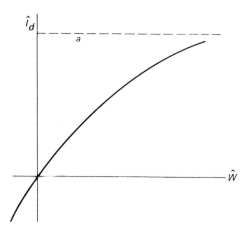

Figure 8.2

$$\frac{1}{W}\frac{dW}{dt} = \hat{W}$$

is represented on the horizontal axis and the rate of change of investment on the vertical axis.

At the origin $\hat{I}_g$ is positive, because $\hat{W}$ is zero but the rate of increase of productivity is positive; $\hat{I}_g$ increases when $\hat{W}$ decreases, and vice versa. However, in the former case $\hat{I}_g$ increases at a decreasing rate, owing to the frictions referred to before.

At the origin $\hat{I}_d$ is zero, because $\hat{W}$ is the only source of demand for consumption goods; $\hat{I}_d$ is increasing when $\hat{W}$ increases. Again $\hat{I}_d$ is increasing at a decreasing rate.

The relationship between the rates of change of investment and of wages, when wages are considered only as costs, can be expressed by a function of the type:

$$\hat{I}_g = a - hb^{\hat{W}}, \tag{9}$$

where $a > h > 0$ so that, when $\hat{W} = 0$, $\hat{I}_g > 0$ and where $b > 1$; a represents the straight line toward which $\hat{I}_g$ is tending for $\hat{W} \to -\infty$.

The relationship between the said rates of change, when wages are considered only as income, can be expressed by a similar function:

$$\hat{I}_d = a(1 - c^{\hat{W}}), \tag{10}$$

where $c < 1$ when $\hat{W} = 0$ and $\hat{I}_d = 0$ and a represents the straight line toward which $\hat{I}_d$ is tending for $\hat{W} \to \infty$.

The unified relationship represented in figure 8.3 is

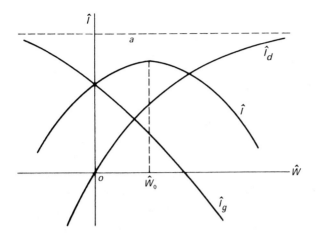

Figure 8.3

$$\hat{I} = 2a - hb^{\hat{W}} - ac^{\hat{W}}. \tag{11}$$

At the origin we should have

$$\frac{d\hat{I}_d}{d\hat{W}} > -\frac{d\hat{I}_g}{d\hat{W}}$$

so that, recalling all the conditions previously mentioned, $\hat{I}$ reaches its maximum at the right of the origin, and more precisely when

$$\frac{d\hat{I}_d}{d\hat{W}} = -\frac{d\hat{I}_g}{d\hat{W}}$$

It must be observed that the changes in wages do not only have the effects on investment that have been mentioned: if we would consider the said effects in a general model, the net outcome would be uncertain. It seems, however, that in this case the *ceteris paribus* clause is not misleading. In fact the equations presented in the previous section belong to a broader theoretical model that I have used to build up an econometric model for the Italian economy (Sylos-Labini 1974, ch. 1). I made several simulations with this model by taking $\hat{W}$ as an independent variable and observing the effects of its changes on the rate of change of investment. The results are fully consistent with the hypothesis that the demand and the profit effects on investment of $\hat{W}$ are the prevalent ones and that the behavior of $\hat{I}$, when $\hat{W}$ changes, can be represented by an equation such as (11); indeed, the stimulus to work out an equation of this type came by observing the results of a number of simulations made with that model to study the effects of changes in $\hat{W}$.

8.4 The Optimum Rate of Profit

The preceding analysis can bring us to the conclusion that—given the increase in productivity—there is an "optimum" rate of wage increase that maximizes the positive effects and minimizes the negative effects on investment of the dynamics of the cost of labor. It is "optimum" in the sense that it maximizes the rate of accumulation. The "optimum" rate of wage increase implies an "optimum" rate of profit, which, for the sake of realism, is to be conceived as the modal value of a variety of profit rates. The optimum rate of wage increase, $\hat{W}_0$, will be equal to the rate of productivity increase in a closed economy in which the prices of raw materials are assumed to be constant. In an open economy the income effect can be supplemented by foreign demand, so that the rate of wage increase can be smaller than the rate of increase of productivity without negatively affecting the rate of increase of total effective demand. Indeed, in such a situation the cost of labor tends to decrease with a consequent increase in the international competiveness and in the growth of exports. On the other hand, a wage increase more rapid than productivity depresses both profits and exports, and their growth, but does not affect negatively the rate of profit and international competitiveness if the raw materials prices fall sufficiently.

Figure 8.3 does not aim at solving an equilibrium problem. It only illustrates the proposition that, as far as the cost of labor is concerned, the growth process can proceed at a sustained rate provided, the rate of wage increase does not diverge too much from the optimum rate. If $\hat{W}$ is to the left of $\hat{W}_0$, the rate of profit is "too high," and effective demand is increasing "too slowly"; the opposite is true if $\hat{W}$ is to the right of $\hat{W}_0$. In either case sooner or later a crisis will interrupt the accumulation process. Therefore the rate of wage increase will not remain stable but will fluctuate, and it will not remain stable even if, for a period, it does not diverge very much from $\hat{W}_0$, because the economic fluctuations do not depend only on the dynamics of the cost of labor. However, if and as long as $\hat{W}$ does not diverge very much from $\hat{W}_0$, the fluctuations will, *ceteris paribus*, be relatively moderate. (Here I neglect the question of relative variations in the rates of profits in different countries and of capital movements caused by such variations.)

8.5 Keynes on Wage Cuts

As is well known, Keynes considers what I have called the demand effect and the profit effect of a wage cut on the level of activity from a peculiar angle and with peculiar assumptions, among which we find constant technology and widespread unemployment. According to Keynes (1936), a wage cut is not likely to push up the level of activity because it tends to determine not only a price reduction but also a redistribution of income in favor of profits, with a probable diminution in the propensity to consume. It is true that the said redistribution tends to raise the marginal efficiency of capital, but such a rise is short-lived if consumption diminishes. (This is one of the few instances where Keynes gives a hint to the possible consequences of a redistribution of income.) If we drop the assumptions of constant technology and widespread unemployment and consider not only the reduction but also the increase of wages, then the range of the possible consequences of wage changes on the level of activity appears to be much broader than that envisaged by Keynes, and it is no longer possible to generalize, as Keynes does, though cautiously, about the algebraic sum of the two contrasting effects.

8.6 The Dynamics of the Labor Cost and the Business Cycle

If we concentrate our attention on the dynamics of the cost of labor, we can observe that in the now advanced capitalist countries the rate of change of wages has followed in general the fluctuations in economic activity. However, if we compare the said dynamics of the past century and until the first world war with the experiences after the second world war, we notice at least two important differences (the interwar period, characterized by the Great Depression, is a special case which I will discuss separately). The first difference is that in the past the rate of money wage change was often positive but was sometimes negative, whereas in our times it is always positive. Second, in the past the fluctuations of that rate regularly followed the fluctuations in economic activity, whereas now the correspondence is far from being close. This is not the place to discuss the reasons for such differences, which are associated with a series of structural changes, among which I would mention the downward price rigidity, the power acquired by the trade unions, the much larger scope of government intervention in economic life, and the much larger international economic integration. Here I will limit myself to a few remarks concerning the role of the changes in the cost of labor in the process of accumulation by distinguishing between the business cycle and the trend of output.

Let us consider first the business cycle, and let us refer in particular to the business cycle of the past rather than to that of the present. In the ascending phases of the cycle—recovery and prosperity—the wage rate increased progressively, in line with the fall in unemployment. In recession and in depression that rate decreased. In the ascending phases the problem of effective demand became increasingly easy to solve. But the problem of the share of profits made its appearance and then became increasingly serious, especially toward the top of the boom when wages were increasing very rapidly. To reduce such pressure, industrialists speeded up the process of mechanization. But if such a behavior alleviated the pressure of labor cost, by the same token it made more serious the problem of the market because it implied a slowing down of the rate of increase of the wage rate and of the wage bill. Eventually the boom ended in a slump; as a rule the turning point was characterized by a profit squeeze, due to the rapid increase both in wages and the rate of interest.

8.7 Marx and the Business Cycle

As is well known, the Marxian analysis of the business cycle has been interpreted in two ways. Both interpretations recognize that, according to Marx, the whole cyclical fluctuation is conditioned by movements of the "industrial reserve army" and by technical progress. However, the first interpretation emphasizes the tendency to underconsumption and therefore the so-called "realization problem" as the main source of the recurrent crises. The other emphasizes the tendency of the rate of profit to fall, due to the increasing composition of capital; this tendency can be offset only temporarily. It is paradoxical to observe that nobody, it would seem, has offered an interpretation similar to the one outlined here, combining "dialectically" the two tendencies. And yet such an interpretation would clearly have been the most appropriate for those who claim to accept a Marxian type of analysis.

8.8 The Optimum Rate of Profit and the Great Depression

The process of accumulation, which is a cyclical process, does not proceed in all capitalist countries and in all periods at the same pace. It is my contention that one of the determinants of the trend of output of that process is given by the behavior of the cost of labor. In certain periods the rate of wage increase tends to be systematically "too low" (always through fluctuations), thus determining an excessive increase in profits; the reverse tends to happen in other periods. In periods of the former type the increase in investment, during the ascending phases of the cycle, tends to be higher than in the latter periods, but the crises tend to be more serve.

It might seem strange that an expansion of profits can be such as to prepare the ground for particularly severe crises. But it is so. The Great Depression which began with a collapse of the U.S. economy in 1929 was preceded, and in a sense "caused" by, a period of an excessive expansion of profits. In fact the

Table 8.1
Cost of labor, prices and the distribution of income, 1922–23/1928–29

1. Industrial output	38.4	6. Wholesale prices of industrial goods	−2.1
2. Employment: total	1.5		
wage earners[a]	0.7	7. Average salary	19.6
3. Productivity per hour	37.4	8. Wage bill (billion $)	11 → 11.6
4. Wage per hour	12.0	9. Salary bill (billion $)	2.8 → 3.6
5. Cost of direct labor	−18.5	10. Nonlabor incomes (share in value added)	47 → 53

Changes in Selected Productions, 1922–23/1928–29

Food products, 2%	Textiles, 9%	Residential construction, 46%	Automobiles, 57%	Pleasure craft, 300%	Iron and steel, 33%

a. The small percentage change referring to the number of wage earners can also be applied to the total number of hours, since with the exception of the iron and steel industry, in the period considered the hours worked per week did not change very much.

unprecedented speculative wave on the stock exchange was fed precisely by an extraordinary expansion of profits which could not find an adequate outlet in investment.

Let us reflect on the figures in table 8.1 concerning American industry in the period 1922 to 1929; the values from 1 to 7 in the first section and all the values in the second section are percentage rates of change (*Statistical Abstract of the U.S.* 1934; *Statistical History of the U.S. from Colonial Times to the Present* 1965).

The absolute and relative expansion of nonlabor incomes (profits and property incomes) is caused first of all by the downward rigidity of prices. In fact in the period considered, the prices of raw materials remained practically stationary; the cost of direct labor fell by almost 20 percent, while the prices of finished products fell very little.[3]

These figures show that in that period in the American economy the market for the products bought by wage earners was clearly increasing very slowly, owing to the very modest increase in the wage rates and the wage bill. (This slow increase shows that in that period the trade unions were very weak, a phenomenon that deserves careful scrutiny.) Salaries and the salary bill were increasing less slowly, thus providing a market for certain categories of goods, including residential buildings and automobiles (which in that period were quasi-luxury goods). Nonlabor incomes were increasing very quickly, but such an increase provided a market mainly for "luxury" goods, such as villas, pleasure craft, and the like. To a considerable extent, those incomes were invested; but at home the investment opportunities were increasing very slowly. Therefore those incomes were invested to some extent abroad (up to 1927) and to an increasing extent in speculative activities, namely in the stock market which experienced a gigantic boom and eventually collapsed.[4]

These observations concerning the behavior of different categories of incomes, though fragmentary, are consistent with the view that the great prosperity of the twenties did not significantly affect more than 30 percent of the population, mostly businessmen, managers, and some of the salary earners; as a rule small farmers, blue-collar workers, and irregularly employed workers only obtained modest benefits, if any, during the "new era" (see Fano 1976).

8.9 The Present Situation and the Prospects

At present from the point of view of the dynamics of labor cost, we are living in a period in which the process of accumulation in the advanced capitalist countries is meeting with obstacles that are opposite to those that emerged in the twenties in the American economy: manufacturing profits have been falling for several years, through various fluctuations, and are now "too low." This seems to be the situation in most capitalist countries; it is certainly the situation in the British and the Italian economies. The main impulses behind this trend are, first, the sustained increases in the cost of labor and, second, the explosion in the price of oil and many other raw materials. Underlying these impulses we find economic and political factors: the increasing bargaining power of the trade unions, on the one hand, and of several underdeveloped countries producing raw materials, on the other. (The latter power is conditioned and enhanced by the relative scarcity of several natural resources, in the face of an acceleration of demand, due mainly to the international spread of economic growth.) It is true that in the important case of oil the major international oil companies played an appreciable role in the price explosion. But unlike what used to happen in the past, their role has been neither exclusive nor prevalent: the role of the producing countries has not been inferior; certainly in administering the oil price since 1973, it is the role of the producing countries that has been prevalent. In any case in the advanced capitalist countries the general conditions are such as to allow only a relatively slow rate of growth; at the same time they are such as to rule out the probability of a major depression in the foreseeable future.

8.10 Smith and Ricardo on Profits

A brief remark is to be made about the history of economic analysis. Adam Smith looked with favor on the tendency of the rate of profit to fall, at least up to a certain level, whereas David Ricardo looked on such a tendency with great concern. This difference derives, I think, not only from different analytical constructions but also from the different times and conditions when the two great economists wrote. In Smith's time legal privileges and institutional barriers to entry of new productive units were still widespread and were determing high prices and high profits in several branches of economic activity. In his view the dismantling of such privileges and barriers would have meant falling prices, falling profits, and a more rapid expansion of demand and production. Ricardo was living in a period in which those privileges had been considerably reduced and in which the prices of agricultural products were rapidly rising, principally as a consequence of the French Revolution and the Napoleonic Wars. This rise was determining an increase in money wages and rents and a fall in profits; Ricardo was concerned about the negative effects on accumulation of a protracted fall in profits.

Compared with the model presented here, Smith was envisaging a situation in which profits as a rule were "too high," and Richardo a situation in which profits were tending to become "too low"; the economic processes behind those tendencies were very different from those of our times.

8.11 Problems of Optimization in a Dynamic Context

The preceding argument applies to the manufacturing industry. As I mentioned in chapter 7 (section 7.7), a profit reduction in this sector differs inherently from comparable profit declines in the banking and commercial sectors in the sense that it may have more damaging effects on the process of growth; it is even possible that a profit decline of comparable intensity in the commercial sector may have a positive effect on growth, if there are no accompanying bankruptcies, since the costs to firms engaged in strictly productive activities will be lower. In other words, the optimum rate of profit differs in the different sectors. In certain activities it is zero; indeed, as activities with zero profit cease, the means of production employed in those activities can be used in more advantageous ways for the economy as a whole. The optimal rate is zero in the purely speculative activities, and such activities perform no economic function whatsoever, not even indirectly. They give rise to a redistribution of wealth rather than an increase of wealth. Several financial activities that have developed recently in certain Latin American countries belong to this category. In these countries the *real* rate of interest—an expression of the *real* gain obtainable from a large number of financial investments—has reached the astronomical figure of 40 percent or more, and this in a period of economic stagnation. Strictly speaking, those activities that produce luxury goods in Sraffa's sense belong to the same category. (The problem may be also viewed differently if we take into account a luxury commodity's possible *social* function, as in the case of monetary incentive or a prize; however, this concern is more for a sociologist than an economist.) There are yet luxury goods that imply not simply redistribution but the dissipation of wealth and human energies, for instance, hard drugs. Then too the optimum rate of profit is zero; but should it be positive—and even high—the effect is entirely negative for the economy as a whole.

The optimum rate of profit, as we have seen in section 8.5, corresponds to the optimum rate of increase of wages. These are all "optima" of a dynamic type—they refer to the process of growth. Economists have discussed at length various optima of the static type, beginning with the problem of the optimum allocation of resources (for the economy) and of the specific means of production (for a firm). Much more important than such optima are those of the dynamic type. The optimum rate of increase of wages belongs to this category, in the sense that wages, as we must recognize, are not only costs but also an important source of effective demand. Another important component of effective demand is given by public expenditure; here too we need to consider the optimum rate of expansion (see chapter 5, section 5.6). This optimum rate depends, among other things, on the kind of expenditure and on the way it is financed: a growing unproductive expenditure—be it military or social—in the long run will generate even more difficulties, increasingly raise inflation or squeeze out private investment or both. And these difficulties may determine a slow down and even a paralysis in the process of growth. Things are different when rising public expenditure has a productive character. Even if it leads to a deficit, such expenditure contributes to the growth of national income and hence, in the long run, of fiscal receipts, so the public deficit will tend to decrease.

The distinctions between profits favorable and unfavorable to the growth process, between commodities that are necessary to the perpetuation of the productive process and luxury goods, and between productive and unproductive activities are connected with the distinction between productive and unproductive labor proposed by the classical economists and reproposed anew 30 years ago by Alberto Breglia in a short and important article.

Among the economic forces of growth, excluding social and institutional factors which are treated by other scholars, two are particularly relevant: profit and demand. However, both have an optimum level or an optimum rate of increase, below or above which those forces weaken. And further, both must be considered in terms of substance: certain kinds of profits or demand expansions simply cannot represent weaker forces of growth but rather negative forces, forces of decline and not growth.

Notes

1. I express my thanks to my colleague Gioacchino D'Ippolito for his help in the mathematical elaborations presented in this section.

2. From equation (7) we get

$$\frac{dI}{dt} = I_d \frac{dI_g}{dt} + I_g \frac{dI_d}{dt}$$

and

$$\frac{1}{I}\frac{dI}{dt} = \frac{1}{I_g}\frac{dI_g}{dt} + \frac{1}{I_d}\frac{dI_d}{dt},$$

which can be written in the simple form given as equation (8).

3. These observations should be read in the light of the proposition put forward in section 8.3, that is, the markup increases when the direct cost falls and decreases when the direct cost increases. Now I wish to add that the shift is not only partial but also asymmetrical. It is always less than 100 percent, but it is much less than this level when the direct cost decreases; it is almost 100 percent when the direct cost increases.

4. As far as I know, only two economists have noticed and attached importance to some of the phenomena mentioned here—(downward rigidity of prices, slow increase of wages, insufficient growth of investment)—without, however, trying to explain them by means of a theoretical model; they are Luigi Einaudi (1934; reprint 1937) and Galbraith (1955).

References

Breglia, A. (1953). Profitti sterili e profitto fecondo. *Giornale degli economisti* (March–April).

Einaudi, E. (1934). Debiti. *Riforma sociale*, Nos. 1–2. Reprint 1937. In *Nuovi saggi*. Turin: Einaudi.

Fano, E. 1976. I paesi capitalistici dalla prima guerra mondiale al 1929. In *La crisi del capitalismo negli anni 20*. Ed., M. Telò. Bari: De Donato.

Galbraith, J. K. 1955. *The Great Crash, 1929*. Boston: Houghton Mifflin.

Keynes, J. M. (1936). *The General Theory of Employment, Interest and Money*. London: Macmillan, ch. 19.

Statistical Abstract of the U.S. 1934. Washington. D.C.

Sylos-Labini, P. 1969. *Oligopoly and Technical Progress*. Rev. ed. Cambridge, Mass.: Harvard University Press, ch. 3.

Sylos-Labini, P. 1974. *Trade Unions, Inflation and Productivity*. Lexington, Mass.: Lexington Books.

Statistical History of the U.S. from Colonial Times to the Present. 1965. New York: Fairfield Publishing Co.

9   Keynes's *General Theory* and the Great Depression

The fear of a another severe depression in some way comparable to the one of the thirties has revived the debate on what factors determined it. Keynes's *The General Theory of Employment, Interest, and Money* (1936) has long been seen as a result of a powerful analytical effort to explain those factors and to find a way out of the depression, yet it may be useful to present some critical reflections on the Keynesian conception of this subject.

Let us start with certain methodological considerations.

9.1 Three Types of Criticism of the Models of Economic Theory

A theoretical model can be criticized from the standpoint of its internal consistency or with reference to the hypotheses on which it is based. Such hypotheses in their turn can be criticized because they did not apply even for the period in which they were put forward or because, though valid then, under changed conditions they are no longer valid; this is likely to occur rather often, since economic theory is historically conditioned. Thus we can distinguish between hypotheses that have to be rejected because they are irrelevant irrespective of the period considered and hypotheses that have become untenable for historical reasons.

The model worked out by Keynes in his *General Theory* has been criticized on these three grounds. As regards its internal consistency, Alvin Hansen, for example, raised a criticism concerning the influence of changes in income on the rate of interest. Hansen's commentary is logically well founded if we interpret the Keynesian system in terms of simultaneous relations, but not, if we interpret it in terms of causal sequences.[1] However, the greater part of the other criticisms belong to the second and third types. I myself advanced criticisms of both types at different times referring to (1) the essentially psychological character of the assumptions upon which Keynesian theory is founded, (2) the assumption that the quantity of money is exogenous, and (3) the hypothesis that both the product and labor markets react in the same way to variations in demand (Keynes supposed that increases in demand do not determine significant variations either in prices or wages up the level of full employment).[2]

The first two criticisms I mention here are to a large extent independent of historical changes; the third is not. More precisely, as far as the product markets are concerned, already at Keynes's times it was important to distinguish between the markets of agricultural and mineral raw materials and the market of industrial products. In the short run, which is the one that Keynes refers to, in the agricultural and raw materials markets prices depend on demand and supply, whereas in the industrial products market prices vary with costs and are largely independent of demand variations as long as resources are not fully utilized. As for the labor market, since its inception distinctions have been appropriately made between the so-called manual and intellectual occupations; some economists, however, including Keynes, have reasoned as if such a distinction were not important. The great increase that has taken place since the second world war in the average per capita income in industrialized countries has, among other things, made possible a considerable extension in subsidies to the unemployed, and accordingly workers in advanced countries have increasingly shown a tendency to refuse unpleasant and repetitive jobs. To some extent such jobs have been partly transformed into automated operations or partly entrusted to workers coming from relatively backward countries. Consequently today it is necessary to distinguish between three types of jobs: unpleasant and repetitive jobs of a prevailingly manual kind, manual jobs with an increasingly specialist component, and predominantly intellectual jobs, especially in offices. In the labor markets of the first kind compensations (wages) are moderately sensitive to variations in the demand for labor, especially if the immigration of foreign workers is free. In the labor markets of the second kind compensations (again wages) are much less sensitive to variations in the demand for labor: only great fluctuations in this demand can affect those compensations. In the labor markets of the third kind compensations (salaries) are sensitive to demand variations to an only very limited extent, if at all—I refer always to money compensations. The well-known Phillips curve, which has been rightly considered fully compatible with the Keynesian theory, has been always related to wages in the strict sense, not to salaries. However, owing to the bargaining power acquired by the trade unions, for several decades unemployment has no longer been the only factor or necessarily the principal factor in the determination of wage changes. Since the first world war another important factor, even in the short run, has been the cost of living. Therefore, rather than an individual Phillips curve, we have to think in terms of a "family" of Phillips curves. In recent times, owing to the great increase in average per capita income, to the extention and increase in subsidies to the unemployed, and to the further strenghtening of trade unions, not even the two variables unemployment and the cost of living are enough to explain wage changes, so the Phillips curve has further lost its explanatory power. At the same time the share of workers receiving salaries, which are largely independent of the variations in the demand for labor, has increased considerably.

Keynes considers the labor market to be relatively homogeneous, but with the proviso that when the economy is approaching full employment, the increase in the demand for labor meets with "bottlenecks" that determine the increase in the compensations for certain categories of workers. For reasons partly discussed before, the Keynesian assumption concerning the homogeneity of the labor market could be considered acceptable in his own time and soon after the war; today, however, it is no longer acceptable. Let us have a closer look.

According to Keynes, the quantity of employment can be made homogeneous "by taking an hour's employment of ordinary labour as our unit and weighting an hour's employment of special labour in proportion to its remuneration; i.e., an hour of special labour remunerated at double ordinary rates will count as two units."[3] This criterion, which is in fact followed by the classical economists, presupposes that at least in the short run relative wages are constant.[4] Of course in the past, when wages were not much higher than the subsistence level, this corresponded closely enough to reality. Today, however, because workers in industrialized countries tend increasingly to refuse the unpleasant and repetitive jobs, the relative wages in unpleasant jobs tend to rise even in the short run; and Keynes's criterion no longer holds. The increase in the relative wages in those jobs can at least partially be avoided if firms hire foreign workers, but then, when the demand for labor rises, immigration and not employment will rise. If we count the immigrants too, the volume of employment rises, but the volume of unemployment does not fall.[5]

9.2 Two Reference Models

Unlike the criticisms pertaining to internal consistency, criticisms of the hypotheses could be made convincing if only the critics would indicate, at least schematically, some viable alternative. I shall try to set such a standard by reducing to symbols a very simplified version of the Keynesian model and proposing an alternative model founded on partially different hypotheses. I shall show that it is worthwhile to adopt these hypotheses in order to analyze in a more valid way certain problems treated by Keynes, including his interpretation of the Great Depression. The first model considered consists of a system of simultaneous equations. Thought it is doubtful that such a method can give a correct interpretation of Keynes's theory, for our purposes there seem to be no difficulties in adopting it. The second model, in which the variables are dated, cannot be treated by a system of simultaneous equations, since that would imply static interdependence.

Model 1: The Keynesian Model

Keynes's relations can be interpreted in the following way:

1. Income

$Y_w = C_w + I_w.$

2. Consumption

$C_w = a_1 + b_1 Y_w.$

3. Investment

$I_w = a_2 + \dfrac{b_2 G^*}{K^*} - c_2 i.$

4. Rate of interest

$i = a_3 - b_3 M_w + c_3 Y_w.$

5. Employment

$N = a_4 + b_4 Y_w.$

6. Price level

$P = a_5 W.$

7. Wages

$W = \bar{W}.$

The symbols used are Y = income, C = consumption, I = investment, G = total profits, K = capital, i = rate of interest, M = quantity of money, W = wage rate, N = dependent employment, and P = price level. The star indicates expected values; the subscript indicates that the variable is expressed in wage units (e.g., $Y_w = Y/W$).

For income, besides relation 1, the following relation applies:

$Y_w = \alpha N$ (relation la),

which can be obtained from $Y = \alpha WN$ on the assumption that income distribution does not change and hence money income and the total wage bill vary in the same proportion ($\alpha > 1$).

Relations 6 and 7 apply in conditions of widespread unemployment. When full employment is approached, however, the following relations apply:

for prices

$P = a_6 W + b_6 N$ (relation 6a),

for wages

$W = a_7 + b_7 N$ (relation 7a).

(Note that relation 7a is equivalent to the Phillips relation).

Model 2: An Alternative Model

I propose a model composed of these relations:[6]

1. Investment

$$I = a_1 + \frac{b_1 G}{Y_c} + c_1 UT - d_1 i.$$

2. Prices (rate of change)

$$\hat{P} = a_2 + b_2 \hat{W} - c_2 \hat{\pi} + d_2 \widehat{RM}.$$

3. Profits (share)

$$\frac{G}{Y_c} = a_3 + b_3 P - c_3 W + d_3 - e_3 \widehat{RM}.$$

4. Utilized capacity

$$UT = a_4 + b_4 C + c_4 I + d_4 E.$$

5. Consumption (current price)

$$C_c = a_5 + b_5 W + c_5 OI + d_5 N.$$

6. Consumption (constant price)

$$C \equiv \frac{C_c}{P}.$$

7. Cost of living

$$\hat{V} = a_6 + b_6 \hat{P}.$$

8. Employment

$$\hat{N} = \alpha \hat{C} + \beta \hat{I} - \hat{\pi}.$$

9. Wages

$$\hat{W} = a_7 + b_7 \hat{N} + c_7 \hat{V} + d_7 \, TUP.$$

10. Income

$$Y = C + I.$$

11. Rate of interest

$$i = \bar{\imath}.$$

The new symbols are UT = degree of utilized capacity (in percent), RM = raw material prices, π = productivity per worker, E = exports, OI = nonwage incomes, V = cost of living, and TUP = trade union pressure. The cap over a variable indicates a rate of change. Variables Y, C, and I are expressed in terms of constant prices, excepting those with subscript c, which are expressed in terms of current prices.

In the first model the given variables are the rate of expected profit, G^*/K^*, which expresses the state of long-term expectation; the wage rate, W, and the quantity of money, which is exogenously fixed by the monetary authority.

In the second model the given variables are productivity, raw materials prices, the "other incomes," trade union pressure, and exports, and the rate of interest, which is fixed exogenously by the monetary authority.

The differences between the first and the second model concern the equations of investment, prices, and employment. Moreover neither profits nor utilized capacity appears among the equations of the first model, and the quantity of money is not included among the variables.

The equation of investment constitutes the most fundamental difference between the two models. In the second model it depends, among the other determinants, on income distribution and, more precisely, on the profit share. Conceivably, this difference may not appear relevant since the variations in the rate of profit and those in the share of profits are proportional, if we assume that in the short run the capital-output ratio (K/Y) is constant, which is a reasonably realistic assumption, and if we admit, as Keynes seems to be inclined to do, that expectations often are of an extrapolative character (i.e., the behavior of the current rate of profit can be taken as an index of the expected rate of profit). In fact it is on this point that the difference between the two models becomes especially important. In the second model the rate of profit does not depend in any essential way on psychological factors (the state of long-term expectation) but on the interaction between prices, wages, and productivity, which in effect is conditioned by various impulses including imports, especially of raw materials, and socioeconomic conflicts that affect wages. But the main difference is that in the second model the antithetical role of wages is brought out: an increase in wages stimulates investment, pushing up the demand for consumption goods, and hence investment (relations 9, 5, 6, 8, 4, and 1), but an increase in wages tends to reduce the share of profits, with the fall in profits affecting investment negatively (relations 9, 2, 3, and 1).[7] Whether the positive or the negative effect tends to predominate will depend on the intensity of the initial impulse and on the value of the coefficients. All this means that the problem is one of determining an optimum rate of increase in wages and, correspondingly, an optimum level for the rate of profit.

9.3 The Great Depression of the Thirties

The diagnosis of the Great Depression that can be derived from *General Theory* can be criticized particularly for its psychological assumptions and the assumption concerning the relative homogeneity of both the product and the labor markets.

The question of the psychological hypotheses is strictly linked to the question of expectations, or better, a part of it. To avoid misunderstandings, I wish to point out that it is not my intention to deny the relevance of subjective factors. However, if the economist does not want to usurp the job of the psychologist and if he wants to avoid spurious or circular reasoning, he must be able to explain *why* certain expectations rather than others are formed. Those impulses from areas lying outside his field of study, he is entitled to treat as given data. The criticism arises when expectations are taken as the prime mover, or else when, as is more frequently the case, the reasons at the basis of expectations are given in vague terms and not really explained.

Keynes attributes the stock exchange crash of 1929 and the ensuing economic crisis to a sharp fall in the marginal efficiency of capital, which in turn expresses the state of long-term expectation. The state of expectation depends not only on psychological factors but also on other factors, especially on the size and composition, actual or foreseen, of capital goods and consumers' tastes. However, Keynes imparts such importance to psychological factors to feel the need of warning the reader: "We should not conclude from this that everything depends on waves of irrational psychology."[8] Rational or irrational, the psychology Keynes is talking about leaves those waves unexplained. And since the trade cycle, according to Keynes, depends on the cyclical variations in the marginal efficiency of capital, in the final analysis the Keynesian explanation of cycles and crises, and therefore of the spectacular crisis of 1929, enters into the category of spurious explanations. This does not imply that the Keynesian analysis of the Great Depression is of no value. The fact is that this historical event posed to the economists questions of various kinds: (1) why the stock exchange crash that started the Great Depression took place, (2) why the depression turned out to be so long (question of underemployment equilibrium) and (3) how effective could be the measures proposed to overcome the depression, in particular a wage cut, an expansionary monetary policy, and an expansionary fiscal policy.

To the first question, Keynes answers by referring to the marginal efficiency of capital and to the variations in the state of expectation. As I have said and will show better later in this chapter, this is the most unsatisfactory answer. To the second question, he answers with his analysis of effective demand (there is no mechanism ensuring that the intersection point between the aggregate demand and supply functions corresponds to full-employment income). To the third question, Keynes answers with various arguments suggesting that neither a wage cut nor an expansionary monetary policy can be a way out of a depression; he maintains, instead, the necessity of an expansionary fiscal policy in the form of a decisive increase in public expenditure, even beyond the level of receipts: the deficit, indeed, acts as a support of total demand.

I will devote a few comments only to the first question concerning the reasons for the stock exchange crash that marked the beginning of the Great Depression.[9] Keynes's answer comes out clearly in the following quotations:

> If I may be allowed to appropriate the term *speculation* for the activity of forecasting the psychology of the market, and the term *enterprise* for the activity of forecasting the prospective yield of assets over their whole life, it is by no means always the case that speculation predominates over enterprise. As the organisation of investment markets improves, the risk of the predominance of speculation does, however, increase. In one of the greatest investment markets in the world, namely, New York, the influence of speculation (in the above sense) is enormous.
>
> Speculators may do no harm as bubbles on a steady stream of enterprise. But the position is serious when enterprise becomes the bubble on a whirlpool of speculation. When the capital development of a country becomes a by-product of the activities of a casino, the job is likely to be ill-done. The measure of success attained by Wall Street, regarded as an institution of which the proper social purpose is to direct new investment into the most profitable channels in terms of future yield, cannot be claimed as one of the outstanding triumphs of *laissez faire* capitalism.[10]

9.4 An Alternative Diagnosis

I maintain, in contraposition to the thesis of Keynes, that the Wall Street crash, which came at the end of a true frenzy of speculation and created some important preconditions for the depression, should be attributed instead to three "objective" reciprocally interacting factors: the extraordinary changes in the distribution of income, the effects of certain great innovations, and deep-rooted changes in the market structure manifest in the spread and the strenghtening of oligopolies and monopolies.

It is advisable to start with a consideration of the rigidity of industrial prices with respect to demand, which became fully evident after the first world war. It was then that large corporations emerged as a result of the concentration process that asserted itself in several important branches of economic activity starting with the last two decades of the past century. Within certain limits these corporations are capable of influencing prices. A comparable situation appeared in those branches in which, mainly as a consequence of the development of the mass media and advertising, product differentiation became pronounced. Prices in all these markets have become less and less sensitive to demand variations; rather they vary with costs and, in particular, with direct costs: demand affects output rather than prices. In those countries where foreign competition is not very important, as in the United States, the diminution of prices can be remarkably less than the diminution in direct costs.[11] This is precisely what happened in the years preceding the stock exchange crash (see table 9.2 in the appendix, columns 3, 2, 4, 8, and 9). The margin over direct costs in industry rose and total profits rose both for this reason and because of the expansion of output, that had two positive effects on profits: the diminution in total unit cost, owing to overhead costs, with the consequent increase in the net margin over total cost and the multiplication of this margin by an increasing number of units produced and sold.

Such a process appeared to be particularly pronounced in the public utilities industries, especially in electricity and railroads which in the United States were (and are) private but subject to public controls. These controls had been introduced before the first world war with the purpose of avoiding, or at least of moderating, price increases in those two important sectors and containing profits. After the war the paradoxical consequence of those controls had been to strengthen the market power of the firms operating in those two sectors and to raise profits even more than would otherwise have been the case. As a matter of fact the said controls had been introduced in a period of rising prices: the objective was to slow down or even to prevent price increases. After the war trends changed: the price of oil fell considerably, thanks to the extraordinary advances in the technology of geological prospecting, to the discovery of new oil fields, and to the innovations in the methods of extraction. Oil of course was a very important source of energy for electricity and railroads. At the same time the fall in the price of oil determined that in the price of coal. Moreover in those sectors the cost of labor tended to fall as well. Total average costs then were falling to a notable extent, but controls tended to keep both electric and railroad tariffs stable: the result was a rapid increase in profits in both sectors.

A similar phenomenon, though somewhat more limited, took place in other industries: in general, prices of raw materials were stable; money wages increased to a small extent ($+14$ percent from 1922 to 1929), but as a result of technological innovations of various kind, productivity in industry rose considerably, 30 percent.[12] Despite this, "by some weird and unexplained magic" (Einaudi's words) industrial prices remained stable, with a considerable increase in industrial profits (see table 9.2 in the appendix, columns 3, 4, 8, and 9).[13] In fact the relative stability of prices depended on the market power of a relatively large number of firms—"spontaneous" or "artificial"—that in the previous two or three decades had rapidly increased. Thus the gross margin rose, overhead costs per unit tended to fall and total profits to rise, owing to the increase in both the net margin and output. The overall result is a truly extraordinary shift in income distribution, a shift favoring primarily profits but increasing other incomes as well (see table 9.2 in the appendix, column 10). *It is precisely this phenomenal shift in the distributive shares that is at the origin of the Wall Street crash and not the unexplained exhaustion of a wave of optimism, followed by an equally unexplained wave of pessimism.* Waves of this kind do take place, but it is necessary to identify the impulses generating them. In the case we are considering, the impulse was generated by the large profits which, moreover being on the rise, were determining expectations of further increases.

Many economists believe that in the capitalist system an increase in profits, however criticizable from the point of view of social justice, is favorable to economic development. But this problem must be posed in different terms. Smith had rejected, and rightly so, such a view. The truth is that in every given situation, as I have already noted, there is an *optimum* in the share and in the rate of profits, especially in the industrial sector. A decreasing rate, at least after a certain point, acts as a brake on accumulation, as has been so often maintained, but an increasing rate normally indicates a fall in the share of income going to dependent labor. This brings about a weakening in the rate of increase in the demand for consumption goods and, indirectly, the demand for investment goods; the whole process of development is slowed down. The consideration of incomes other than profits and wages in industry, among which we find the incomes of managers and those of the self-employed, does not appreciably affect the sequence we have just considered.

In its essential lines such a sequence and its contradictions can be seen in the alternative model presented earlier. An increase in wages has a positive effect on investment (relation 1) through the increase in the demand for consumption goods (relation 5) and in the degree of capacity utilization (relation 4), assuming employment as constant. On the other hand, an increase in wages has a negative effect on investment if prices do not increase at all or do not increase adequately; hence it determines a fall in profits (relations 2, 3, and 4). An opposite sequence tends to take place if wages fall or—in this case the analysis is more complex—if productivity increases, wages and employment remaining the same (relations 8, 5, and 1 are to be considered to start the analysis).

From the empirical standpoint during the twenties we find in the United States various indications of an exceptionally high rise of profits and other nonlabor incomes (see table 9.2 in the appendix, column 10).[14] As for the behavior of output, it should be noted that the output of mass consumption goods such as good and textiles increased only to a limited extent, similarly the wage bill (see in the appendix table 9.1, column 5 and table 9.2, column 5); from 1922–23 to 1928–29 the output of food increased by 2 percent and that of textiles by 9 percent. By contrast, the output of durable consumers' goods such as automobiles and residential buildings—goods that in those times were demanded principally by relatively high income earners—increased much more rapidly; we must observe, however, that the rapid expansion in the said sectors took place from 1922 to 1926; after that year it tended to dwindle (table 9.1, columns 3 and 6). Although disaggregated data are not available, we can presume that in the building industry the main increase in demand was for houses and cottages by the middle and upper classes, especially in the new satellite districts whose creation was stimulated primarily by the diffusion of automobiles.[15] With the gradual exhaustion of the investment opportunities which was the consequence of the variations mentioned earlier, investable funds coming from profits and from the other rapidly increasing incomes flowed in the first period—until 1927—toward other countries, even in the shape of high-risk loans.[16] In the second period—1927 to 1929—they flowed into the stock exchange, especially through purchases of shares whose quotations were rapidly rising precisely because profits were rising. After a certain moment the rise becomes explosive because, together with the funds coming from profits of the productive sector, there were those coming from banks and from speculative profits.[17] The wave of speculation is to be seen in these terms and not in the purely psychological terms discussed by Keynes.

9.5 Conclusions

At the origin of the whole process, then, there was the huge redistribution of income that combined with and reflected also the other two great changes: those in the market structure and those that can be attributed to technological innovations.[18] As already noted, the distributive shift did not only favor profits, particularly industrial profits, but also other incomes: those of the self-employed outside agriculture and the compensations of managers, especially those who directly or indirectly shared in the profits of the average and large firms. All in all, however, the prosperity of the twenties did not concern more than 20 or, at most, 30 percent of the income receivers; the others, obtained very modest benefits during the "new era."[19]

The whole Keynesian construction—I repeat—and not only the analysis of the trade cycle and of crises is based on psychological hypotheses. Indeed, as is well known, the three pillars of this construction are given by the state of long-term expectation, the propensity to consume (expressing a "fundamental psychological law"), and liquidity preference. Having made this choice, Keynes considers it natural to assume as given technology, the distribution of income, and the market structure ("the intensity of competition"). It is precisely those three factors that, in my judgment are essential to understanding the conditions that determined the Great Depression and, more generally, to interpreting the main lines of evolution of modern capitalism.

It may appear then that he who accepts such an approach is bound to reject the whole Keynesian system. Yet this is not so if we recognize that the relevance of the assumptions depends on the problems one considers. Thus if we put aside the problem of the origin of the Great Depression and examine different problems, such as the analysis of the mechanisms governing the variations in effective demand, the choice of assumptions of one kind or another becomes much less important, or even irrelevant in the sense that the psychological hypotheses can be substituted with assumptions of a different kind without irreparable damages to the system. Naturally, the analysis should then be partly modified and integrated, since in such a process we are made to realize that the psychological hypotheses are masking an analytical vacuum; the very prescriptions of economic policy are likely to be modified. It is possible, however, to walk together with Keynes for a relatively long part of the way.

Appendix: Some Data Concerning the Period 1922 to 1933

Table 9.1
Production

	Industrial production	Electricity	Consumers goods Durable	Semidurable	Nondurable	Building	Railroads (carriages)
	1	2	3	4	5	6	7
1913–14	80	41	60	17	46	62	255
1922	100	100	100	100	100	100	100
1923	120	116	146	131	116	121	182
1924	113	125	130	122	102	135	227
1925	127	139	176	141	113	149	218
1926	133	154	143	149	116	158	254
1927	133	166	143	132	117	155	182
1928	140	177	156	144	117	150	136
1929	153	192	185	154	119	148	200
1930	127	188	143	105	97	112	136
1931	100	179	86	80	78	82	27
1932	80	162	47	49	56	46	15
1933	100	169	50	56	60	39	—

Sources: U.S. Department of Commerce, *Historical Statistics of the United States—From Colonial Times to 1970*, Washington D.C., 1972. U.S. Department of Commerce, *Statistical Abstract of the United States*, Washington, D.C., 1934 and 1937.
Notes: Column 1 includes manufacturing industry; column 3 includes automobiles, and column 4 shoes, apparel products, and tires.

Table 9.2
Prices and Wages

	Prices			Wages				Output per man-hour	Cost of labor per unit	Income distribution
	Agricultural products	Raw materials	Finished products	Hourly	Total	Total salaries	Trade union membership			
	(1)	(2)	(3)	(4)	(5)	(6)	(7)	(8)	(9)	(10)
1913–14	76	71	70	47				75	62	
1922	100	100	100	100			4.0	100	100	29.0
1923	105	103	103	106	11.0	2.8		98	108	(48)
1924	106	102	100	110				105	105	
1925	117	111	104	110	11.0	3.0		113	97	
1926	110	104	104	110				114	96	
1927	106	101	98	110				117	93	
1928	112	103	99	110				124	90	
1929	112	102	98	114	11.6	3.6	3.4	130	88	33.5
1930	95	88	91	112				132	84	(54)
1931	65	68	80	104	6.9			137	76	
1932	50	57	73	90				130	70	
1933	54	59	73	90	6.6	1.6		136	66	

Sources: U.S. Department of Commerce, *Historical Statistics of the United States—From Colonial Times to 1970*, Washington, D.C., 1972. U.S. Department of Commerce, *Statistical Abstract of the United States*, Washington, D.C., 1934 and 1937. For column 10 in addition to the sources just mentioned, see M. A. Copeland, "Determinants of Distribution of Income," *American Economic Review* (March 1947).

Notes: 1922 = 100 except in columns 5, 6, 7, and 10. Columns 3, 4, 5, 6, 8, and 9 refer to manufacturing industry. Columns 5 and 6 in billion $ and column 7 in millions (1939: 9; 1970: 21). Column 10 in percent share of income going to the highest 5 percent of income receivers (33.5 percent in 1929 falls to 17 percent in 1972). Numbers in parentheses give estimates of the percent share of income going to the highest 20 percent of income receivers (54 percent in 1929 falls to 43 percent in 1972).

Notes

1. See A. H. Hansen, *A Guide to Keynes* (McGraw-Hill, New York, 1953), ch. 8; L. L. Pasinetti, *Growth and Income Distribution—Essays in Economic Theory* (Cambridge University Press, 1974), ch. 2.

2. The works in where I have raised the criticisms recalled in the text are the following: "The Keynesians," in *Banca Nazionale del Lavoro Quarterly Review* (November 1949); *Oligopoly and Technical Progress*, 2nd ed., (Harvard University Press, Cambridge Mass., 1969), p. 214 (orig. Ital. ed. 1956); *Lezioni di economia*, vol. 1: *Macroeconomia* (Edizioni dell'Ateneo, Roma, 1979); "Rigid Prices, Flexible Prices and Inflation," *Banca Nazionale del Lavoro Quarterly Review* (March 1982).

3. J. M. Keynes, *The General Theory of Employment, Interest and Money* (Macmillan, London, 1936), p. 41.

4. Smith: "Though pecuniary wages ... are very different in the different employments of labour ..., yet a certain proportion seems commonly to take place between ... the pecuniary wages in all the different employments of labour.... Though in many respects dependent upon the laws and policy, this proportion seems to be little affected by the riches or poverty of [the] society; by its advancing, stationary or declining condition; but to remain the same or very nearly the same in all those different states" (*Wealth of Nations*, Cannan, ed., Methuen, London, 1961, p. 71). Ricardo: "The estimation in which different qualities of labour are held, comes soon to be adjusted in the market with sufficient precision for all practical purposes and depends much on the comparative skill of the labourer, and intensity of the labour performed. The scale, when once formed, is liable to little variation" (*Principles*, Sraffa, ed., Cambridge University Press, 1951, p. 20).

5. For Great Britain (but similar considerations apply for many other industrialized countries) a very partial index of the change can be given by the share of foreign workers in total employment: about 2 percent in 1931 (400,000 out of 18 million workers), between 8 and 9 percent in 1981 (a little less than 2 million out of 21 million). (The estimates are derived from the 1931 and 1981 censuses.)

6. It has been derived from a broader model originally published in 1967 ("Prices, Distribution and Investment in Italy, 1951–1966: An Interpretation," *Banca Nazionale Quarterly Review*, December 1967; reprinted in *Trade Unions, Inflation and Productivity*, Lexington Books, Lexington, Mass., 1974). This model is now being revised and enlarged. For relations 2 and 3 see chapter 7.

7. See chapters 7 and 8.

8. Keynes, *General Theory*, p. 162.

9. As for the second question, I only wish to mention that the Keynesian analysis is not wrong but insufficient; in my judgment, it should be modified along the lines that I suggested in chapter 5 and, more at length, in my monograph on oligopoly (2nd ed., 158–160). The essential point is this: in modern conditions a fall in demand provokes a sharp fall in production rather than in prices and an even sharper fall in employment.

10. Keynes, *General Theory*, pp. 158–159. See also *The Collected Writings of J. M. Keynes*, Vol. 9, (Macmillan, London, 1973): "Essays in Persuasion," "The Great Slump of 1930," and "The Consequences of the Collapse of Money Values."

11. See chapter 7.

12. One could ask whether, to explain such an extraordinary increase in productivity, the analysis presented in chapter 4 could be used. A precise answer cannot be given, since some of the essential statistical series are lacking. From the available data it appears that the said analysis can in fact be useful. However, it is necessary to take into account that the cost of labor had considerably increased during the war (see table 9.2 in the appendix) and that in the twenties, among other things, a process of gradual absorption of the previous great leap took place.

13. L. Einaudi, "Debiti," *Riforma sociale* (January–February 1934); reprinted in the volume *Nuovi saggi* (Einaudi, Turin, 1937); the same phenomenon was noticed later on—but again not explained—by J. Schumpeter (*Business Cycles: A Theoretical, Historical and Statistical Analysis of the Capitalist Process*, McGraw-Hill, New York, 1939, pp. 809–810). In his book *The Great Depression* (Macmillan, London, 1935, pp. 48–9) Lionel Robbins writes, with reference to the twenties:

... it was the more or less stable condition of the price-level which blinded contemporary observers to the real nature of what was going on at the time.... When productivity is increasing, then, in the absence of inflation, we should expect prices to fall. Now the period we are examining was a period of rapidly increasing productivity. The comparative stability of prices, therefore, so far from being a proof of the absence of inflation, is a proof of its presence.

This phenomenon, whose definition today appears very paradoxical (an inflation with stable prices!), is attributed by Robbins to the policy of cheap money. He considers it as a cause of "profit inflation," discussed repeatedly by Keynes in his "Treatise on Money" (*The Collected Writings of J. M. Keynes*, Macmillan, London, 1971, vol. 5, which constitutes vol. 1 of the "Treatise," pp. 140, 151, 249, 263–271, 283–284; vol. 6 pp. 143–145, 190, 197); he quotes a rather long passage in which Keynes states that "a genuine profit inflation some time between that date [the end of 1927] and the summer of 1929" (vol. 6, p. 170). Apart from the period mentioned—there are clear indications that the "profit inflation" started several years earlier—it is a pity that in his *General Theory* Keynes completely neglected that important cue!

14. See also J. A. Schumpeter, *Business Cycles*, p. 831, and that important article by R. R. Keller, "Factor Income Distribution in the United States during the 1920's: A Reexamination of Fact and Theory," *The Journal of Economic History* (March 1973).

15. Let us remember that the output of automobiles in 1929 (4.5 millions) was exceeded only in 1949 (5.1 millions).

16. See J. K. Galbraith, *The Great Crash* (Houghton Mifflin, Boston, 1961). The foreign capital issues (government and corporate) publicly offered in the United States rose from 100 in 1972 to 175 in 1927; in the next two years they fell (from 175 to 88).

17. The Stock Exchange index rose from 100 in 1922 to 168 in 1926 and then jumped up to 370 in 1929.

18. The main lines in this interpretation are already contained in my monograph *Oligopoly and Technical Progress* (1st Italian ed. 1956; rev. American ed., Harvard University Press, 1969, pp. 127–128, 142–143, 156–157). Later on I reconsidered the question in my short essay "On the Optimum Rate of Profit" (chapter 8 of this volume). Recently I have noticed that an American historian, who clearly did not know my monograph, a few years ago has proposed an interpretation similar to my own (Keller, "Factor Income Distribution in the United States during the 1920's"). I should warn the reader that the analysis concerning the paradoxical consequences of public controls and tariffs of public utilities (strengthening of market power and rapid increase of profits) has been put forward for the first time by this author.

19. See E. Fano, "I paesi capitalistici della prima guerra mondiale al 1929," in *La crisi del capitalismo negli anni '20*, ed. by M. Telò (De Donato, Bari, 1976).

Index